Art at the Rockface
The Fascination of Stone

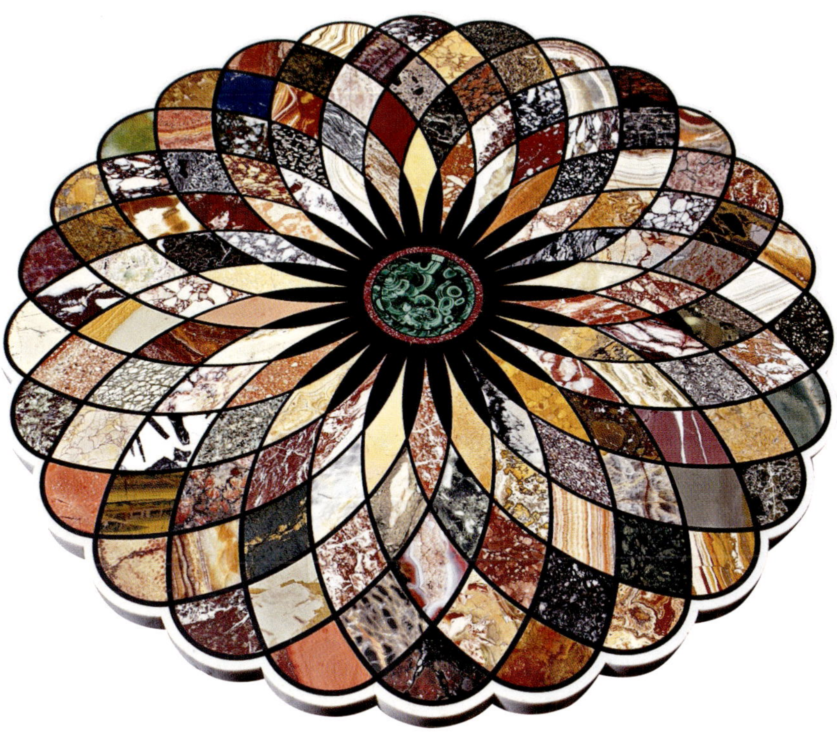

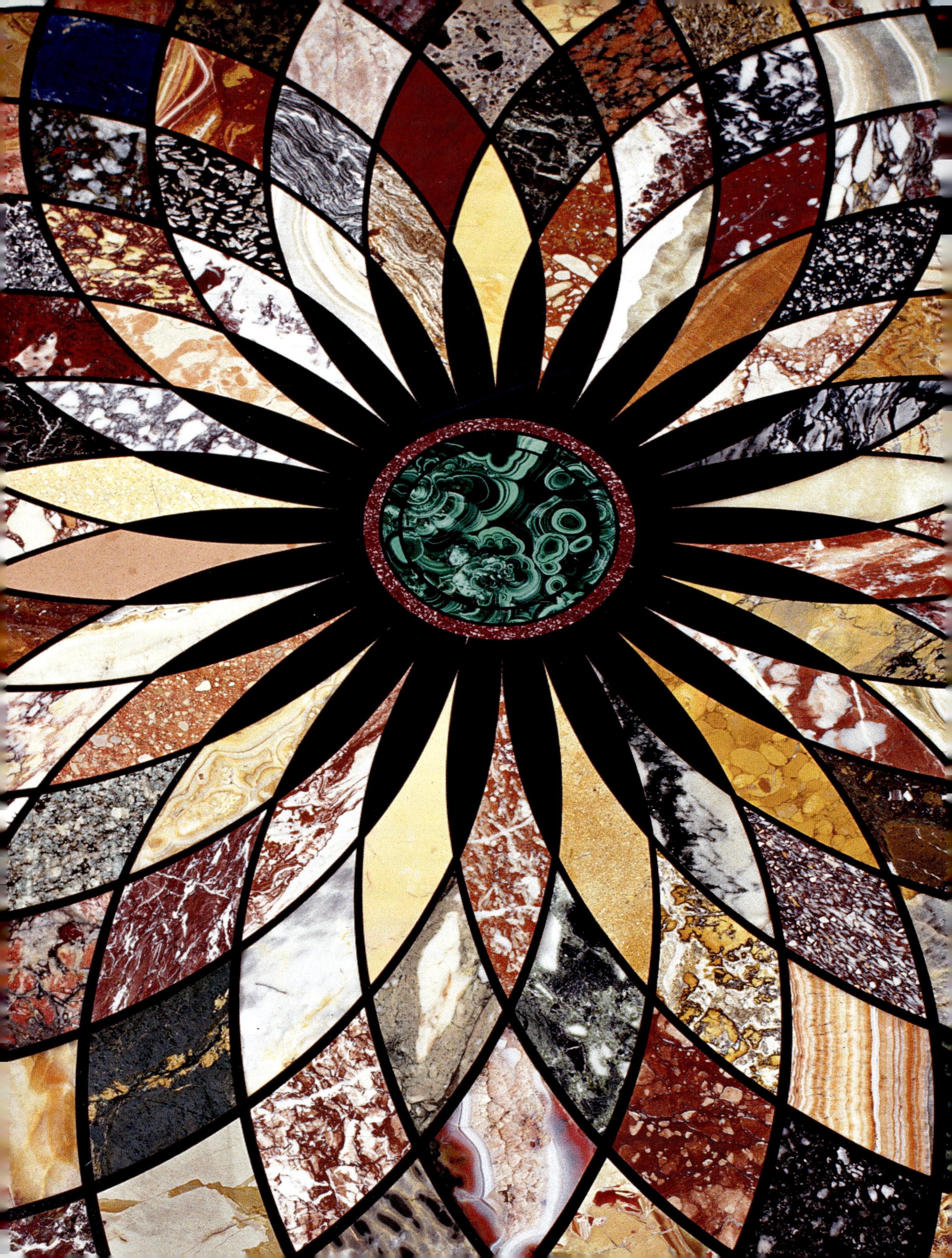

Art at the Rockface
The Fascination of Stone

WITH A FOREWORD BY ANDREW SMITH

EDITED BY ANDREW MOORE AND NIGEL LARKIN

With contributions by

FRANCESCA VANKE ALTMAN
GIORGIA BOTTINELLI
NICHOLAS THORNTON
NORMA WATT

NORFOLK Museums & Archaeology Service

SHEFFIELD GALLERIES & MUSEUMS TRUST

Philip Wilson Publishers 2006

The publication of this book accompanies an exhibition at Norwich Castle Museum & Art Gallery (22 May – 3 September 2006) and Millenium Galleries, Sheffield (23 September – 7 January 2007).

First published in 2006 by
Philip Wilson Publishers
109 Drysdale Street
London
N1 6ND

Distributed throughout the world
(excluding North America) by
I.B. Tauris & Co. Ltd
6 Salem Road
London W2 4BU

Distributed in North America by
Palgrave Macmillan, a division of
St Martin's Press
175 Fifth Avenue
New York NY 10010

Designed by Peter Ling
Printed in Italy by Printer Trento

ISBN: 0 85667 612 8 (hardback)
IBSN: 0 90310 179 3 (paperback)

Esmée Fairbairn Foundation

Bringing great art to the East — East Anglia Art Fund

Illustration, half-title page, frontispiece and p. 11

Collector's Table with scalloped edge Design (detail), 1829

WORKSHOP OF GIACOMO RAFFAELLI, ROME
Carrara marble, *pietre dure* and ancient and modern marbles
91.5 x 100 cm diameter
Trinity College, Cambridge

This is a magnificent example of the art of *pietre dure,* a painstaking technique of inlaying cut and shaped marble and semi-precious stones. Such artworks were highly prized both for their level of craftsmanship and for the luxurious nature of the materials. This particular example is not only an extraordinarily patterned and coloured work of art, it is also a classic study piece intended for intellectual and scientific scrutiny, containing over 133 separate stones cut and polished for comparative purposes. Purchased by Daniel Pettiward in 1829, it was accompanied by a detailed list describing each of the stones and their origin. The florally spiracular design is far more elaborate than that of most such tables collected on the Grand Tour and must have been a challenging piece to execute. It is as useful for those wishing to learn about stones and geology now in the twenty-first century as it was when it was made.

The workshop of Giacomo Raffaelli operated from 92 Via del Babuino, in Rome. The certificate of sale consisted of ten pages listing the sources of each of the stones encircling the central one of 'Siberian Malachite' and described the table in these terms:

> *Of a Magnificent Table in white Carrara Marble for 'Dejeuné' purposes, in a new Geometric shape composed of twenty-six interwoven Ellipses with a shared centre, encrusted with choice Pietre Dure, Ancient and Modern Marbles, and so that it can be beneficial to the understanding and study of the Stones, here are added their Specification, Denomination and Provenance....*

Daniel Pettiward was ordained Deacon at Norwich in 1789 and was Rector of Great Finborough, Suffolk from 1798–1833. Trinity College, Cambridge was his *alma mater* and in addition to the marble table, he gave Trinity College Library some 5,000 books, many of them of an antiquarian nature and also related to the Grand Tour (Trinity College Library, MS Add.a.151). NL

Contents

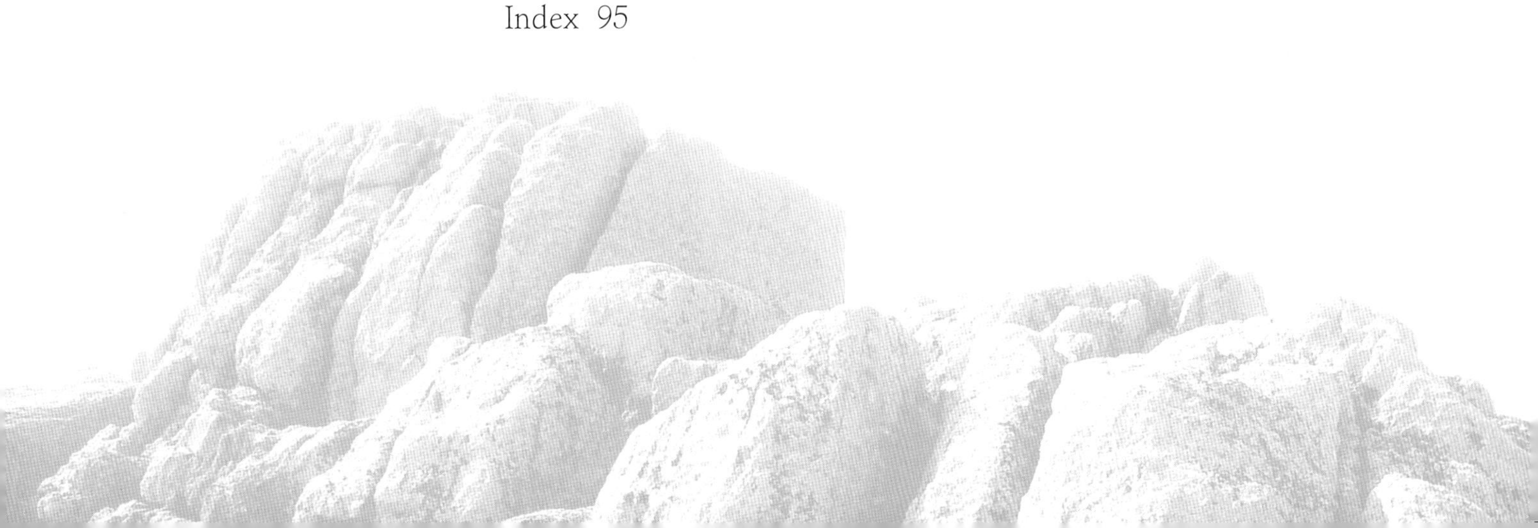

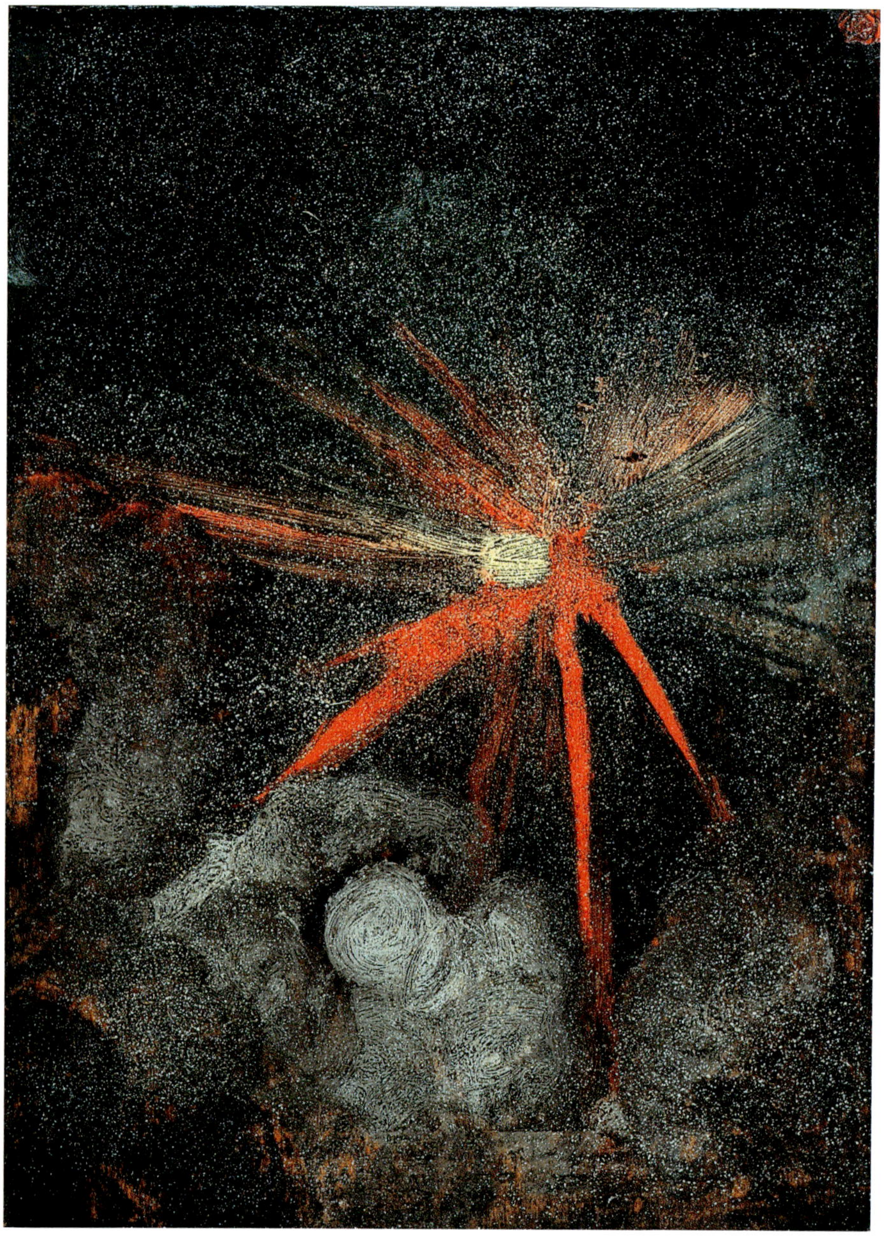

A Heavenly Body, c. 1496

ALBRECHT DÜRER (1471–1528)
Oil on wood, 23.1 x 17.4 cm

National Gallery, London. Bought with the assistance of the Heritage Lottery Fund, the National Art Collections Fund and Mr J. Paul Getty Jr through the American Friends of the National Gallery, 1996.

This painting of a heavenly body in the night sky appears on the reverse of the devotional panel painting by Dürer of *Saint Jerome* (see p. 71). Dürer, celebrated for his study of nature, here extends his scientific approach and depicts a cosmological event to affirm celestial portent, a theme consistent with the image of the Saint on the front of the panel. The red star-like light and streaking golden disc has been thought to be an eclipse or meteor, but it is almost certainly a comet. Dürer's image is probably derived from woodcuts of comets published in the *Nuremberg Chronicle* of 1493 and he again included a similar image in the sky of his engraving of *Melencolia 1* (1514). Early scientific investigation of comets was centred on Nuremburg during his childhood and the astronomer Bernhard Walther was a family friend. Indeed, after Walther's death Dürer bought his house, the upper floor of which was an observatory (M. Bailey, 'Dürer's Comet', *Apollo*, March 1995, 29–32).

Dürer's interest in cosmography suggests a specific meaning for his image of Saint Jerome kneeling before a crucifix. Dürer could well be referencing the third stage of *Melancolia rationalis*, which encompasses theology and the divine secrets (E. Panofsky, *Albrecht Dürer*, 1943, I, 168). The evening sky on the front gives rise to the divine portent on the reverse. This combination mirrors the Saint's learned status as a Father of the Church, but also Dürer's own intellectual curiosity.

In 1497 the artist was also working on his woodcuts of the Apocalypse. The specific text to which Dürer alludes may be the description of the Last Judgement in the Book of Revelation, when 'there fell a great star from heaven, burning as if it were a lamp' (Revelation 8, 7–12). However, his contemporary woodcut of *The Martyrdom of St Catherine* bears a closer resemblance to this astral body than his woodcut depiction of the falling stars of the Apocalypse. AM

Foreword

BETWEEN 1969 AND 1972, twelve human beings set down on the surface of the moon. Hundreds of millions of people watched and listened as they dropped to the surface, then proceeded to explore this alien world. It was an extraordinary human story which fired the imagination and set pulses racing. Yet if you'd asked anyone at NASA what the astronauts' most important task was, they would have replied as one: it was to bring back rocks. The rocks, it was felt, held the keys to our own self-knowledge.

This is why *Art at the Rockface* makes such perfect sense to me. When I came to write a book about the surreal adventure of the Apollo project, I was determined that it would be about people rather than geology, but separating the two turned out to be impossible. On Apollo 15, the fourth mission to land, for instance, Jim Irwin happened upon the crystalline 'Genesis Rock', a 4.15 billion-year-old relic of primordial crust formed in Moon's infancy – in geologic terms, mere moments after the solar system was born. It just sat there on a rocky pulpit at the edge of a crater, as if on an outstretched hand, waiting for him, and he later insisted that in that moment he heard the voice of God in his ear. When he returned home, he quit NASA to found a ministry. Irwin knew exactly what William Blake meant when he spoke of seeing 'a world in a grain of sand'.

Indeed, perhaps the most profound discovery to emerge from the space programme arose from a small incident which has hardly been remarked upon. When Apollo 12 landed in November 1969, one of its minor objectives was to retrieve a camera from an unmanned probe NASA had sent up a short while before. This the crew did, and when the device was examined back on earth, it was found that a technician had sneezed into it during its manufacture, leaving traces of streptococcal bacteria upon it – and that the bacteria had unexpectedly survived in the void of space. This meant that the 'panspermia' argument – that primitive life might have arrived on earth aboard a meteorite, a *lump of rock*, was feasible. In light of this, Henry Moore's repeated urge to carve the image of mother and child in stone has a kind of primal logic, as does Michelangelo's belief that his sculpture involved releasing what was already contained in the rock, or the ancients' propensity to find gods in it.

All of which is simply a way of saying that, while this thrilling exhibition might at first glance look to be about geology, its true subject is us, our secret longings and search for meaning through the miracle of time and of the universe itself. My own first thought as I pondered the exhibits concerned disbelief that no one had done it before. My second took me back to a holiday on the north coast of Brittany; to a particular place where, as the tide recedes, what previously appeared to be a series of grassy mounds just offshore become huge, looming figures, as dramatic as anything you might see in an art gallery. At the time, I remember gasping 'My God, they're like sculptures.' Yet if *Art at the Rockface* teaches me one thing, it's that I should have said 'My God, sculptures are like *them*.'

ANDREW SMITH

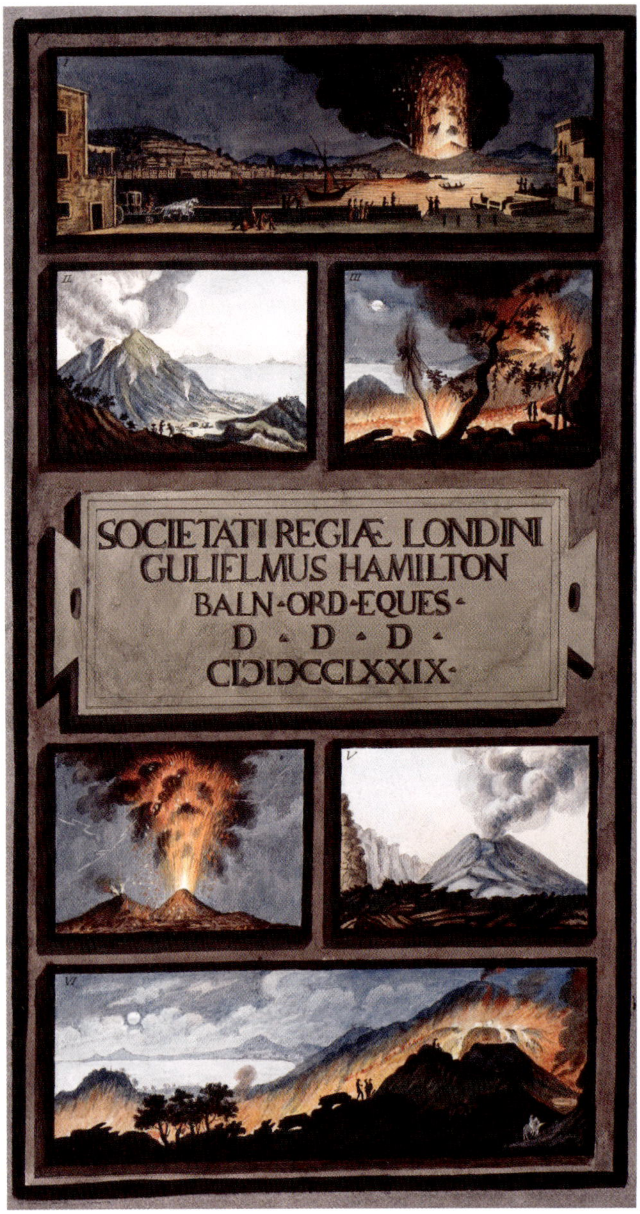

Campi Phlegraei

Frontispiece to the 1779 Supplement to *'Campi Phlegraei, Observations on the Volcanoes of the Two Sicilies, As They have been communicated to the Royal Society of London' by Sir William Hamilton, Naples, 1776*, 1779
PIETRO FABRIS (1740–92)
Etching and watercolour in printed book
46 x 34.4 cm
Courtesy of the Trustees of the Natural History Museum, London

Sir William Hamilton (1730–1803) arrived in Naples in 1764 as the British envoy to the court of Ferdinand IV, King of the Two Sicilies. Shortly after his arrival nearby Vesuvius began to erupt and Hamilton, a collector, scholar and keen natural historian, studiously recorded its activity, together with that of Etna and the region. He watched Vesuvius erupt on several occasions and climbed the unpredictable volcano over seventy times, making notes and collecting specimens as he went. His studies were subsequently published in the Philosophical Transactions of the Royal Society, London.

Hamilton produced a very grand publication in 1776 entitled *Campi Phlegraei, Observations on the Volcanoes of the Two Sicilies.* This contained fifty-four beautifully executed hand-coloured etchings of scenes depicting fiery eruptions and smoking vents as well as detailed depictions of rocks and lava specimens. This monumental work is still considered the most lavishly illustrated treatise ever published about volcanoes. Pietro Fabris (fl.1756–84), an artist living in Naples, was specifically employed by Hamilton to illustrate the work. At the time this was the very best scientific publication available on volcanic activity and it secured Hamilton's name as an early pioneer of vulcanology. Three years later a supplement with five hand-coloured plates was published, showing the eruption of August 1779.

In the eighteenth century Naples was one of the largest cities in Europe. It was famous for its natural beauty, artistic riches and the antiquities that were being unearthed from the nearby Roman cities of Herculaneum and Pompeii, buried since 79 AD. by volcanic ash. All these factors, as well as the presence of the intellectual and hospitable Hamilton, were more than enough reason for Grand Tourists to include Naples in their itinerary. The extraordinary images of volcanic activity in this publication added greatly to the reputation of Naples as an attractive and exotic destination. NL

Introduction & Acknowledgements

NOTHING ILLUMINATES the brevity of human life for us more clearly than our understanding of the planet on which we live. Artists over the millennia have responded to the geological environment surrounding them and have preserved a record of our relationship with the earth as a source of inspiration.

This book examines the principal ways by which artists have explored the geology of landscapes and the forms within individual stones in their quest for truth. In the writings of Leonardo da Vinci we learn that his exploration of the environment parallels his study of the human body: the study of geology has been as long-lived for man as his fascination with his own body, in life and death. Those who sculpt with the chisel, grind pigments, create landscapes, fashion jewellery or work with graphite are connecting directly to the rock beneath their feet. Early people drew or painted on the rockface and fashioned flint by which to live. More recently humankind has selected stone to build and sculpt, often making symbols for worship and we have consistently conferred values, properties and meanings upon selected stones.

The study of stone in art cannot be separated from that of the forces that have made the Earth. At times a belief in the sacred has informed artists' desire to make art. To cite just one example, in Japan Mount Fuji has a central, essential presence which is both geological and sacred within Japanese society, being host to numerous Shintō and Buddhist deities. Indeed, Fuji is the focus of the Shugendō sect of Buddhism founded in the ninth century, which venerates not only mountains but mountain-climbing. A similar sense of the spiritual finds parallels in Chinese culture and in Western culture. Today artists are among those inspired to explore form and meaning in ways that invite a contemplative and sometimes explicit spiritual response. Equally, other non-spiritual themes remain common to different cultures, notably those of study or transformation, myth and memory, all fundamental to our sense of ourselves. These themes are the foundation upon which this study of the fascination and meaning of stone in the history of art is built.

Conceived as a companion to the exhibition *Art at the Rockface* (Norwich Castle Museum & Art Gallery 22 May–3 September 2006; Millennium Galleries, Sheffield: 23 September 2006–7 January 2007), six thematic chapters echo those of the exhibition. The colour plates and descriptive texts discuss approximately half of the total number of works of art in the exhibition, aiming to explore the themes in more depth than is possible in a visit to an exhibition. The breadth and diversity of the artworks selected for this publication aim to highlight the range of ideas that were presented by the exhibition, rather than to provide a full record of the entire show. Norwich Castle Museum & Art Gallery was delighted to win the top award offered by the Esmée Fairbairn Foundation's Regional Museums Initiative programme to make this concept a reality, in association with Sheffield Museums and Galleries Trust. We have greatly enjoyed working with our colleagues in Sheffield and have received considerable support from national and regional museums and galleries, as well as private collections, as the project has developed. By lending to the exhibition, owners jointly encouraged an engagement with the works of art and geological specimens in an entirely new way. Many contributors responded directly to the initiative of the Esmée Fairbairn Foundation by supporting this thematic approach to understanding the wealth of regional as well as national art collections.

It is important to record those numerous institutions and individuals who were lenders to the exhibition. Without their support this book would not have been possible. Our thanks go to: Her Majesty the Queen; Art Space Gallery, London; Birmingham Museums and Art Gallery; Bolton Museum, Art Gallery & Aquarium; Ivor Braka Ltd, London; Gary Breeze; Bristol Museums and Art Gallery; The British Council, London; The British Museum, London; Julian Cooper; Thomas Joshua Cooper; Courtauld Gallery, Courtauld Institute of Art, London; Cresswell Heritage Trust; Eastnor Castle Collection; The Fitzwilliam Museum, Cambridge; The Gilbert Collection, London; The Goldsmiths Company, London; The Guild of St George, Sheffield; Harris Museum and Art Gallery, Preston; Jacqueline Hassink; Haunch of Venison, London; Houldsworth, London; James Hyman Fine Art, London; Tania Kovats; Clare Langan; Leeds City Art Gallery; The Library and Museum of Freemasonry, London; Lord Leicester and the Trustees of the Holkham Estate; The Museum of London; Tadayuki Naitoh; The National Gallery, London; The National Portrait Gallery, London; The Natural History Museum, London; Nottingham Castle Museum and Art Gallery; Paul Rosenbloom; Royal Academy of Arts, London; Salisbury and South Wiltshire Museum; Scott Polar Research Institute, Cambridge; The Sedgwick Museum of Earth Sciences, Cambridge; Tate, London; Towneley Hall Art Gallery & Museum, Burnley; Trinity College, Cambridge; Victoria and Albert Museum, London; Watts Gallery, Guildford; Winsor Bishop Ltd, Norwich; World Museum, Liverpool; York Museums Trust (York Art Gallery) and Emily Young. In addition, we thank those who wish to remain anonymous. Photography credits and copyright acknowledgements are given on page 93.

We particularly wish to thank our contributing authors and colleagues, Francesca Vanke Altman, Giorgia Bottinelli, Nicholas Thornton and Norma Watt, whose contributions have immeasurably enriched the insights of this publication. We are also grateful to Andrew Smith for contributing the Foreword. Writers, mountaineers and even astronauts are fascinated by the geology of our planet. For his best-selling book, *Moondust: In Search of the Men who Fell to Earth*, Andrew Smith interviewed all those lunar astronauts who participated in the Apollo programme, including the twelve who have walked on the moon (one of whom became a painter of moonscapes). His work well demonstrates the universality of the theme of this book. In addition, a number of individuals have generously provided information and expertise. We are grateful in particular to the following for their help with research and development: Martin Barnes; Frances Carey; Tim Clark; Diane Clements; Caroline Cook; Simon Dell; Edwina Ehrman; European Regional Development Fund; Susan Foister; Matthew Gale; Anne Goodchild; Rica Jones; Caroline Krzesinska; Lafarge Aggregates; David McKitterick; Tessa Murdoch; Venetia Porter; Louise Pullen; Jane Roberts; Judy Rudoe; Fiona Salvesen; Nicholas Savage; Chris Stephens. Finally, we would like to express our appreciation of Anne Jackson, Peter Ling, Philip Wilson and his publishing team.

ANDREW MOORE
NIGEL LARKIN

Painting with Stone

Mere colour, unspoiled by meaning and unallied with definite form, can speak to the soul in a thousand different ways

OSCAR WILDE, 'THE CRITIC AS ARTIST', *INTENTIONS*, 1891

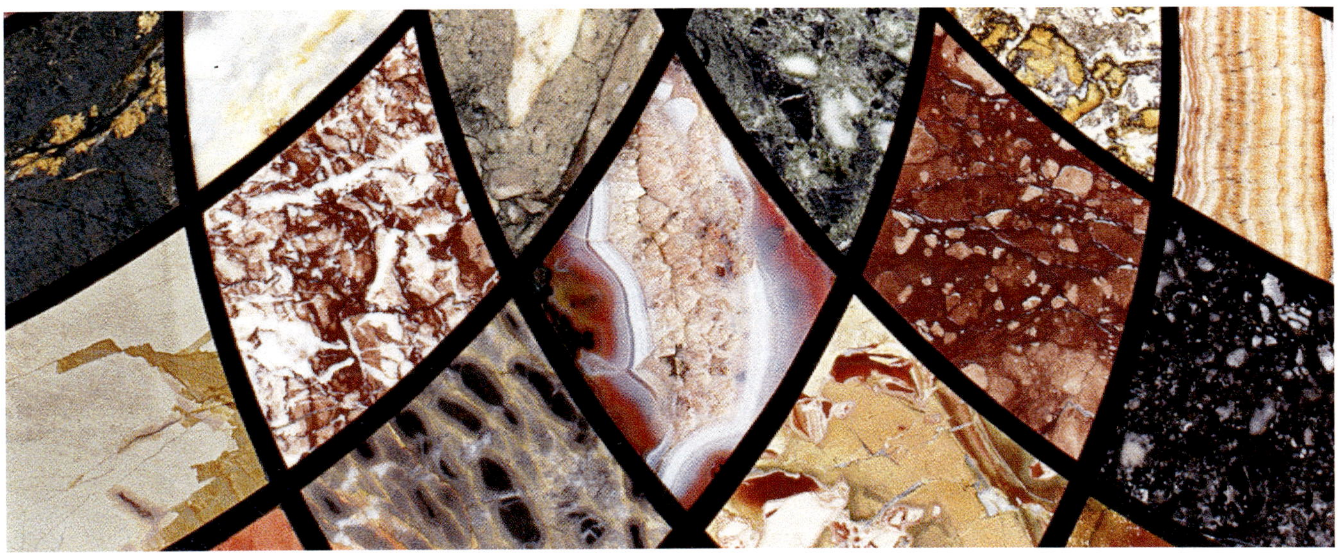

Introduction

There is a direct and intimate association between the worlds of art and geology that provides a colourful tale encompassing prehistoric shamanism, medieval alchemical experimentation, poisonings and long-distance trade. Quite apart from sculpting stone, engraving rockfaces and extracting metals for jewellery and statuary, mankind has consistently looked to the geological landscape of his surroundings to provide not only a canvas on which to paint, but the very colours to paint it with. The tradition of using minerals as pigments has continued unbroken since early humans first coloured their bodies with ochres as early as 70,000 years ago, followed by painting rock shelters and the walls of caves so eloquently from around 40,000 years ago. Although plant extracts, the remains of insects and beetles and even ground-up Egyptian mummies have occasionally been used as pigments in the past, minerals have been – and remain – the most vital ingredient in pigment manufacture.

All the paintings of the world, including the greatest of masterpieces, were once only pigments waiting on a palette. In its simplest form a pigment is a finely powdered mineral, sometimes mixed with another, and usually mechanically bound to the chosen surface with a fluid medium. This 'binder' can also enhance the colour and promote its longevity. As in prehistoric times, indigenous cultures today use many types of binders: water, wax, egg yolk, spit, urine, animal fat, bone marrow, blood, plant resins and, in the case of Maoris, the oil from shark's liver.

The colours on a palette or in a work of art can only be created from substances available at the time. These are determined by local geology, historical trade routes and current technology. The combined

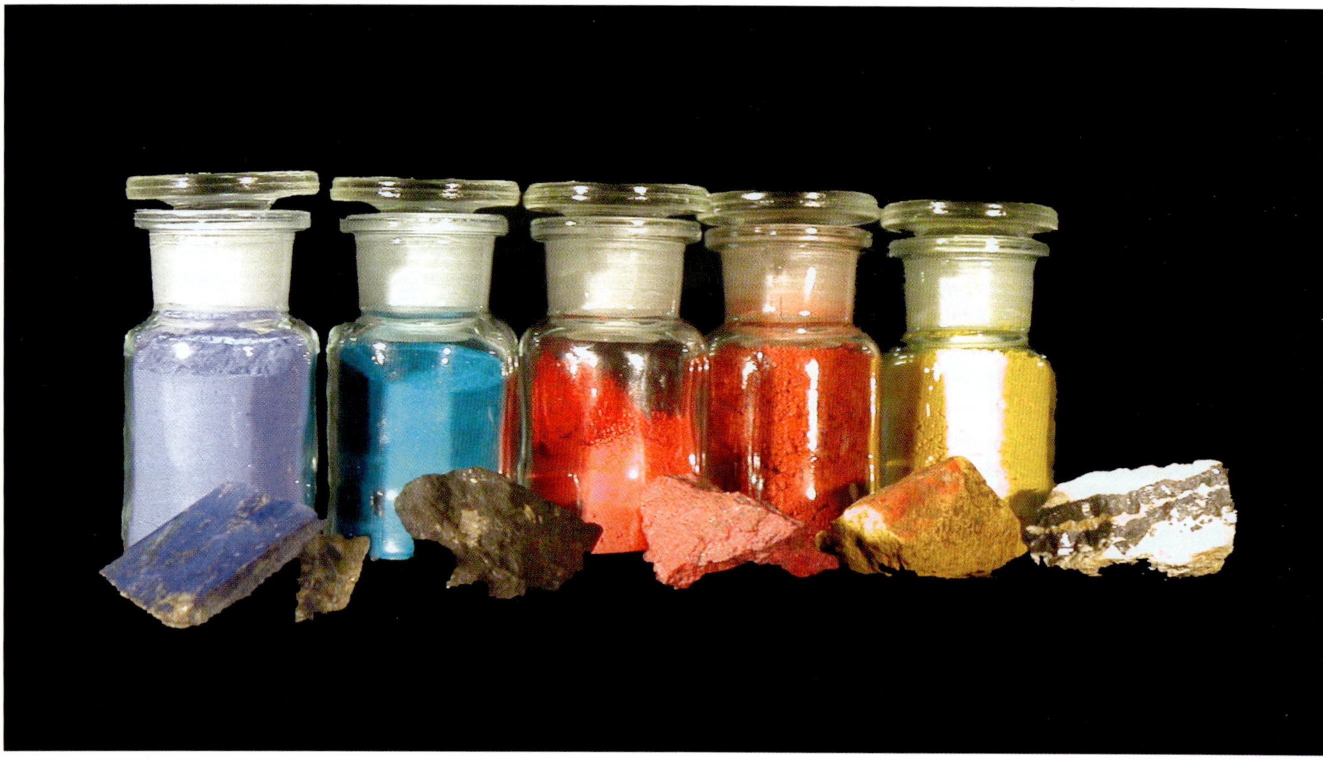

Five important milestones in the history of manufacturing pigments (from left to right): ultramarine, made from lapis lazuli from Afghanistan; verdigris, made from copper sulphate; vermilion, made from cinnabar; red ochre; and chrome yellow, made from lead sulphate.

evolution of these three factors has taken us from utilising the mud beneath our bare feet through the use of oil paints, watercolours and acrylics to employing airbrushes and aerosol cans today. The art lies in an individual's ability to manipulate the materials currently available, often in novel ways. Daring to exploit newly available colours created through experimentation or brought in by trade can both lead fashion and induce criticism. Pliny, for example, worried about new pigments from the East – bright reds and yellows – corrupting the established conservative Roman palette, while Constable and later the Impressionists were criticised for painting only with intense colours.

The Earth Palette

In prehistoric times, and in many indigenous cultures today, colours have been obtained from animal, vegetable and mineral sources to adorn tools, weapons and bodies and to make pictures on bark, cloth or rockfaces. Most colours from botanical sources, although easily accessible, were found to fade quickly but earths, ochres and clays of varied colours from yellows and reds to browns were discovered to be just as accessible and even more stable – indeed, some artworks made entirely of these materials have already lasted for tens of thousands of years.

The oldest known example of 'art' in the world is a 77,000-year-old block of red ochre engraved with repeated lines. Found in a cave in Blombos, South Africa, this block had been carved out of a piece of ochre derived from a deposit several miles away. For the next 70,000-odd thousand years ochre was to be the pigment of choice and ancient examples of rock art utilising ochres are known from every populated continent of the world. More recent bark paintings by Australian Aborigines demonstrate how ochres would have been used on materials less durable than rock which simply have not survived, unlike the exquisitely executed artworks they painted on rockfaces over 40,000 years ago.

Ochres are naturally occurring earths consisting of silica and clay with varying amounts and types of iron oxides, giving a huge variety of yellows, reds, browns, even purples. The reds contain ferric oxide (hemætite, from the Greek *Hæma*, for blood); the yellows contain iron oxide minerals such as goethite, and brown ochres are almost pure limonite. Found with relative ease all over the world, they vary in hue, consistency and permanence. White pigments were made from kaolin clay, chalk or gypsum and black pigments either from manganese nodules, powdered jet, or wood charcoal or soot. Reds, browns, yellows, blacks and whites provide the palette for most indigenous cultures. These colours, for which the earliest mines were created independently many times throughout the ancient world, were not actually necessities, but luxury goods. This clearly demonstrates an appreciation of aesthetics and a culture of visual symbolism deeply held within the human psyche.

Although some ochres are hard and brittle and need grinding to produce a powder, sometimes ochre is oxidized, soft and in a pure enough form that no processing is needed. Ochre 'crayons' of pure pigment cut directly from the earth and simply shaped were discovered in the Lascaux cave in France where some of the most stunning prehistoric artwork in the world has been dated to 20,000 years old. Some of the images were made by spraying the pigment out of the artist's mouth, possibly through a tube such as a bird or animal bone, bamboo or reed, but most were 'painted' directly onto the rockfaces with fingers.

Ochre has been in continuous use for tens of thousands of years and was the mainstay of artwork produced in ancient cultures including Australian Aboriginels, European Cro-Magnons, New Zealand Maoris, Egyptians, Romans, Central Americans, 'Red' Indians, and more recently in all periods of European painting.

Interestingly, much prehistoric European art seems to have been deliberately positioned deep within cave systems that are difficult to access, indicating that the caves themselves had symbolic value and suggesting ritualistic, ceremonial or shamanistic meanings for the artworks. Oral traditions relating to the ancient use and meanings of colours and pigments can still be found in some indigenous cultures today. The Aboriginal bark-painters of Arnhem Land in Australia still utilise ochres quarried from sites of important ritual and political significance, and the acquiring and utilisation of ochre can involve sophisticated rituals. Red ochres are often associated with the blood of ancestor-beings who now reside in the earth, and white clay is used in mourning. In some aboriginal burial ceremonies the body is ritually painted with clan designs after death, then after decomposition the bones are painted with red ochre before being crushed and placed in a painted hollow log coffin left exposed to the elements. Similarly, many prehistoric European burials have included painting the bones of the deceased with red ochre before burial, or burying the dead with lumps of ochre for use in the afterlife. In many cultures the colour red is intimately associated with blood, the most obvious and important of bodily fluids, and therefore perhaps the obvious choice to represent life-force during funerary activities. Red can also be associated with transition as it can represent the pivotal moments of dawn and sunset, dividing day and night and hence symbolically life and afterlife.

Throughout Polynesia, the use of red ochre denotes sacred value and high rank. From the island of Lemnos in the Northern Aegean comes the famous red ochre 'Lemnian earth', used by Odysseus on the prows of his ships, and for decorating Greek vases in antiquity. Originally collected by the priestesses of

Artemis and stamped with a seal of the Goddess, this red earth was supposed to have come from the forge of Hephaestus, the Greek God of Fire. Until the nineteenth century almost all buildings that were decorated were painted with ochres or lime wash as they were the only colours available in large enough quantities. The effect was that such vernacular architecture tended to blend in with the surrounding landscapes on the one hand, or shine conspicuously from a distance on the other. Ochre continued to be used in Europe throughout the Renaissance and the Middle Ages and is still utilized today in industrial quantities.

Creating Colour

No doubt many ancient cultures began to experiment with more than just ochres for their cave paintings, rock art, body art and permanent tattoos, but we know most about the artists of ancient Egypt. The manufacture of pigments was of great importance to the Egyptians because the artists were priests and their artwork devotional and endowed with symbolism and power. They created a wider and brighter range of colours than was previously available, made from minerals found occurring naturally in the surrounding desert. They ground malachite (a basic copper carbonate) into a powder and added sand and salt and heated it in kilns to achieve various hues of green. They were the first people to really experiment with heating and blending minerals in this way to make new colours.

The Egyptians found that by melting sand with copper minerals and chalk and grinding up the result, a blue pigment was made – possibly the very first synthetic, deliberately made pigment. Remaining in use until medieval times, this 'Egyptian blue' was used on the Ishtar gates of Ancient Babylon and can still be seen on the walls of the tombs of the Valley of the Kings today looking as bright as the day it was applied. They also heated quartz, malachite powder and calcium carbonate together to make a pale blue. Green could be made by altering the mixture of malachite and calcium carbonate, but more usually ground malachite was simply used on its own. They also used powdered green malachite for make-up, as well as black lead, but for their devotional artworks their palette included red ochre, carnelian, gold (either the real thing or a substitute made from orpiment, a poisonous arsenic sulphide), orange (realgar, another arsenic sulphide), turquoise, lapis lazuli and malachite greens and blues – a diverse colour range that subsequently inspired many other cultures.

The Greeks knew of the wide range of colours in the Egyptian palette, but generally restricted theirs to just four: black, white, red and yellow. This austere restriction of colours was the favoured palette for classical artists for centuries and was subsequently employed by the Romans, perhaps partly because earth colours including umbers, siennas and greens were so easily available locally in the nearby hills. However, the pigments used freely throughout the Roman Empire (as in Egypt) for cosmetic purposes seem to have been far brighter and included (poisonous) lead sulphide for silvers or greys, malachite for greens, azurite (also a copper carbonate, found as blue prisms and crystal masses) for blues, and hæmatite (iron oxide) for reds.

In classical times, Naples yellow (lead antimonite, found on the slopes of Vesuvius and highly toxic) was extremely popular among painters and its use can be traced back to about 1400 BC. 'Lead white', the finest white pigment used by painters from prehistoric times until the nineteenth century, was made by exposing raw lead to the fumes of vinegar and animal dung. By the second century AD, this was taken further by roasting white lead to make lead tetroxide, which is red, and roasting it again to make a yellow pigment called litharge or massicot.

The Colour Blue

Ultramarine, gold leaf and vermilion were the most prized colours of the European Middle Ages, and each of these had to be mined from the ground and processed. Materials that are rare locally and have to be imported are often seen as precious and beautiful and pigments are no exception. In medieval times pigments were important articles of trade and the brightest, rarest and most exotic were transported great distances. Although blue seems an abundant colour in nature it is quite elusive in geological terms and as it is a primary colour it cannot be made by mixing other pigments together. As a result, the rare blue mineral lapis lazuli was traded from deposits in north-eastern Afghanistan all round the known world to be used as the pigment ultramarine blue. Chiefly a sulphur-containing silicate of sodium and aluminium, when powdered and taken through an elaborate purification process lapis lazuli was regarded as valuable as semi-precious stones, sometimes worth more than its weight in gold. For centuries it was the most precious of all artists' colours and was reserved for the most revered of subjects. Its expense was akin to using gold foil and provided a means of making a devotional offering. Because of this the colour blue came to be considered a devotional colour representing royalty, pure thoughts and heaven. Poorer artists during this period rarely used blues in their paintings as they could not afford them; to own a painting containing blue colours was regarded as a status symbol. Although still expensive, a more affordable 'mountain blue' was extracted from a type of copper called azurite. It was highly prized by the artists of Renaissance Europe and remained the most widely used blue pigment until Prussian blue replaced it in the eighteenth century.

The Medieval Palette

The medieval palette, essentially the same as that used in classical times, was still made by the artists who ground the raw minerals and blended them. They understood that the quality of their art depended on the quality of these materials. These artists found allies in the alchemists, who were not just obsessed with the search for gold but experimented with many types of transformations. They often turned rocks and minerals into interesting new pigments as a by-product, creating a new range of manufactured colours to be utilised by the emerging Renaissance artists.

One example of this can be seen in the use of the bright red mineral cinnabar (Greek for 'of oriental origin'), which forms close to recently created volcanic rocks and hot springs. Cinnabar primarily contains sulphur and mercury and consequently has a sparkling and glittery quality, which encouraged the alchemists to experiment with it in their search for gold. They achieved an unexpected result in a hard, blackish red substance that turned bright red when ground up: vermilion. Although this technique had been employed in China as early as the third millennium BC, this was the first time it had been discovered in the West. The consequent manufacture of vermilion by processing cinnabar became big business (even though it was often bulked-out with brick dust) but slaves who mined the mineral in Spain often died within three years, as it is so poisonous.

The discovery of this intense red livened up palettes considerably, resulting in a compulsion to find equally intense greens and blues. With the discovery of these new colours artists began to mix these with oils, rather than binders such as water or egg. This allowed a greater range of shade and tone to be used, bringing more subtlety to the works of art of the Renaissance. This enabled scenes to be depicted with increased realism. However, many of the traditional pigments looked transparent and less brilliant in oil and the addition of lead white was required to make the colour stronger.

Drawing

Renaissance artists, like cave painters before them, used natural chalks made from mineral pigments dug straight out of the earth and shaped into sticks, ready for drawing. Natural red chalks were very popular from about 1500 to 1900 and were used by, amongst others, Leonardo da Vinci, Michelangelo and Rubens.

The mineral graphite, a mass of flaky carbon crystals, whilst not actually a pigment has an important place in the history of art. Graphite was discovered by artists in the seventeenth century. For hundreds of years charcoal had been the main medium for sketching out compositions before applying paints but it was brittle, smudged easily and could run when paints were applied. Pure graphite held together by firing at high temperatures, however, left behind a good dark line that did not smudge or run, and could be used to create subtleties of shade and depth. Low-quality graphite could be improved simply by the addition of clay. Graphite in the form of pencils subsequently travelled all around the world, valued by amateurs and great artists alike for its immediacy, and was frequently used to capture the essence of foreign landscapes as sketches.

Modern Colour

Many pigments used by artists up until the eighteenth century, whether simply collected directly from the ground or subsequently processed, created problems: they were either poisonous (many contained lead or arsenic) or could easily fade – or both. Emerald green, first made in the early nineteenth century from copper sulphide and copper arsenic, was a brighter green than had hitherto been available. As it could be made cheaply it appeared in household paints and coloured wallpapers as well as on artists' palettes. Unfortunately, dampness caused the mineral pigments to give off a toxic gas, famously poisoning Napoleon in his bedroom whilst imprisoned on Saint Helena.

In the eighteenth and nineteenth centuries modern synthetic pigments began to be produced as by-products of industrial experimentation when pure elements of raw materials were isolated. The ranges of colours available to artists increased dramatically and were more stable, longer lasting, cheaper, more readily available and safer. They were also much purer and brighter, and this helped to stimulate new ways of seeing – indeed, a new artistic movement: Impressionism.

Colour and Light

Partly as a response to the new art of black and white photography, and partly because they could now use premixed paints in tubes (rather than grinding and mixing dry pigment powders with linseed oil themselves), artists could more easily paint outdoors rather than in studios. The Impressionists captured the momentary and transient aspects of sunlight by using short brush strokes of pure unmixed pigments and applying bright colours to convey spontaneity, vitality and joy. This new approach with its modern, vibrant colours never seen before on canvas was deeply criticized at the time, and many Impressionists could only get their work displayed in the *Salon des Refusés.*

Impressionists could not have achieved the same bright, airy and controversial effects without the discovery of new chemical elements such as zinc, chromium, cadmium and cobalt, and the subsequent pigments they spawned including cobalt green, zinc oxide, cerulean blue and cadmium red, orange and yellow – all made from the same family of metallic minerals. Of the palette of twenty colours most frequently used by Impressionist painters, twelve were newly discovered and manufactured.

The first synthetic colour of the Industrial Revolution was Prussian blue, discovered accidentally by Heinrich Diesbach in 1704 whilst trying to formulate artificial crimson with salt, potash and a chemical compound made from blood. But one of the most significant discoveries, made in 1797 by the French chemist Louis-Nicholas Vauquelin, was a new type of lead in a red Siberian metallic mineral called crocoite. He named the new material chromium after the Greek word for colour because this single new element spawned more pigments and a greater colour range than any other single element in history. Most famous of these colours is chrome yellow. A favourite of Van Gogh's, this appeared in many of his paintings including his famous 'Sunflowers' series. In 1817 Dr Friedrich Stromeyer, professor of chemistry and pharmacy at Göttingen University, discovered cadmium, a by-product of zinc smelting which produced yellows, oranges and reds much favoured by Gauguin and Matisse. Cadmium finally displaced one of the longest used pigments, vermilion.

In 1802 the French chemist Louis Jacques Thénard made a new rich blue and the first pure purple pigment, both from cobalt. But a replacement for the time-honoured and expensive deep blue of ultramarine made from lapis lazuli was not found until 1824. Produced by burning sulphur with other minerals and having an almost identical chemical composition, this synthetic substitute replaced lapis lazuli overnight and the colour became available to even the poorest of artists.

It is perhaps a paradox that it was the work of chemists in the industrialized urban world that stimulated artists to work principally outdoors around Europe, capturing the bright, airy and colourful rural landscapes threatened by the industrialised world. The Impressionists were the first artists to be freed from the constraints of a limited palette, so it is perhaps not surprising that many of their paintings are now worth more than their weight in gold. However, the Impressionists were not the only artists to benefit from these new colours. J.M.W. Turner was one of the first painters in England to make use of cobalt blue, emerald green, viridian and chrome yellow, amongst others. The use of these bright new colours resulted in Turner's pictures being criticised as 'colouring run mad'.

Colour Today

In the 1950s Yves Klein noticed that pigments always look their richest and best before use. With the help of chemists, he invented and patented a way of suspending pure, dry, synthetic ultramarine blue pigment in a crystal-clear synthetic resin and compatible solvent as a binder. Unlike traditional binders, the new colourless carrier did not dull the individual particles of the pigment but left them with their original brightness and intensity and a matt, velvety texture. He exhibited his International Klein Blue in a series of monochrome paintings in the 1950s, believing that the colour alone would suffice to communicate his message without the distractions of line and form. A significant number of modern artists believe in the spiritual and symbolic value of pigments and their power to transform. Pigments have played a key role in the work of artists like Anish Kapoor whose early sculptures consisted of shapes covered in pure pigments of red, yellow and blue.

Pigment manufacture is now big business. It is still mineral-based, but involves huge industrial processes. Titanium dioxide, manufactured from the dark titanium minerals rutile and ilmenite, is an essential ingredient in modern paints and has replaced the previously widespread but poisonous 'white lead'. Today the modern artist has a greater range and variety of durable and safe pigments from which to choose than at any other time in history. Yet our palettes and our paintings are still only available to us by the grace of geological history.

Nigel Larkin

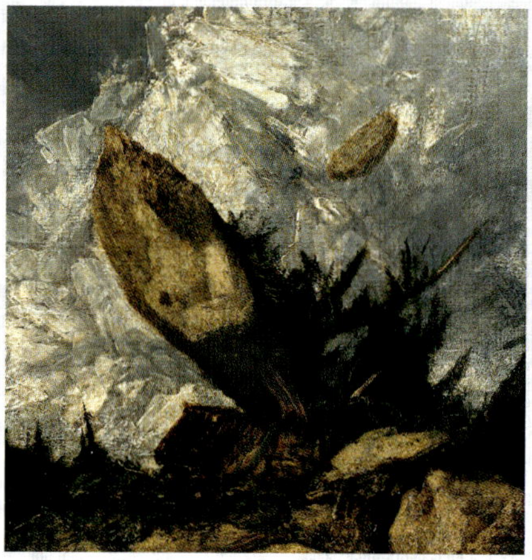

1 The Fundamental Landscape

There is a voice, not understood by all,
Sent from these desert caves

PERCY BYSSHE SHELLEY, FROM A DRAFT OF *MONT BLANC*, 1816

ABOVE:
Joseph Mallord William Turner,
The Fall of an Avalanche in the Grisons (detail)
Tate, London. Bequeathed by the artist 1856

Axehead ➤
c. 6,000 years old
Found at Ashwell, Hertfordshire
Jadeite, length 19.3 cm
P&E 1961.7-3.1
The British Museum, London

THE LANDSCAPES that exert the most power upon the human imagination are those that throughout history have inspired a sense of awe and majesty in the people who have known them from the earliest times. Early man made his home in the rock then built with the stones of that place in which he found himself. Yet the landscape is older than man, beyond the memory of humankind. Geological formations have always had an impact upon the human imagination, while mountains have provided a habitat for the Gods and for monsters that live at the summits, above the clouds. The seas contain landscapes that we can barely imagine and only in the post-Darwinian age do we understand that many of our most distinctive landscape formations were once beneath the seas. Artists have subsequently turned to myth and faith to illustrate the passions that motivate humankind and have also responded to the fundamental nature of stone as a medium for expression.

The works of art selected in this chapter demonstrate the centrality of landscape as possessing a fundamental emotive force that drives humankind to use stone artistically and symbolically and to reproduce great landscapes that echo those of the imagination. Many of these painted works of art have been created with palettes that have included iron oxides, ochres and rubified earths taken from the crust of the earth. The constant flow of materials from one form to another in the geological processes of the natural world is echoed in the acts of transformation performed by the artists – both ancient and modern.

Carved, sculpted, painted and engraved works of art, past and present, are not just testament to the skills of individual artists or the aesthetics of cultures that have long since passed into legend, they are also often testament to the symbolic value that has been conferred upon raw, unfashioned rock. For instance, that which is common locally is often less valued than that which has to be imported from afar and therefore receives greater symbolic status. Beautiful axeheads of laboriously sculpted and polished jadeite were traded all over Europe from their source in the northern Italian Alps over 4,000 years ago. The example pictured here was found in Ashwell, Hertfordshire and must have been greatly prized. Not only is it still in pristine condition and was therefore never used, it is so fine and elegant and represents so many hours of labour that it was probably only ever intended for ceremonial and symbolic functions. Recent research has shown that it was likely to have been made several hundred years before being buried, indicating that it would have passed through the hands of several generations.

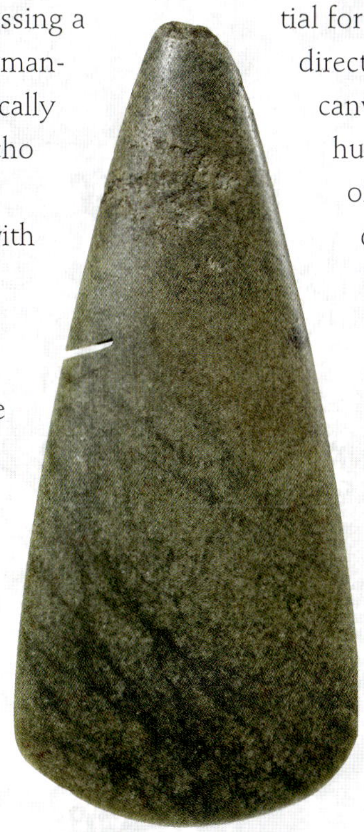

The appreciation of the beauty of stone, its potential for metaphor and its qualities as a medium for direct representation, abstract symbolism or as a canvas for painting and engraving is a universal human trait that goes back tens of thousands of years. With only primitive tools at their disposal, early artists spent incalculable hours at the rockface – carving, sculpting, engraving and painting – to laboriously produce beautiful works of art that were surely luxuries, rather than necessities.

Taking delight in the nature of stone, whether depicted in a serene and genuinely awesome landscape or sculpted and polished and presented as a symbolic abstraction, is a trait that was deeply held by our ancient ancestors to which we still respond readily today.

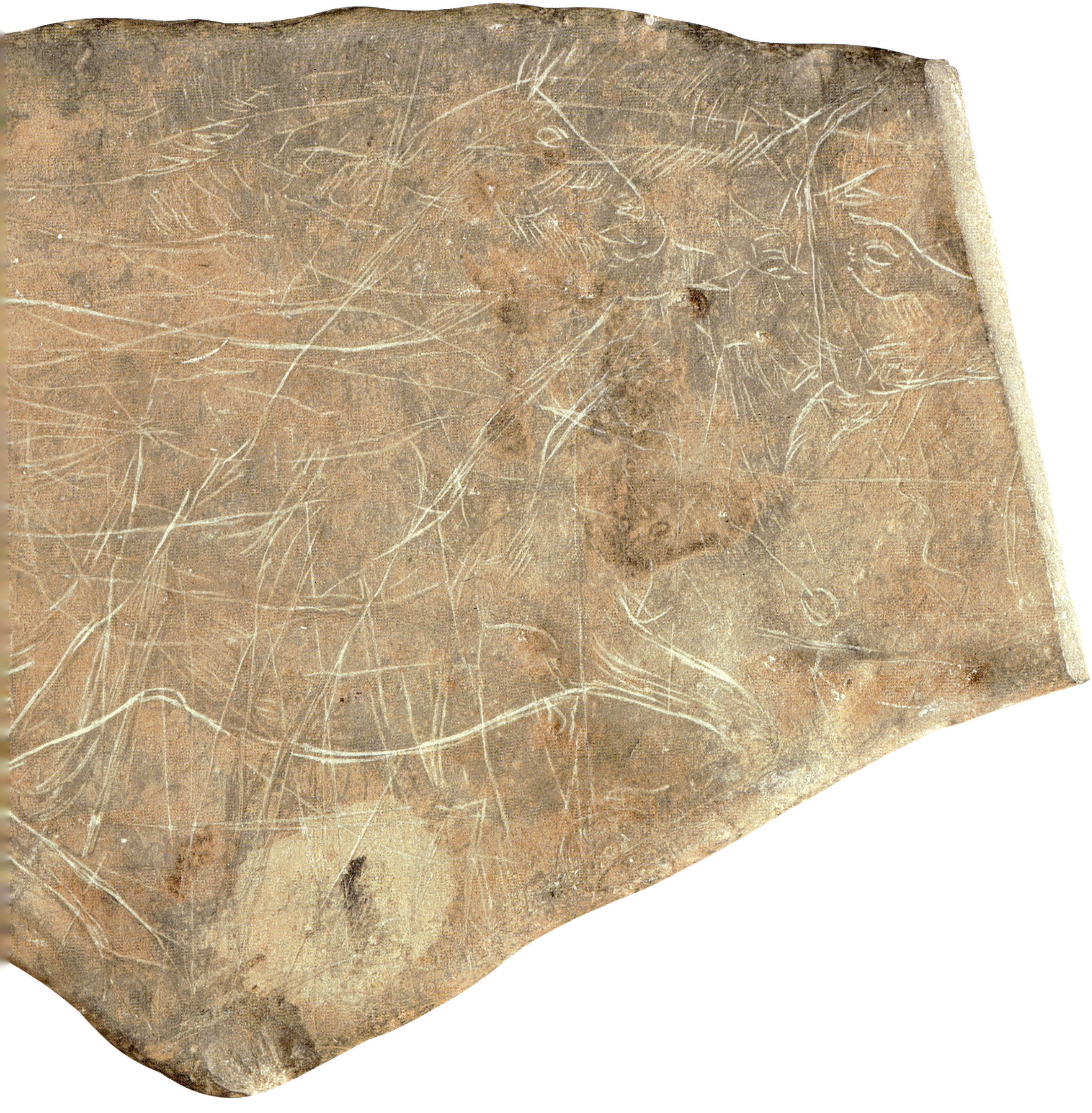

Plaque decorated with Horses

Late Magdalenian, c. 12,500 years old
From the rock shelter of Montastruc, Tarn-et-Garonne, France
Engraved stone, length 16.3 cm

P&E Sieveking 691
The British Museum, London

The faint lines engraved on this rock eloquently describe the preoccupations of life twelve millennia ago. Three horses, full of movement, all face to the right sharing a tail and hindquarters. Beneath them is a female reindeer, impaled by a spear and with legs bent. The animal may be running but more likely is seen from above, lying dead on the ground.

When first engraved, these animals would have looked fresh and white on the grey surface of the limestone. The superimposition of animals is a common feature of Palaeolithic art and this deliberate composition may tell a specific story or call upon particular spiritual powers.

Sophisticated portable rock art such as this is contemporaneous with many of the engravings and paintings that decorate caves and rock shelters throughout Europe, including the newly discovered cave art of Creswell Crags in England. The themes that preoccupied these Magdalenian artists are common to most ancient cultures around the world as can be seen through their artistic legacies. From northern England through Europe to Africa and throughout Australia, Asia, the Americas and far-flung oceanic islands, over the last 75,000 years countless artists have left us a vast canon of images carved, engraved and painted on rock. These were inspired by the natural world they lived in but were possibly used for shamanistic, ceremonial or ritual purposes.

The seventeenth-century philosopher Thomas Hobbes noted famously, 'Life in an unregulated state of nature is solitary, poor, nasty, brutish, and short' (*Leviathan*, 1651, chapter 13). Yet these ancient peoples can be seen to have had a reverence for the natural world around them, a highly developed sense of aesthetics, an intuitive understanding of their materials and a universal desire to create images that were more than transient.

Whilst the exact functions and symbolism of these artworks are difficult for us to decipher through the veil of time, at least these enigmatic images have been preserved through the enduring nature of their medium. We can only guess at the types of other artworks crafted on materials that have not withstood the test of time. NL

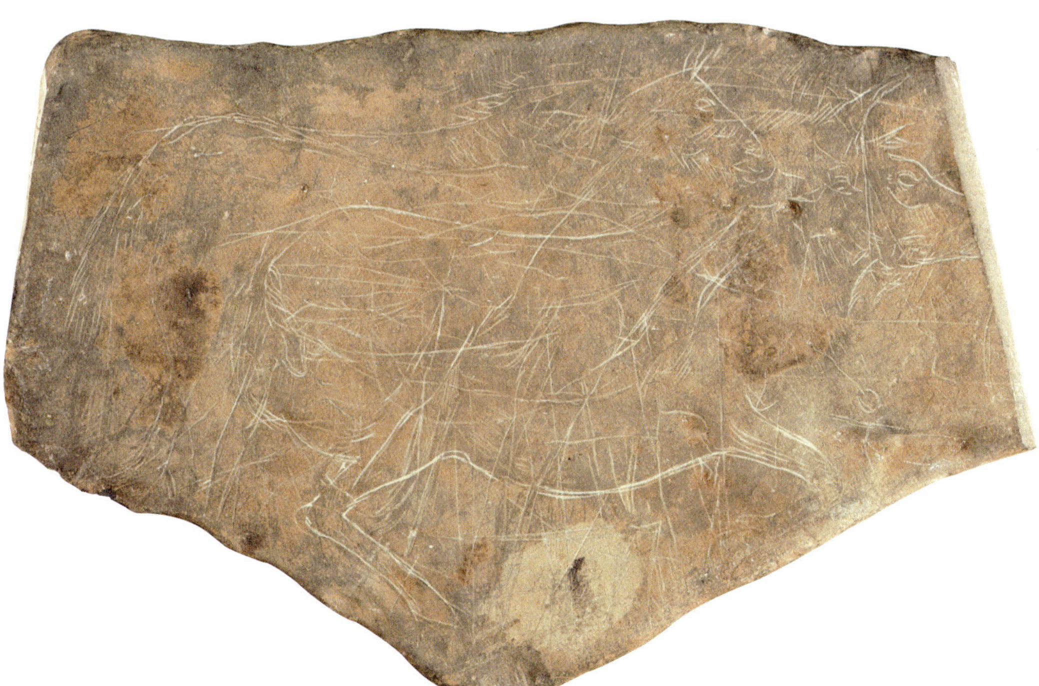

Empedocles leaping into Etna, c. 1660s

SALVATOR ROSA (1615–73)
Oil on canvas, 135 x 99 cm
Eastnor Castle Collection

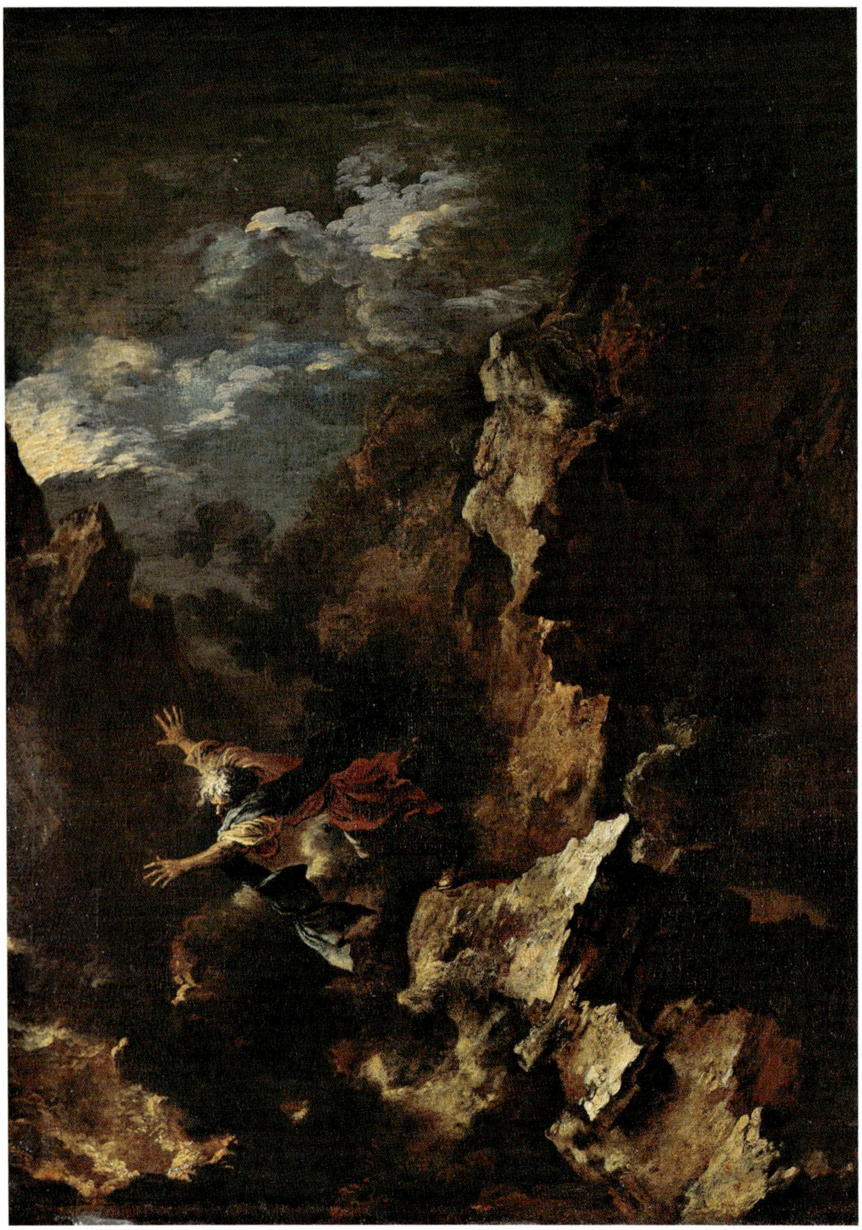

Salvator Rosa is a key figure in the development of a proto-Romantic idea of the Sublime in landscape painting. Rosa was often brought to mind by travellers in the Alps during the eighteenth century and Horace Walpole famously described a journey over the Alps in 1739 as 'precipices, mountains, torrents, wolves, rumblings – Salvator Rosa.' Rosa's paintings of wild and mountainous landscapes led to his being admired for his 'savage' and tempestuous life in the century after his death. His reputation mutated as a fearless champion of artistic genius in the nineteenth century. *Empedocles leaping into Etna*, painted towards the end of his life, reveals Rosa's highly sophisticated response to landscape.

Empedocles (c. 492–432 BC) was a Greek philosopher and statesman born in Acragas (now Agrigento) in Sicily. Although little is known of his life, some 400 lines of his poetry survive which reveal something of his philosophy. He is best known for his belief that matter was composed of four elements: earth, air, fire and water. This theory was to be highly important in the development of science, being adopted by both Plato and Aristotle. Some of his ideas have since been accepted, notably that light travels at a finite speed and that chemical reactions maintain constant proportions. A number of legends developed about his death – his leap into Etna, supposedly an attempt to achieve immortality, being only one.

Rosa depicts the philosopher at the moment he surrenders to the fundamental forces of nature. Rosa, born near Naples, was certainly familiar with Etna, the highest active volcano in Europe, which dominates Sicily and its three seas. In 1669 Etna was to undergo a violent eruption that lasted 122 days, but it is likely that Rosa painted this canvas before that event, when based in Rome. The artist was as much concerned with the philosophies of his subject as with the awesome nature of his legendary death. Rosa's paintings show that he became drawn to the pre-Socratic philosophers, notably Pythagoras and Empedocles, in the process helping to define a new role for the artist, that of freedom of expression. AM

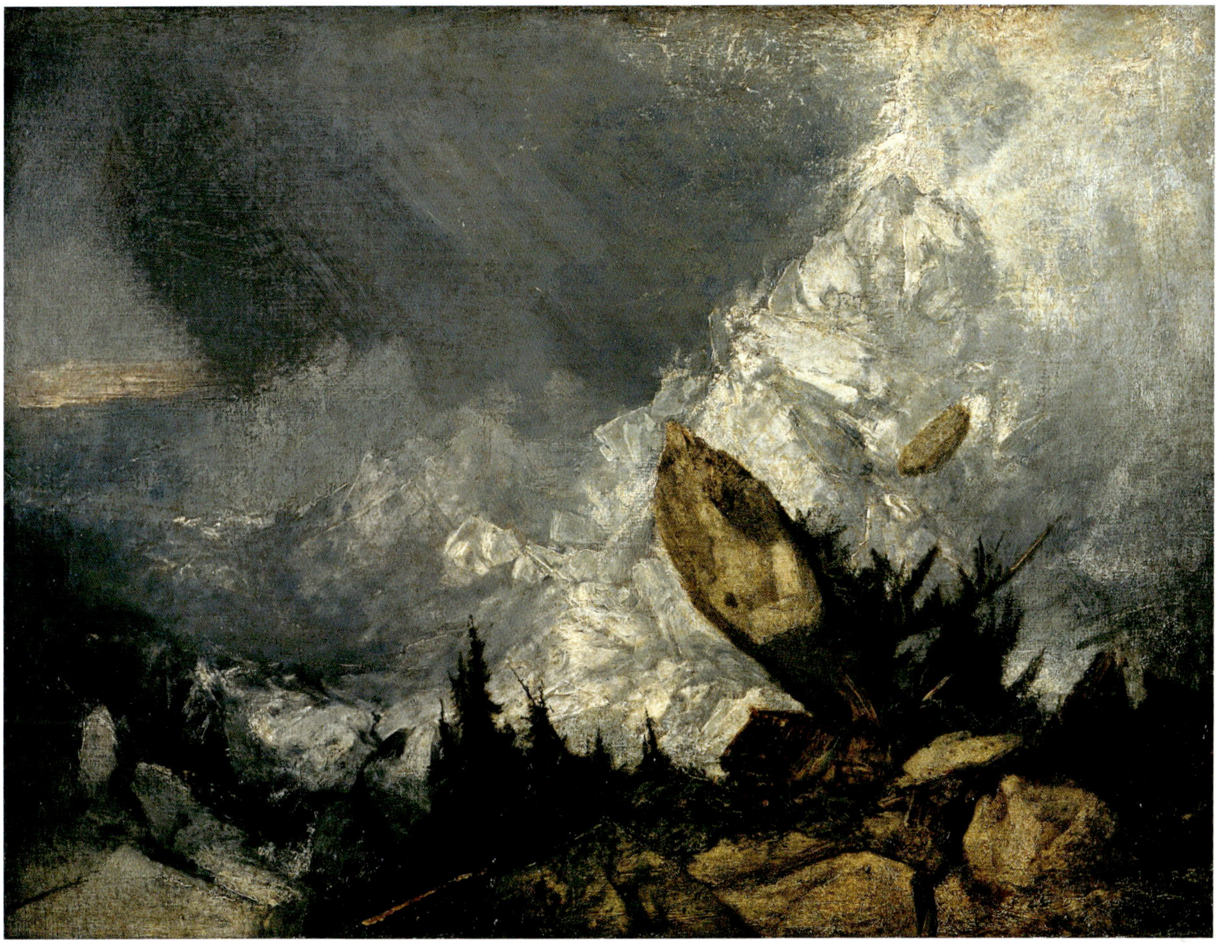

The Fall of an Avalanche in the Grisons

Exhibited 1810
JOSEPH MALLORD WILLIAM TURNER
(1775–1851)
Oil on canvas, 90.2 x 120 cm
Tate, London. Bequeathed by the artist 1856

Turner recorded this disastrous geological event, in which twenty-five people were killed by an avalanche at Selva in the Grisons in December 1808, with a dramatic combination of realism and imagination. We experience the impact and representation of a geological process as inspiration rather than slavish literalism. Turner was directly inspired in art historical terms by the work of Philip De Loutherbourg, one of whose paintings of an avalanche of snow (c. 1800) was in the collection of Turner's patron, Lord Egremont at Petworth. Another patron, Sir John Leicester, also owned a snow avalanche painting by De Loutherburg (c. 1803). Yet, as Ruskin observed, 'No one ever before had conceived a stone in flight' (*Notes on the Turner Gallery at Marlborough House*, 1857). Turner depicts a scene of immense natural violence which is at the same time a terrifying record of geology in action. Here, Turner's subject matter is highly unusual in the history of art, where volcanic eruption or the aftermath of landfall is much more familiar.

The painting possesses an abstract quality which totally involves the viewer. It was exhibited in Turner's Gallery in 1810 with verses of his own composition that echo the *Book of Job* (xiv, 18–19), and emphasized the elemental force of the event:

The downward sun a parting sadness gleams,
Portentous lurid thro' the gathering storm;
Thick drifting snow on snow,
Till the vast weight bursts thro' the rocky barrier;
Down at once, its pine clad forests,
And towering glaciers fall, the work of ages
Crashing through all! Extinction follows,
And the toil, the hope of man – o'erwhelms.

It is uncertain whether Turner visited the Grisons while in Switzerland in 1802, but he would have been familiar with reports in the contemporary press. When he exhibited the painting a contemporary reviewer commented that the painting 'is not in his usual style, but is not less excellent' (*The Sun*, 12 June 1810; M. Butlin and E. Joll, *The Paintings of J.M.W. Turner*, revised ed., New Haven and London, 1984). AM

The Mountains of Thermopylae, 1852

EDWARD LEAR (1812–88)
Oil on canvas, 68.5 x 113.8 cm
Inscribed: *EL 1852*

Bristol's Museums, Galleries and Archives

Edward Lear is best known for his nonsense verse, or limericks. He was also an ornithologist and talented landscape painter who travelled extensively in southern Europe, the eastern Mediterranean, the Middle East and, in 1873–75, India. He published his topographical drawings in a series of volumes of lithographs. Although his work has been regarded as somehow diminished by its topographical earnestness and his devotion to poetical nonsense, his reverence for nature led him in 1852 to seek tutorials from the much younger Pre-Raphaelite artist William Holman Hunt. Lear and Hunt spent part of that summer and autumn at Fairlight on the coast near Hastings, at the time when Hunt was painting highly coloured and symbolic representations of the English landscape. That autumn Lear wrote to thank Hunt: 'I really cannot help again expressing my thanks to you for the progress I have made this autumn ... I am now beginning to have perfect faith in the means employed & if the Thermopylae turn out right I am a P.R.B. for ever' (Staley, Allen, *The Pre-Raphaelite Landscape*, 1973, 153).

Lear was working from sketches made on the spot in 1848 at a place redolent with ancient history. Thermopylae was the site of bitter fighting between the Greeks and the Persians under Xerxes I in August 480 BC. The famous battle of Thermopylae where Leonidas I and his 300 men made a last stand against the Persian army took place in a pass of the mountains of Othys. The mountain pass consists of ancient raised beaches that have been changed into sandstone. Today, historical deforestation and modern siltation has widened the beach strip to an agricultural plain which runs from the cliffs to the sea now several kilometres to the north east, presenting a timeless and inspirational landscape for the artist.

The view looks south over the plain of the Spercheios towards the mountains of Thermopylae. Hunt's advice about colour was particularly important to Lear. He imbues his landscape with a prismatic blue that invests the site with a sense of distance and scale which turns a geological painting of rocks and mountains into an experience of place that goes some way towards expressing its power over the onlooker (RA, London, 1998, 193).
AM

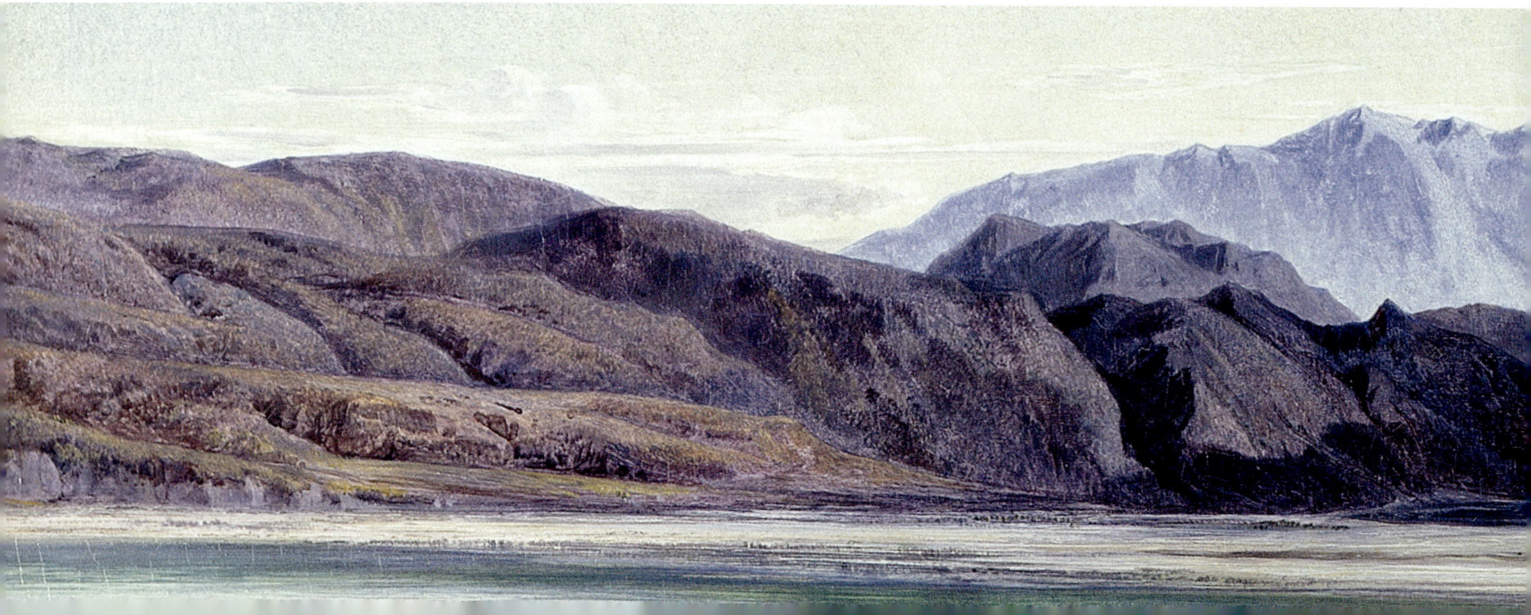

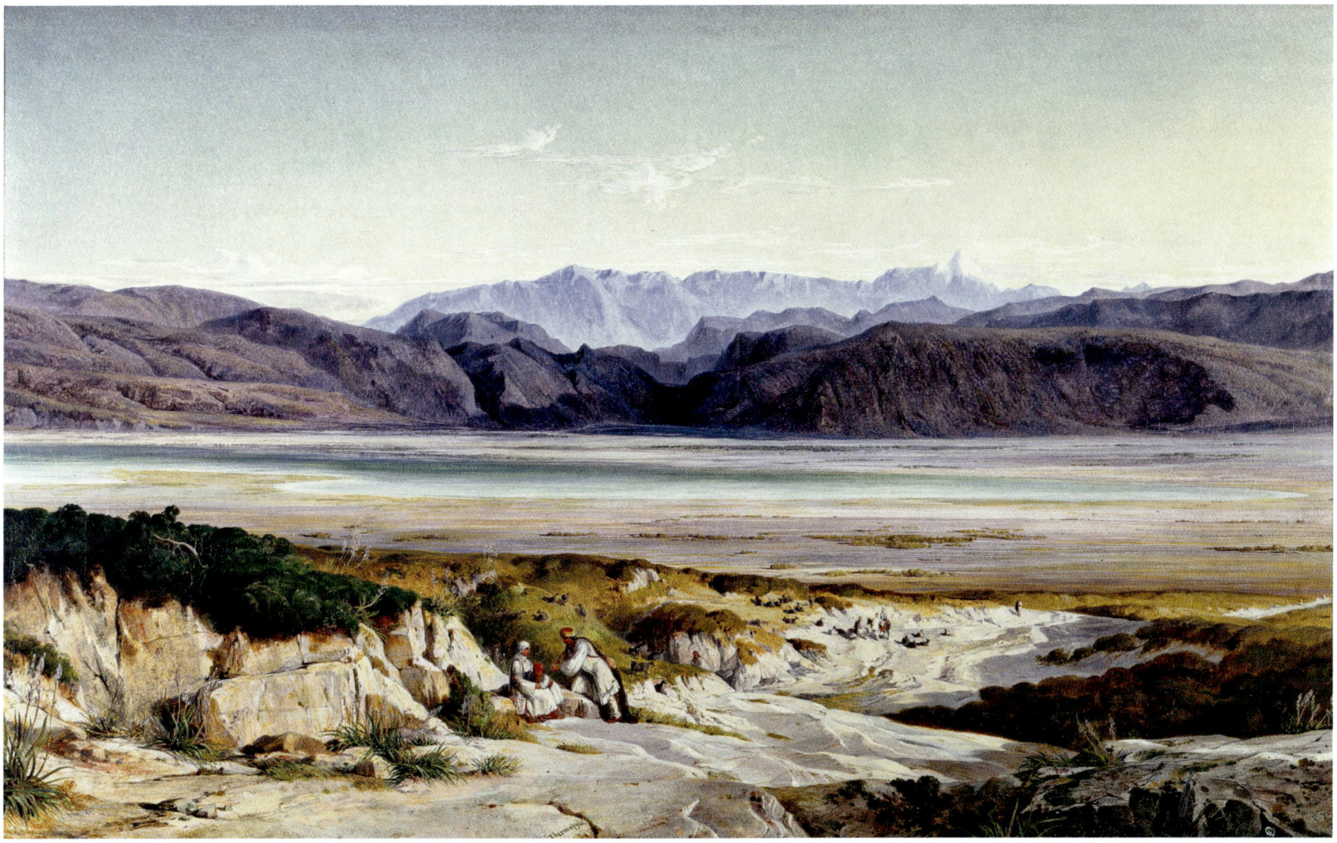

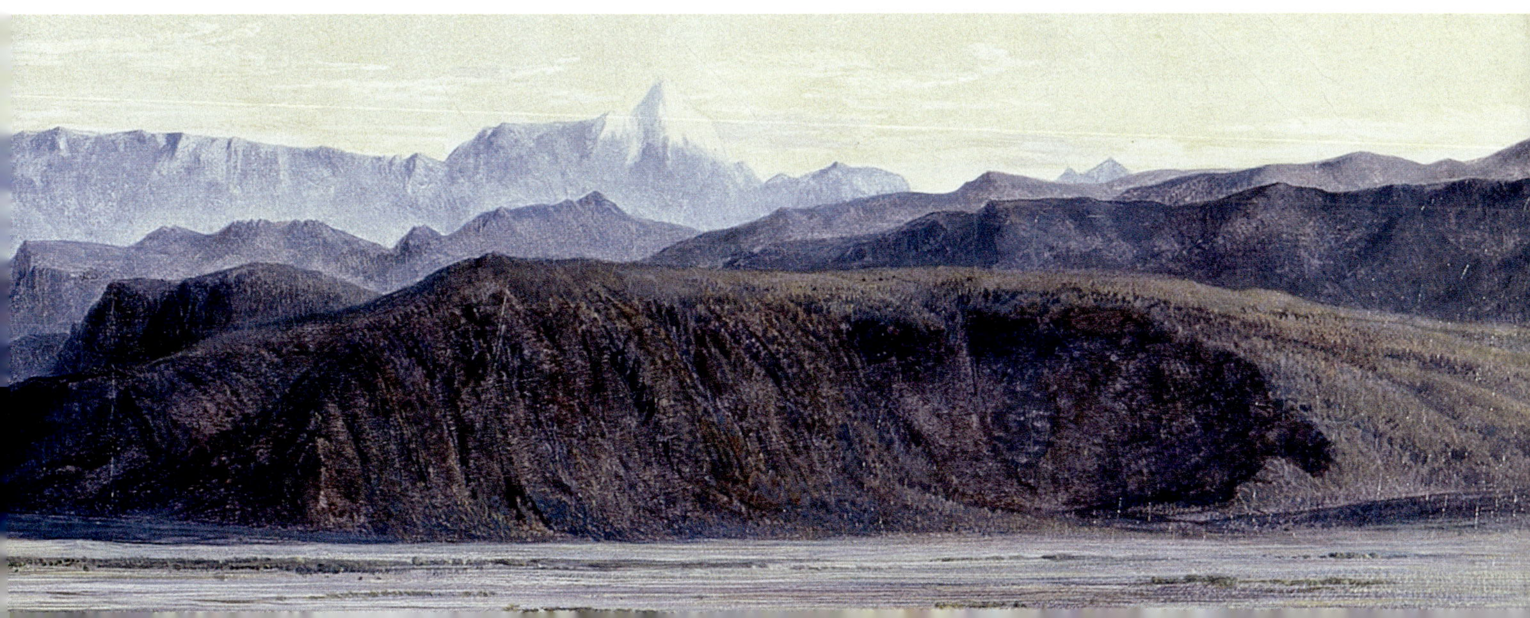

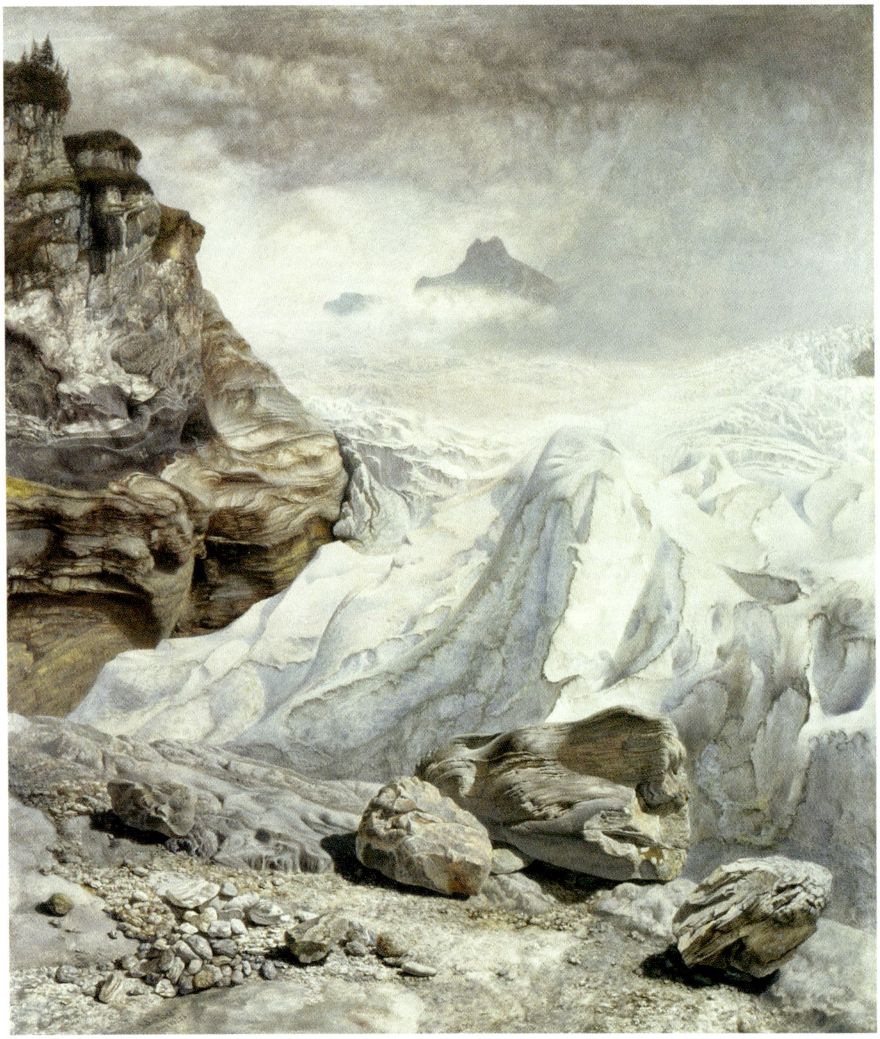

Glacier of Rosenlaui, 1856

JOHN BRETT (1831–1902)
Oil on canvas, 44.5 x 41.9 cm
Inscribed: *John Brett Aug 23 / 56*
Tate, London. Purchased 1946

John Brett sought to represent Rosenlaui in Switzerland with the quality of literal truth that inspired John Ruskin. Brett held a lifelong interest in geology and was motivated to study rocks such as the granite boulder, blocks of gneiss, metamorphic marble and pebbles of the terminal moraine in the foreground of *Glacier of Rosenlaui*. Essentially, he was following Ruskin's admonition that a small stone is a 'mountain in miniature'. A geological understanding of this composition helps us to understand its power, offering a way to appreciate the sublimity of mountains and geological processes that attracted painters even before the concept of the Sublime took hold. Even though the scene is indisputably realistic, it is also the case that Brett composes his subject, notably in the foreground, by staging and lighting his groupings with an eye for dramatic effect. He would have been familiar with the current debate about the literal creation of the world as recounted in *Genesis* and it is unclear whether Brett had any theological motive in his carefully balanced depiction of natural forces.

Brett spent the summer of 1856 at Rosenlaui, having been inspired to visit by reading the fourth volume of John Ruskin's *Modern Painters*, entitled 'Of Mountain Beauty', published in April 1856. While there Brett met John Inchbold, who was working on a painting of the Jungfrau. Brett was inspired by Inchbold's example and wrote in his diary: 'I saw him do a few touches to his jungfrau and there and then saw that I had never painted in my life, but only fooled and slopped and thenceforth attempted in a reasonable way to paint all I could see' (9 December 1856).

For a time Ruskin regarded Brett as his protégé. Brett manages to suggest the enormous power of the glacier as it snakes through the mountains, upending boulders that no man could move. We see the Wetterhorn on the right and the Dossenhorn in the distance. When Dante Gabriel Rossetti took the painting to show Ruskin, the critic and mentor conveyed 'expressions of pleasure and praise' to the artist (Brett's Diary, 9 December 1856). The painting is almost a template of how Ruskin viewed mountains – as manifestations of the creative power of God, 'indispensable to human existence' (*Pre-Raphaelite Vision Truth to Nature*, Tate Britain 2004, no. 86).
AM

Nearing Camp, Evening on the Upper Colorado River, Wyoming, 1882

THOMAS MORAN (1837–1926)
Oil on canvas, 66 x 160 cm
Inscribed lower left: 'THOs MORAN. 1882'
Bolton Museum, Art Gallery & Aquarium

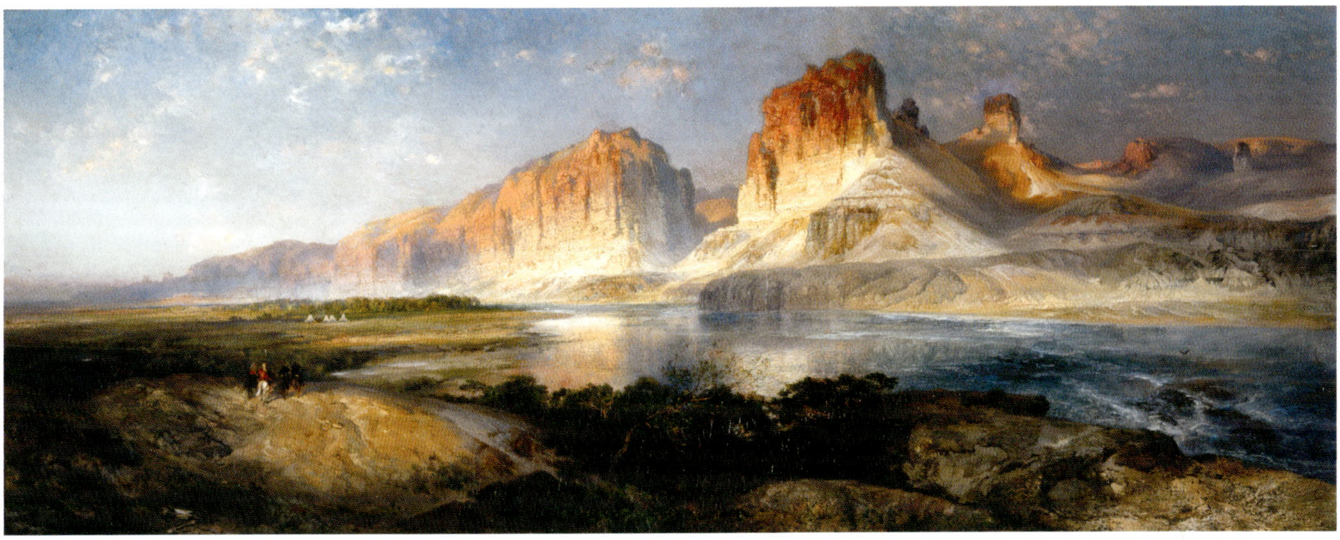

This vivid response by the artist to the challenge of depicting the awesome and spectacular landscape of the American West is a remarkable example of 'American Sublime' painting, a genre that described the attempts of artists to capture some of the most spectacular rock landscapes of the continent (Wilton, A. and Barringer, T., *American Sublime Landscape Painting in the United States 1820–1880*, London, 2002, 248). Born in Bolton, England, Moran moved with his family to Philadelphia in 1844 and became the artist most associated with the opening up of the American West to the railroad and tourism. His early supporters were connected with the move not simply to explore new geographical and geological boundaries, but to establish a new network of railroads and national parks for business and profit, as well as to feed the romantic notions of those living on the East coast, dreaming of exploration westwards.

Moran's first success was to sell his seven- by twelve-foot canvas *The Grand Canyon of Yellowstone* to Congress for $10,000. Of this canvas he wrote: 'My aim was to bring before the public the character of that region. The rocks in the foreground are so carefully drawn that a geologist could determine their precise nature' (Wilkins, Thurman, *Thomas Moran: Artist of the Mountains*, Oklahoma 1966, 69). Moran met with tremendous success, painting enormous canvases, which he exhibited at a time when photography could not compete in capturing the scale of geological features such as the Grand Canyon. The striking colour of the rockface in this picture derives from the red volcanic layer covering the buff limestone, which has leached over time. Their eroded features, sculpted over millennia, enhance the awesome nature of the columnar cliffs or buttes.

Thomas Moran studied in particular the work of J.M.W. Turner and David Roberts, learning from them the power of colour to add mythic status to a scene. The artist was also well aware of his role in feeding the American hunger for their newfound lands. Here, Moran makes no reference to the impact of the burgeoning coal-mining industry that was then spreading in this area in the wake of the Union Pacific Railway. Instead, he chooses to illustrate a group of native Americans on horseback, emphasizing a fantasy of the timeless American outback, dominated and dwarfed by the natural landscape. AM

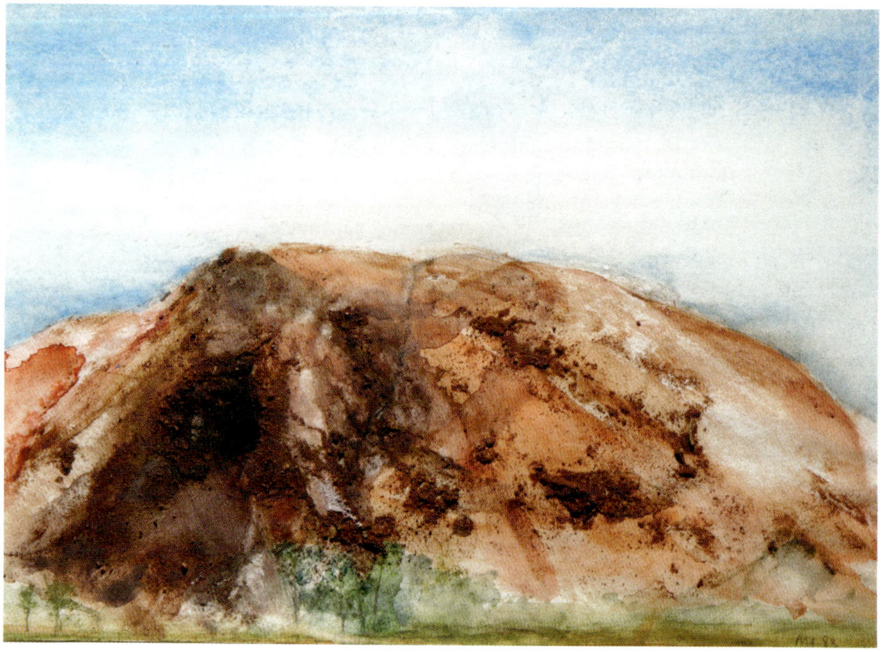

Ayers Rock October '83: Near 'Maggie Springs', 1983

MICHAEL ANDREWS (1928–95)
Watercolour and sand from Ayers Rock,
20 x 28 cm
Private Collection

Ayers Rock, or Uluru, in central Australia is one of the most distinctive and celebrated geological features on Earth. It was created over 400 million years ago when an extensive sandstone bed was subjected to massive geological forces and tilted through ninety degrees. Traces of the original sedimentary processes are still visible on the near vertical ridges that are such a distinctive feature of this huge monolith.

In the late 1960s the British painter Michael Andrews saw a photograph of Ayers Rock in a magazine as an advertisement for Australia. The image stayed with him until 1983, when he was finally able to make his long-awaited pilgrimage to the Rock. He spent nine days in the Uluru National Park, exploring the site, taking photographs and producing a number of watercolour studies including *Ayers Rock October '83: Near 'Maggie Springs'*. The study is topographical, yet clearly communicates Andrews' immediate response to the Rock, the place itself being literally embodied in the watercolour through the addition of local sand to the painted surface.

The photographs and watercolour studies were used as source material for an ambitious series of nine paintings in acrylic. These huge canvases were painted in Andrews's chapel studio in the village of Tasburgh, Norfolk. The artist named the series *Rock of Ages* after the eighteenth-century hymn by Augustus Toplady: 'Rock of ages, cleft for me / Let me hide myself in Thee'. For the Aboriginal people, Uluru is a sacred place. Its surface features reveal mythological narratives, which in turn reinforce the Aboriginal peoples' sense of belonging to the landscape. Andrews' Ayers Rock paintings acknowledge this relationship through their powerful evocation of what Andrews described as the 'interdependence [between] man and the environment' (Paul Moorhouse and William Feaver, *Michael Andrews*, Tate Publishing, London, 2001, p. 34). They both describe and suggest our universal, fundamental experience of landscape. NT

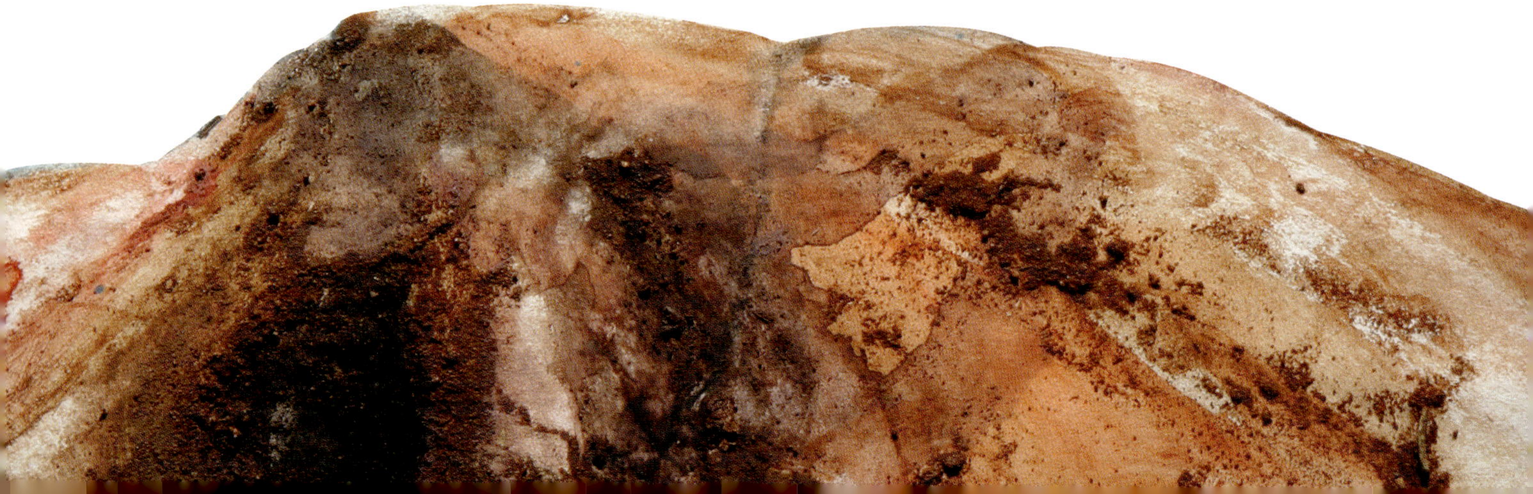

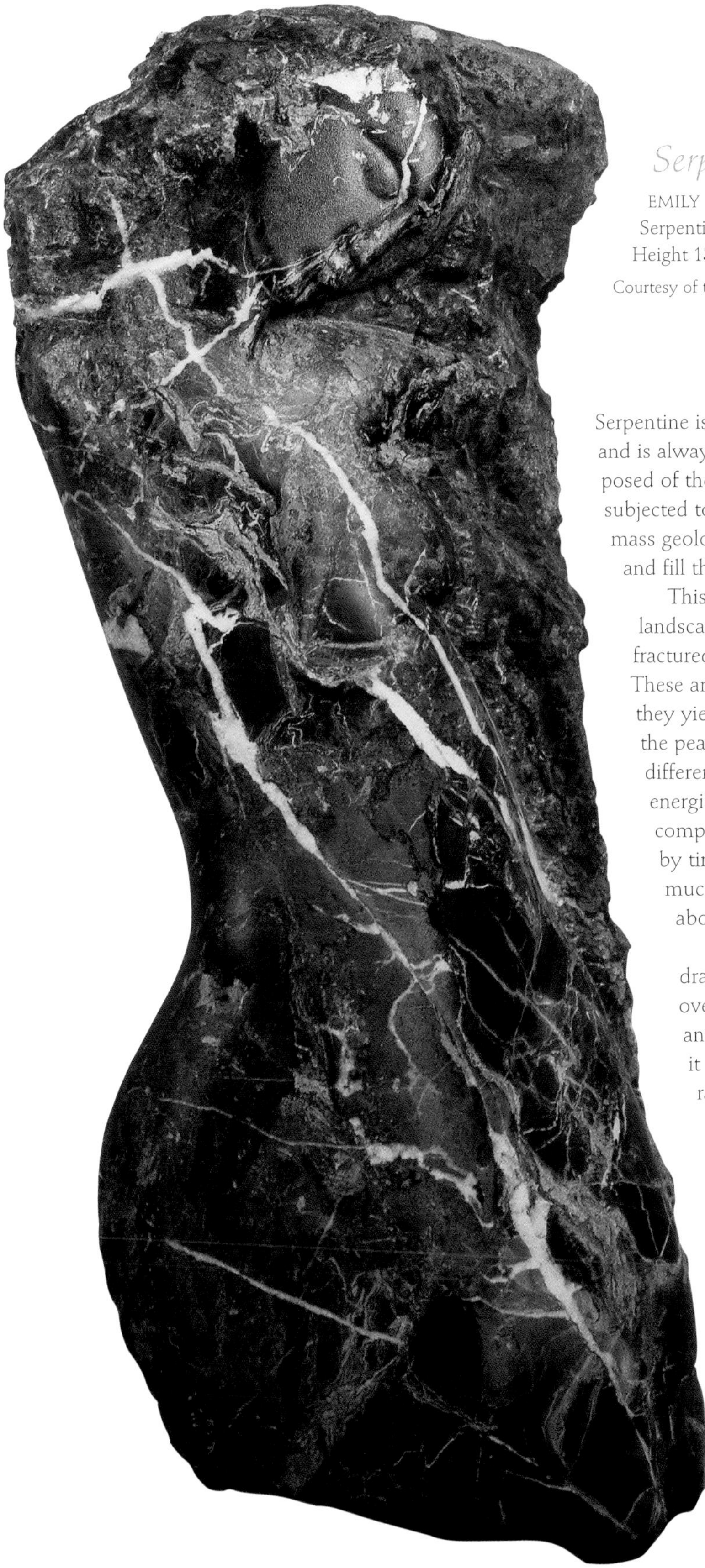

Serpentine Torso, 2005

EMILY YOUNG (BORN 1951)
Serpentine from Carrara, Italy
Height 130 cm
Courtesy of the artist, London

Serpentine is usually found within layers of slate, limestone or marble and is always evidence of a complex and dramatic history. It is composed of the igneous minerals olivine and pyroxene which, when subjected to rising temperatures and pressures due to the stresses of mass geological movements, force their way through older rocks and fill them with a chaos of colourful veins.

This soft elemental figure emerges from the rock like a landscape waking from sleep. The soft, silky, yet dramatically fractured and coloured rock is from the Carrara hills, in Italy. These are more famous for the pure white fine-grained marble they yield, so loved by Michelangelo, which were formed in the peaceful seas of the Jurassic period. That serpentine – so different, so chaotic, colourful and livid, born out of violent energies – can be found in the same hills is testament to the complexity of geological histories. That sculptors divided only by time can work such different rocks so eloquently says as much about the continuum of artistic endeavour as it does about the intrinsic nature of the stone.

Emily Young has said of the raw, unworked block: 'A dramatic geological history of turmoil in those mountains over the past many millions of years has left this wild, rich and complicated stone as its testament.... It had the magic; it talked in a strong, warm voice to me about its beauty and rarity, and so I brought it home to my studio, where we washed it, and saw the swirls, changes and natural lines of drawing that allow one to read into it, to form the familiar lines of humanity, the woman's body, the strong grace of a dancer, powerful, with a kind of sombre wildness that I find heart breaking – it's a quality lost to most of us. This is anthropomorphism, and it's a way into the stone, and its history, through the material and its form, back into the story of the land, our creator, our ancestor, seen now, here, as something like us. And maybe us, as something like it, her.' NL

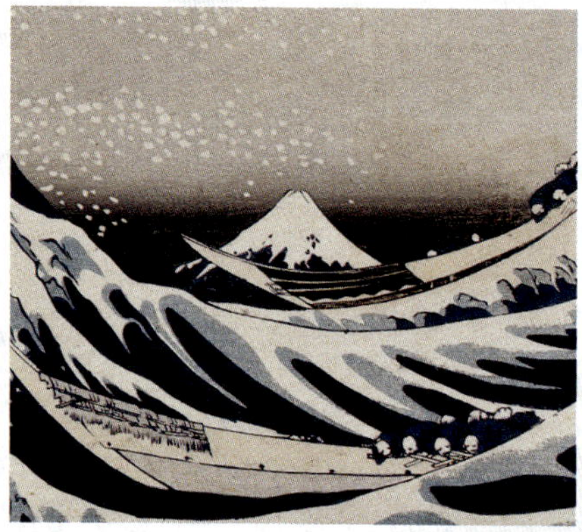

2 Travel and Exploration

For full ten years, since earliest geologic reading, I had thoroughly known the structure and present look of Vesuvius and Monte Somma (but new to me were) the first feeling of being in the presence of the power and mystery of the under earth, unspeakably solemn

John Ruskin, *Præterita*, 1885–89, 35. 288

Above:
Katsushika Hokusai, *The Hollow of the Deep-Sea Wave off Kanagawa* (detail)
Bristol's Museums, Galleries and Archives

Birdman Boulder ➤

Possibly late 18th to mid-19th century
From Orongo, Easter Island
(Rapa-Nui), Polynesia
Volcanic rock, carved in bas-relief
and painted, length 51 cm
Ethno 1920.5-6.1
The British Museum, London

CONFRONTATION WITH NEW LANDSCAPES is made possible through travel. Travellers explore the land for many reasons, including for work and trade, for military or scientific purposes or simply for pleasure. The cultural responses to new landscapes and environments are correspondingly varied. In prehistoric times the search for food and the quest to survive was at the heart of early man's travels and exploration. A direct result of this early mobility was the opening of trade routes and the transport of tools and artefacts which expressed an aesthetic appreciation of form and function.

By the eighteenth century the need to travel and to develop had rather different cause and effect. The Grand Tour of Europe was a prime means by which a young and cultured gentleman might complete his education. While his quest included the artefacts of civilization, he was also confronted by changing landscapes, often of the most awesome nature. Throughout the centuries travellers, including artists, were tested by the beauty, horror and sublimity of the landscapes through which they passed. Later expeditions had scientific enquiry as their quest, while in more recent times mountaineers have sought to attain the peaks as expressions of personal quest and endurance.

Responses to new landscapes and cultures have also led to the desire to collect artworks indigenous to the newly found lands. Whether considered personal souvenirs, scientific specimens, curiosities of anthropological interest or even military or national trophies, works of art from every genre in every culture have been appreciated, studied, collected (even stolen) and traded. As well as discovering the new landscapes of the physical world, early travellers were navigating uncharted realms of new cultures, faiths and ideologies.

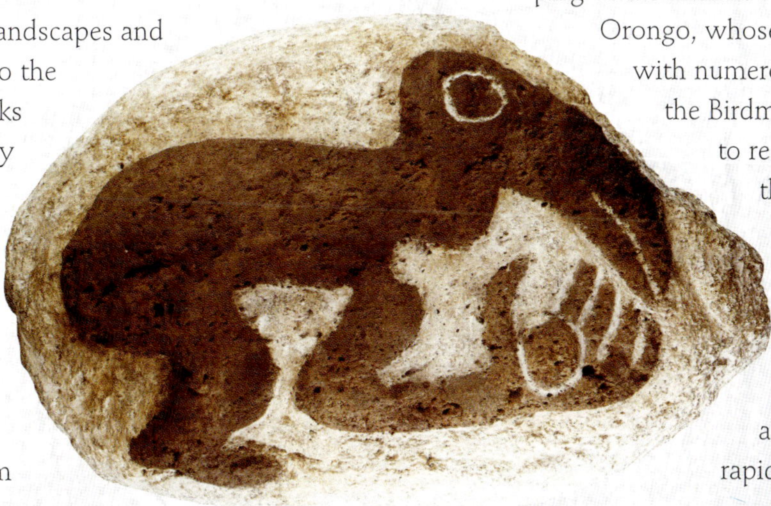

Easter Island (Rapa-Nui) in the Pacific Ocean, with its famous and iconic lines of giant sculpted heads, provides an eloquent example of the lengths to which we will travel, in the process making our mark upon the landscape. The original settlers canoed or rafted across 1,000 miles or more of ocean from east Polynesia some 1,700 years ago. Rapa-Nui, the most isolated occupied island in the world, is home to thousands of carved boulders, engraved rock faces, petroglyphs and statues. The iconic statues, dragged across the landscape from their quarries to be erected, weigh an average of fourteen tonnes, with some up to 150 tonnes.

This volcanic boulder with a carving in low bas-relief outlined in white paint depicting a 'Birdman' holding an egg was collected from Easter Island by Katherine Routledge, an important pioneer in archaeological and ethnographic research on Easter Island. She and her husband sailed there on their yacht in 1914 and her work included the excavation and mapping of the ancient ceremonial centre of Orongo, whose basalt rocks are carved with numerous figures relating to the Birdman Cult. She was able to record information about this cult while it was still possible to do so. Since the arrival of Christianity the cult had declined, and memories of the associated rituals were rapidly fading.

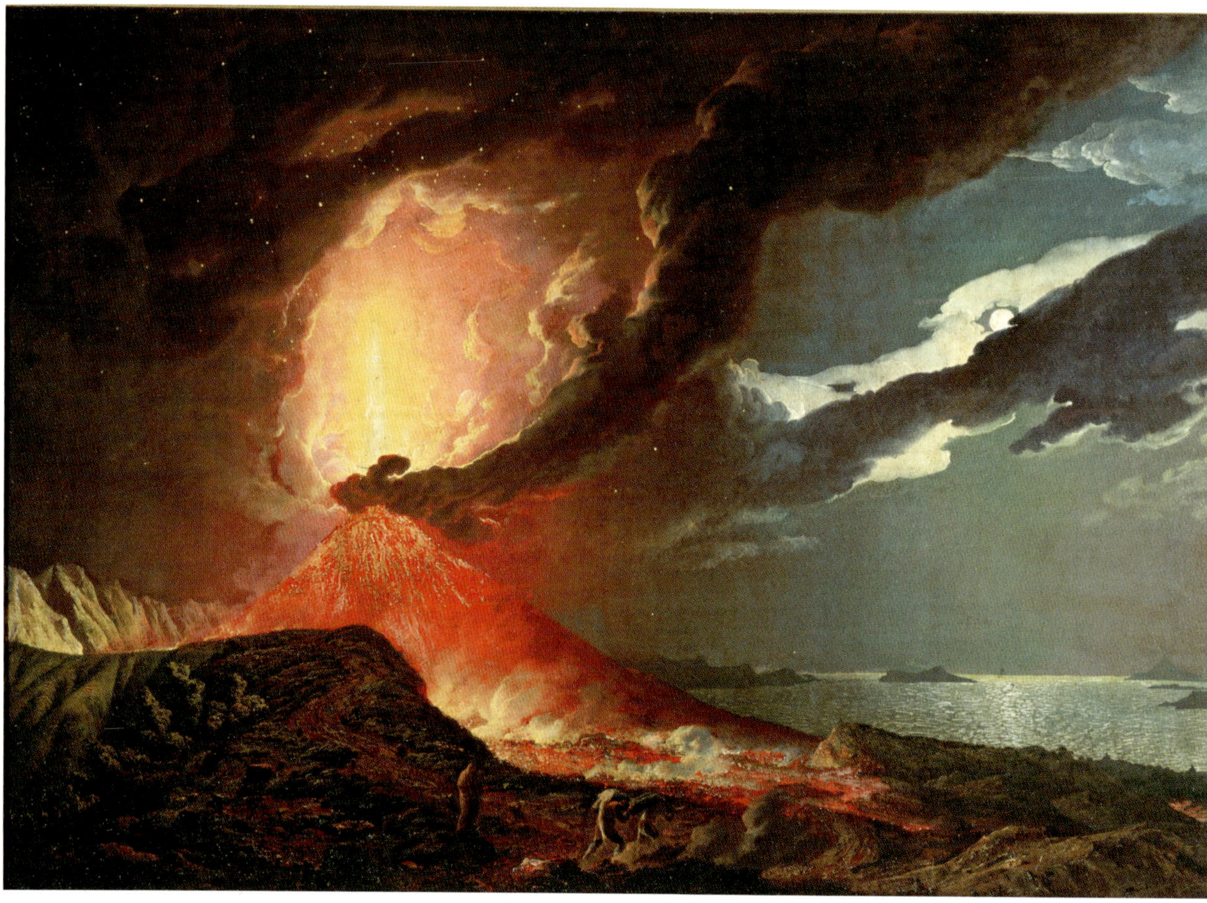

Vesuvius in Eruption, with a View over the Islands in the Bay of Naples, c. 1776–80

JOSEPH WRIGHT OF DERBY (1734–97)
Oil on canvas, 122 x 176.4 cm

Tate, London. Purchased with assistance from the National Heritage Memorial Fund, National Art Collections Fund, Friends of the Tate Gallery, and Mr John Ritblat 1990

The awesome nature of Vesuvius was a lure to travellers in the eighteenth century. Joseph Wright of Derby made his excursion there from Rome in October and November 1774, a trip which inspired over thirty paintings of Vesuvius in eruption. Wright never did see an actual eruption, the last prior to his visit being in 1767. Since that time, however, Sir William Hamilton, British Plenipotentiary in Naples, reported that 'Vesuvius has never been free from smoke, nor ever many months without throwing up red hot SCORIAE ... usually follow'd by a current of liquid Lava' (W. Hamilton, *Campi Phlegraei*, 1779, supplement, 2). The mountain underwent a major eruption in 1777 and Wright's painting may have been influenced by contemporary reports as well as his own experience.

Joseph Wright here focuses upon the event of eruption and thanks to recent research we now know that he used powdered sulphur, a material not normally associated with painting, for the final application (over vermilion) of yellow lines of lava-flow at the apex of the cone. Wright would have enjoyed the literal equation between a volcanic mineral and its painted form: he counted amongst his friends geologists and scientists such as John Whitehurst (1713–88). Interestingly, the ground (or priming) of the canvas is composed of calcium sulphate (gypsum) in oil, a common usage in Italy, as opposed to chalk, used typically north of the Alps. This raises the strong possibility that the picture was painted in Italy (S. Hackney, R. Jones and J. Townsend, ed. *Paint and Purpose: A study of technique in British art*, London 1999, 59 and note).

The view is painted from the foothills of Vesuvius, with the promontory of Sorrento to the left, the island of Capri to the right and, thanks to artistic licence, the islands of Ischia and Procida are also visible. Wright specialized in light effects and here contrasts the mysterious lunar light with that of the dramatic sulphurous eruption. In the foreground the body of a victim of the Earth-shattering event is carried away, accompanied by a mourning woman, in a contemporary parallel to the death of the elder Pliny in AD 79 (Judy Egerton, *Wright of Derby*, Tate London, 1990, no. 102). AM

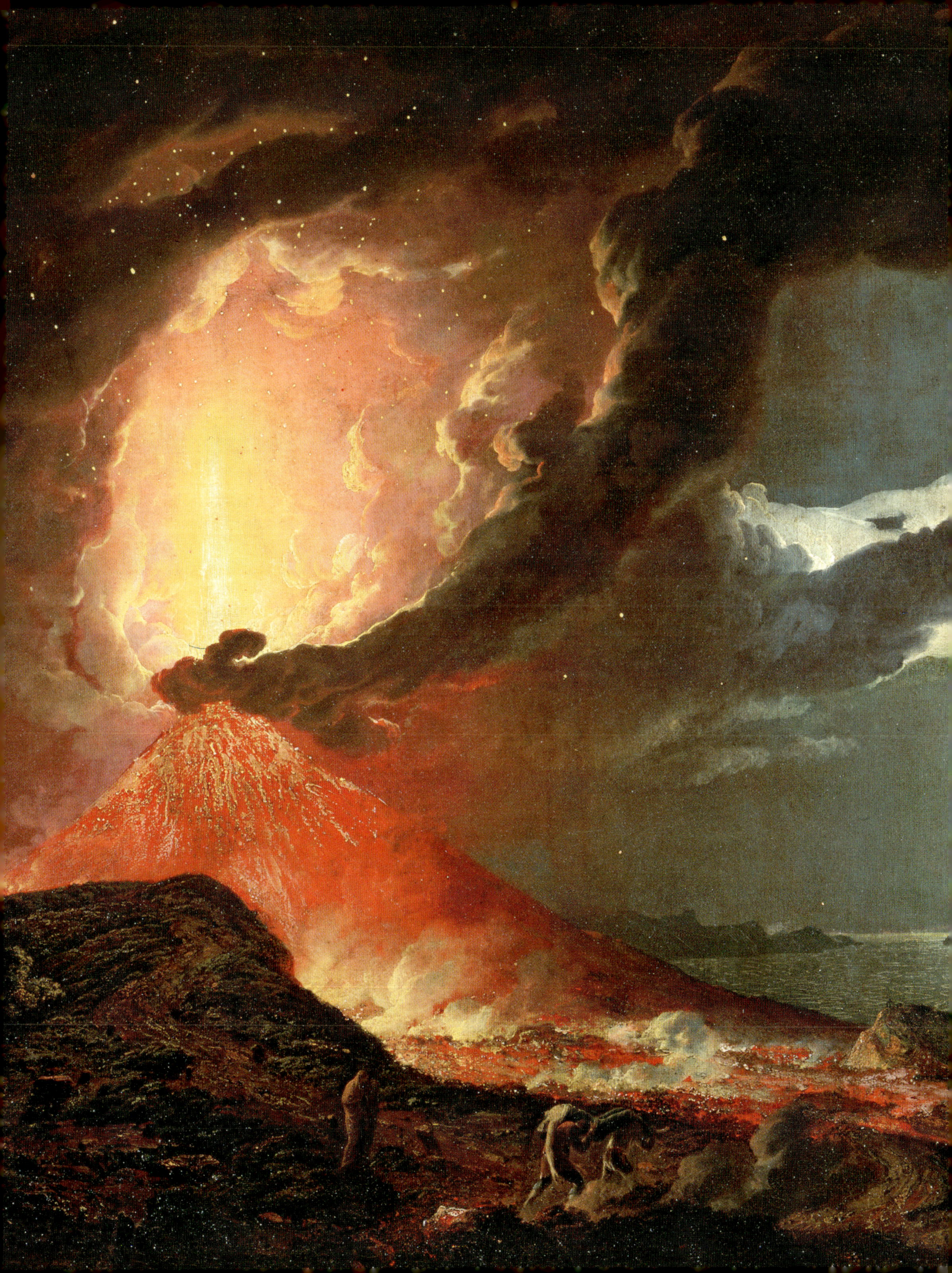

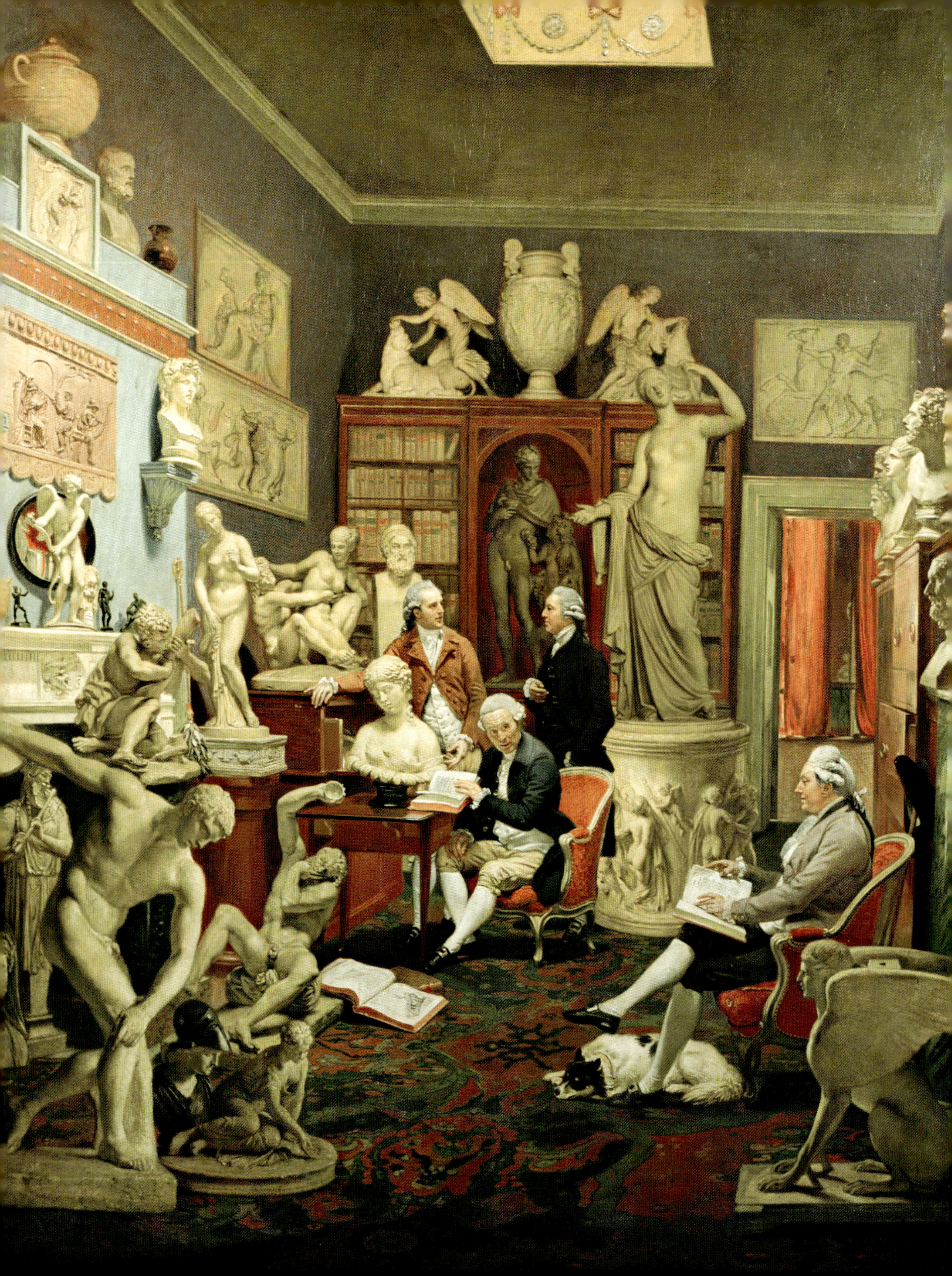

Charles Townley's Library at 7 Park Street, Westminster, 1781–83

JOHANN ZOFFANY 1733–1810
Oil on canvas, 127 x 99 cm

Towneley Hall Art Gallery & Museum, Burnley Borough Council

This celebrated image of Sir Charles Townley (1737–1805) in his library surrounded by his superb collection of busts of sculpted marble, which was destined for the British Museum, is not all that it seems. Townley had been impressed by Zoffany's painting of the Medici collection of paintings, implausibly gathered together at one time in the Tribuna Gallery, Florence, together with a gathering of tourists. This painting had been lent by King George III for exhibition at the Royal Academy in 1780. Townley subsequently commissioned Zoffany to produce a portrait of his spectacular collection of marbles, similarly gathered together in one place. In reality, the collection was arranged throughout Townley's house.

However, the painting is not only a celebration of Townley's collection, but also a metaphor for the obsessive nature of collectors of marbles in the eighteenth century. Divorced from their original contexts, the marbles collectively represent the mania of private collectors for ancient carved stone, here all depicted by Zoffany as perfect examples, without cracks or imperfections, belying their origins. In fact, many ancient stones were unearthed in a shattered state and cleaned and reconfigured in studios such as that of the prolific restorer Bartolomeo Cavaceppi, to provide newly minted and fashionable celebrities from the Greek and Roman worlds.

Excavations under the shadow of Vesuvius at Herculaneum and then Pompeii fed the fashion for classical interiors back in England. In Townley's case, we see a scholarly approach as, seated to the right, he discusses the stones in the context of classic texts with antiquarian friends, beneath the bust of Homer (*Art Treasures of England: The Regional Collections*, Royal Academy of Arts, London, 1998, 86). AM

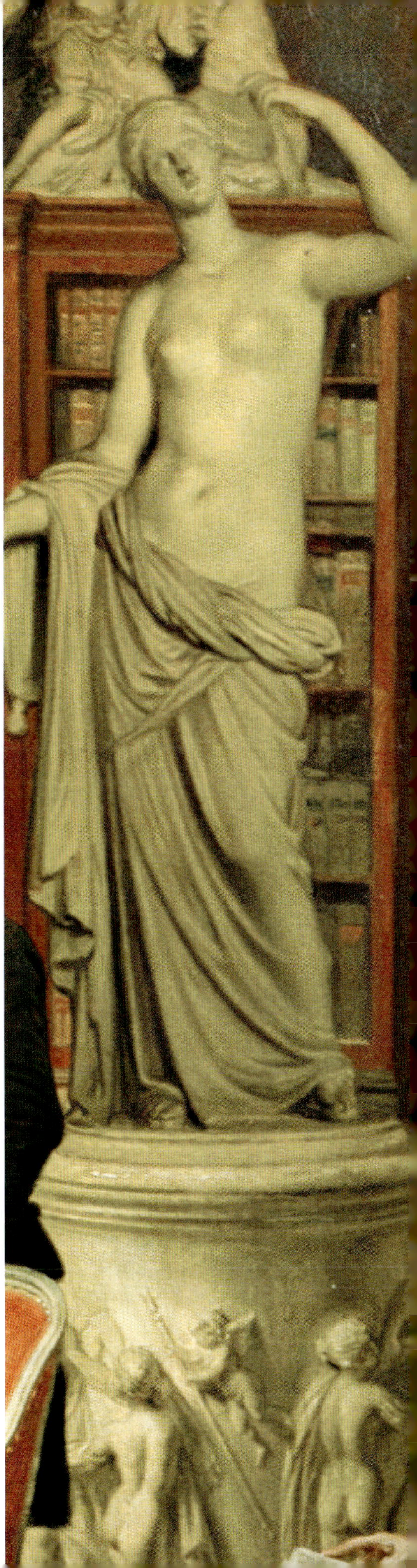

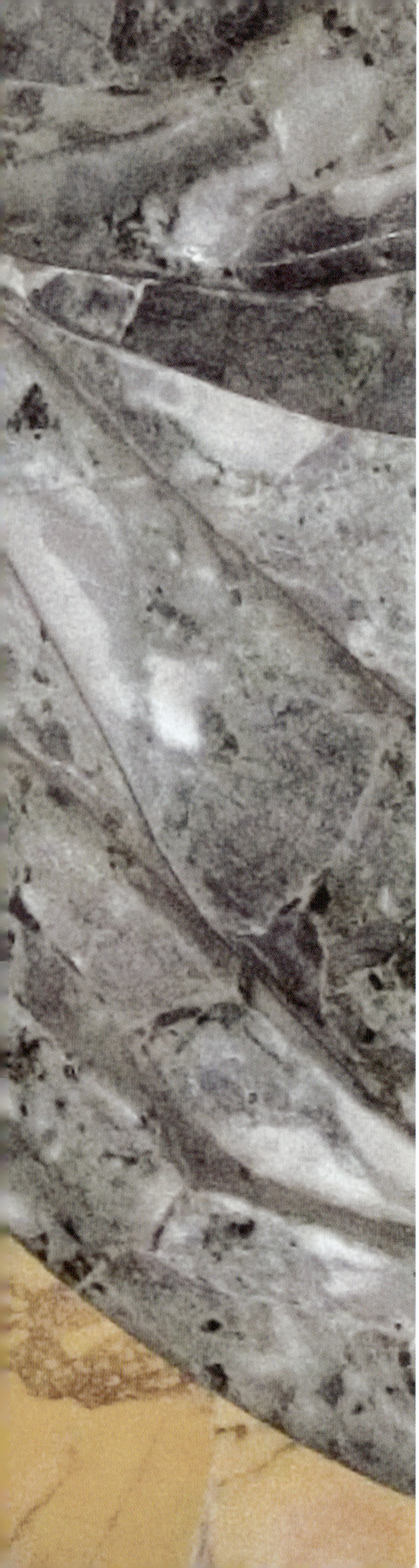

Portrait of the Emperor Marcus Aurelius mounted on a Post-Antique Bust of Variegated Marble, 160–180 AD

Marble, 91 x 73 x 37 cm

Lord Leicester and Trustees of the Holkham Estate

Sculpted marble from classical times has consistently been admired for almost two millennia. Such marbles gained meaning from their subjects, but also from their context. Thomas Coke was an early English tourist who was remarkable for having travelled as a teenager on the longest European tour from England on record, from 1712–18. Having collected a good number of marbles he created a sculpture gallery in his newly built 'temple to the arts' at Holkham in Norfolk. These were dispersed around his new home in a manner that invited discussion of the classical figures and made learned reference to each other. He also employed agents to add to his collection on his behalf. His bust of the Emperor Marcus Aurelius was purchased by Matthew Brettingham from Gavin Hamilton in Rome in 1752 for seventy crowns, presumably to complement that of the Emperor's co-ruler, Lucius Verus, which Coke had bought himself thirty-six years earlier. Brettingham also bought at the same time the only other variegated marble bust at Holkham, presumably offered as a decorative counterpart.

The bust is a notable example of the use of variegated coloured marbles, a highly fashionable and expensive use of polychrome stones over a core of tufa rock, known as 'lapis albanus'. In the early eighteenth century the locations of the ancient quarries were unknown and it became commonplace to use antique pieces in the restoration of excavated antique sculpture. Here the bust has a cuirass of 'giallo antico', with insertions of 'breccia rossa e gialla' (bottom right); a deep red marble neck piece of 'rosso antico' (possibly from Cape Tainaron – or Matapas – in the Peloponnese, southern Greece); a right shoulder of 'cipollino rosso' (possibly from Lasos, Turkey), and a military cloak of 'breccia Africano' fastened with a fibula of alabaster (Angelicoussis, Elizabeth, *The Holkham Collection of Classical Sculptures*, Monumenta Artis Romanae XXX, Mainz 2001, 128–29).

Marble is metamorphosed limestone consisting primarily of calcite, sometimes dolomite and sometimes a combination of both. Pure calcite is white, but mineral impurities add colours in variegated patterns. The presence of hemætite produces reds, serpentine adds greens, limonite gives yellows and diopside gives hints of blue. Because marble can take a high polish it is favoured for fine statuary and architecture. The term 'marble' is often extended to include any rock composed of calcium carbonate that takes a polish, and it includes some ordinary limestones. AM

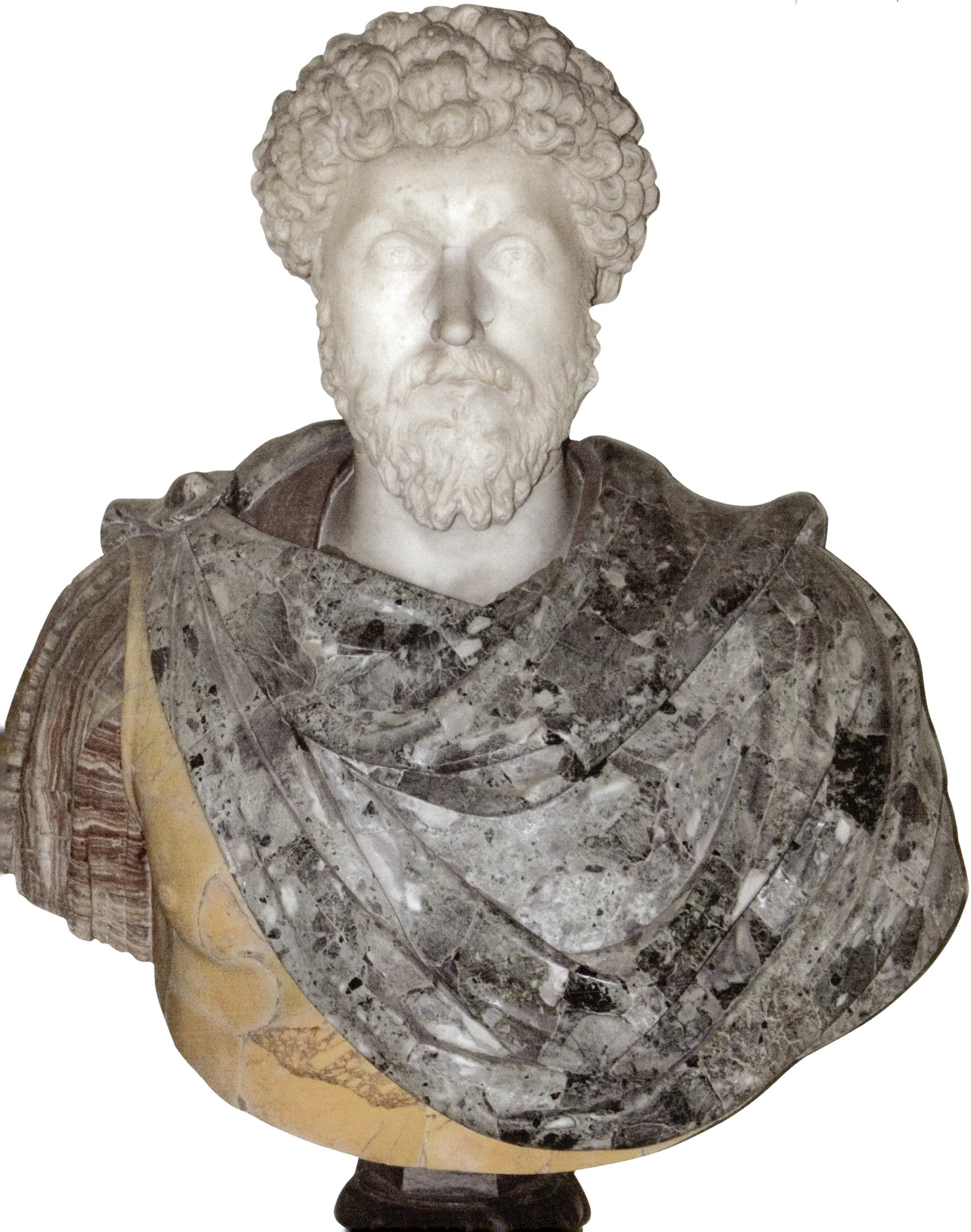

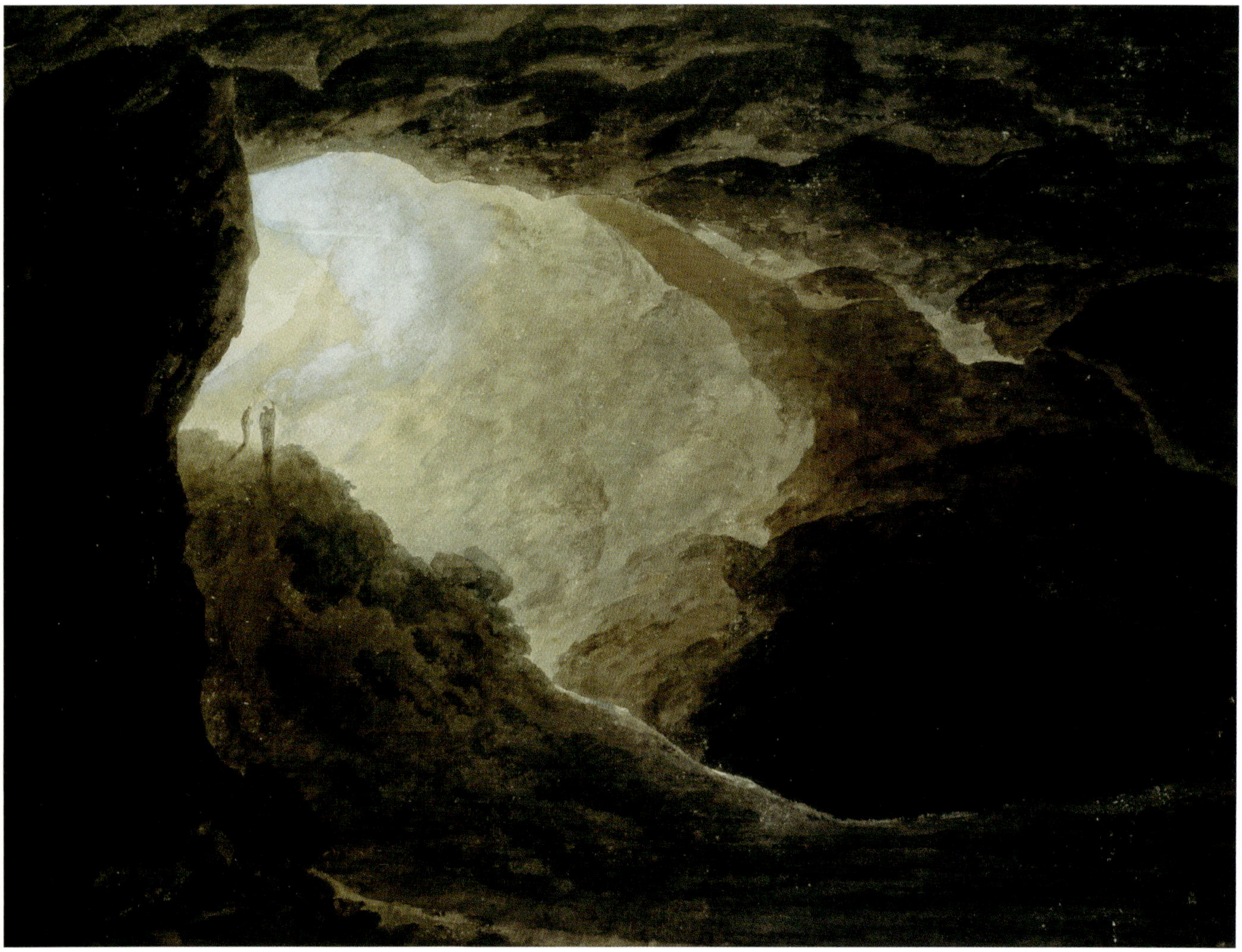

Cavern in the Campagna, 1778

JOHN ROBERT COZENS (1752–97)
Pencil, watercolour and bodycolour on laid paper on original mount, 41.5 x 61 cm
Signed and dated on mount lower left: *John Cozens – 1778*; lower right *cavern in ye campagna*

Victoria and Albert Museum, London

For an artist who had such a profound influence on watercolour painting in Britain, Cozens rarely painted his native landscape. In common with many artists of the period, travels in Europe dominated his work. His first journey was in 1776, when he travelled through Switzerland to Italy, eventually arriving in Rome where he remained for over two years. Here he met up with the many British artists, such as Thomas Jones and William Pars, who congregated there to work and study and to exchange ideas.

From a villa outside Rome, Cozens made extensive excursions. He roamed the plains and hills of the Campagna, sometimes riding on an ass, making sketches to work up later into watercolours. The Campagna, the countryside which surrounds Rome, is the product of volcanic action. Ash and debris from the eruptions built up a series of gently sloping stratified deposits comprising a variety of tufas (cemented ash). For centuries these tufas and pozzolana, a volcanic sandy rock, were quarried for building materials resulting in a series of narrow, low caverns.

It was here that Cozens painted *Cavern in the Campagna*, one of the most original watercolours of the late eighteenth century. With a typically refined colour scheme and simplicity of design, he expresses the haunting grandeur of nature. The light blue of the sky contrasting with the subtle depth of tone of the cavern, small figures added to give scale and the eerie effect produced by smoke from the guide's torch, combine to create the type of poetical composition which so inspired Turner and caused Constable to declare Cozens' work 'all poetry' (ed. R. B. Beckett, *John Constable's Correspondence*, vol. VI, Suffolk Records Society, 1968, 72). NW

The Hollow of the Deep-Sea Wave off Kanagawa, 1829–33

KATSUSHIKA HOKUSAI (1760–1849)
Signed: 'Hokusai aratame Iitsu hitsu' ('From the brush of Hokusai changing to Iitsu')
Colour woodblock, 24.7 x 37.6 cm
Bristol's Museums, Galleries and Archives

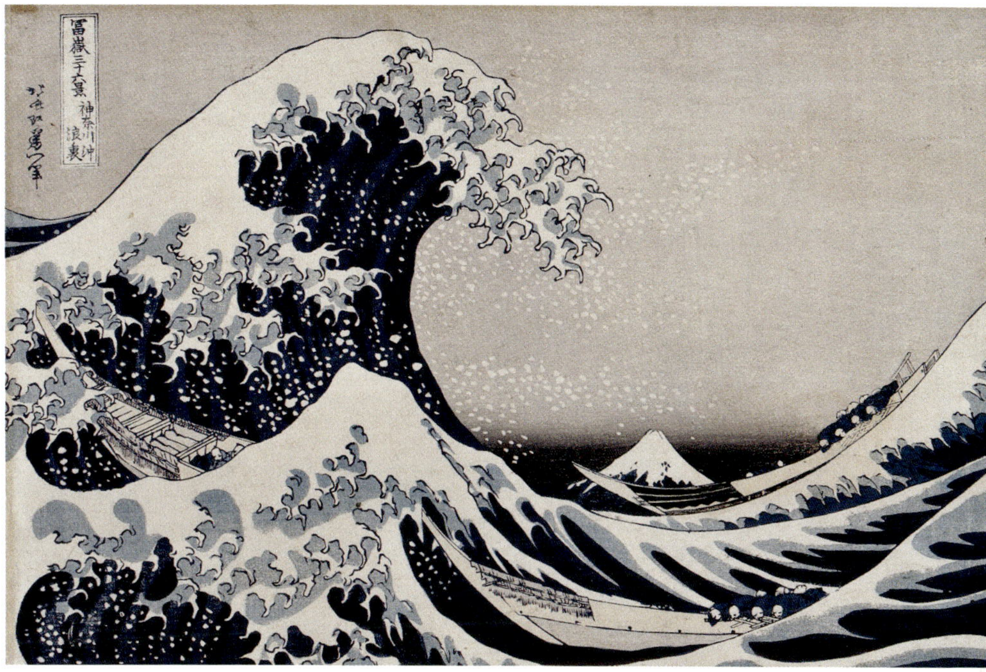

This iconic image demonstrates the centrality of the sacred mountain of Fuji in Japanese culture even though the mountain is not immediately obvious. Mount Fuji is not simply in the background, but at the pivotal point of the composition, just as Fuji is central to Japan's spiritual philosophy: the mountain stands as the still point at the heart of natural forces and man's perilous journey.

Fishermen are braving the elements in three boats, while the crest of the breaking wave in the foreground mirrors the silhouette of the mountain. The earliest record of Fuji's centrality as a symbol of Japanese devotion and identity is in a collection of writings (*Man'yōshū* or *Ten Thousand Leaves*) dated 720 AD. The luminous presence of Mount Fuji was particularly associated with the journey and pilgrimage on the Tōkaidō road *en route* between Edo and Kyoto. For the ageing Hokusai there was also a talismanic symbolism in Fuji, a name the characters of which can be read as 'not death' (Clark, T., *100 Views of Mount Fuji*, London, 2001).

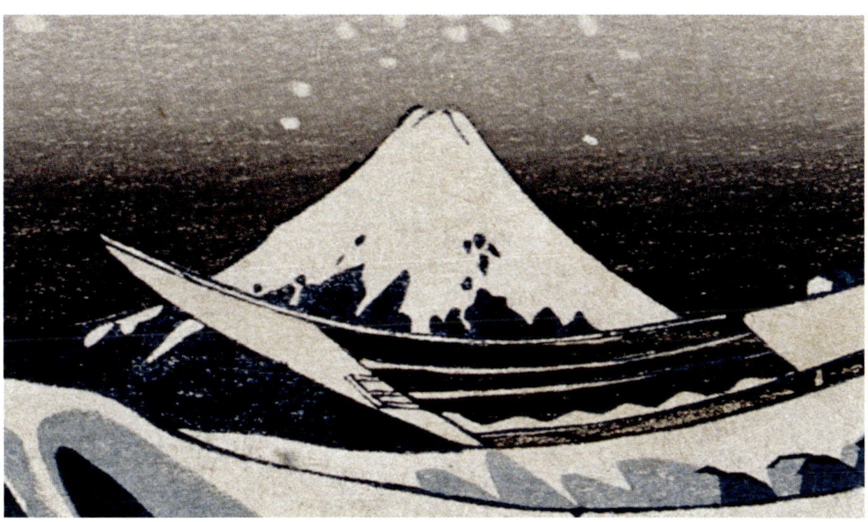

This is among the most inventive images of Fuji in the series of *Thirty-six Views of Mt Fuji* created by Hokusai in the years 1830–33. These depict Fuji from every vantage point and feature the first modern, artificially manufactured colour, Berlin blue, originally made by the colour maker Diesbach of Berlin in about 1704. Diesbach accidentally formed the blue pigment when experimenting with the oxidation of iron. The pigment was available to artists in the West by 1724, but was newly introduced to Japan from China in the late 1820s, initiating the fashion for prints featuring this deep, rich pigment so well suited to the depiction of water and sky. The introduction of this pigment can be seen as a significant influence on the increasingly realistic depiction of landscape in Japanese art, before the country opened its borders to a flood of direct Western influence. AM

Delabole Spiral, 1981

RICHARD LONG (BORN 1945)
Slate, 28 stones, 34.5 x 240.5 x 228.5 cm
Sheffield Museums and Galleries Trust. Presented by the Contemporary Art Society, 1984

Since the 1960s Richard Long's work has explored humankind's relationship with the natural environment. Walking through the landscape he charts his progress using maps, text and photography. Particular places or stages on walks are often marked by sculptural interventions, constructed in a minimal way from materials found locally to the site and arranged in lines or simple geometric shapes. As an extension to working directly in the landscape, Long also collects natural materials from a particular place in order to arrange them in the interior spaces of galleries.

In *Delabole Spiral,* twenty-eight roughly quarried pieces of slate from the Delabole Quarry in Cornwall have been arranged in a spiral on the floor. The quarried stone retains its natural appearance and has received little or no modification, other than having been balanced on its flat, narrow edge. As Long himself explained: 'It's enough to use stones as stones, for what they are. I'm a realist' (*Richard Long: Walking in Circles,* exhibition catalogue, South Bank Centre, London, 1991, 45). In part, Long's work can be viewed as an extension, or natural conclusion, to the idea of 'truth to materials', which dominated approaches to sculpture and stone in the early decades of the modernist movement.

An early use of the spiral in Long's work is the indoor sculpture *A Line the length of a straight walk from the bottom to the top of Silbury,* 1970. This work records a walk up Silbury Hill – a man-made Neolithic earth mound adjacent to the Avebury stone circle in Wiltshire. The line seems to mirror the internal chalk structure of the mound, yet can also be related to the mysterious spiral petroglyphs carved on natural rocks and megaliths in the Neolithic period. Long's use of this universal spiral symbol connects *Delabole Spiral* to a prehistoric past when people necessarily had a closer, more direct relationship to their natural environment, yet still revealed this human need to make their mark or inscribe their presence on the landscape. NT

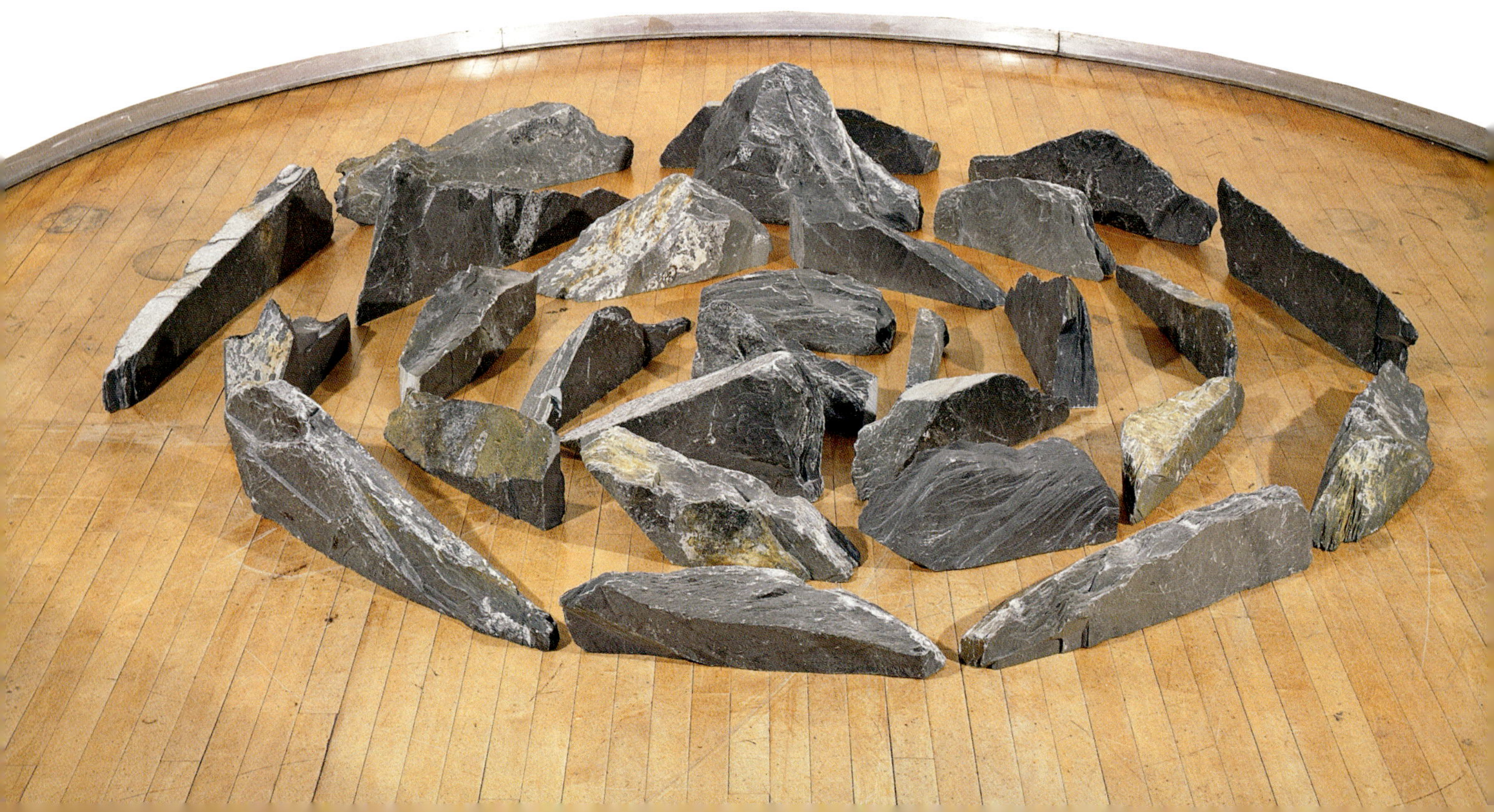

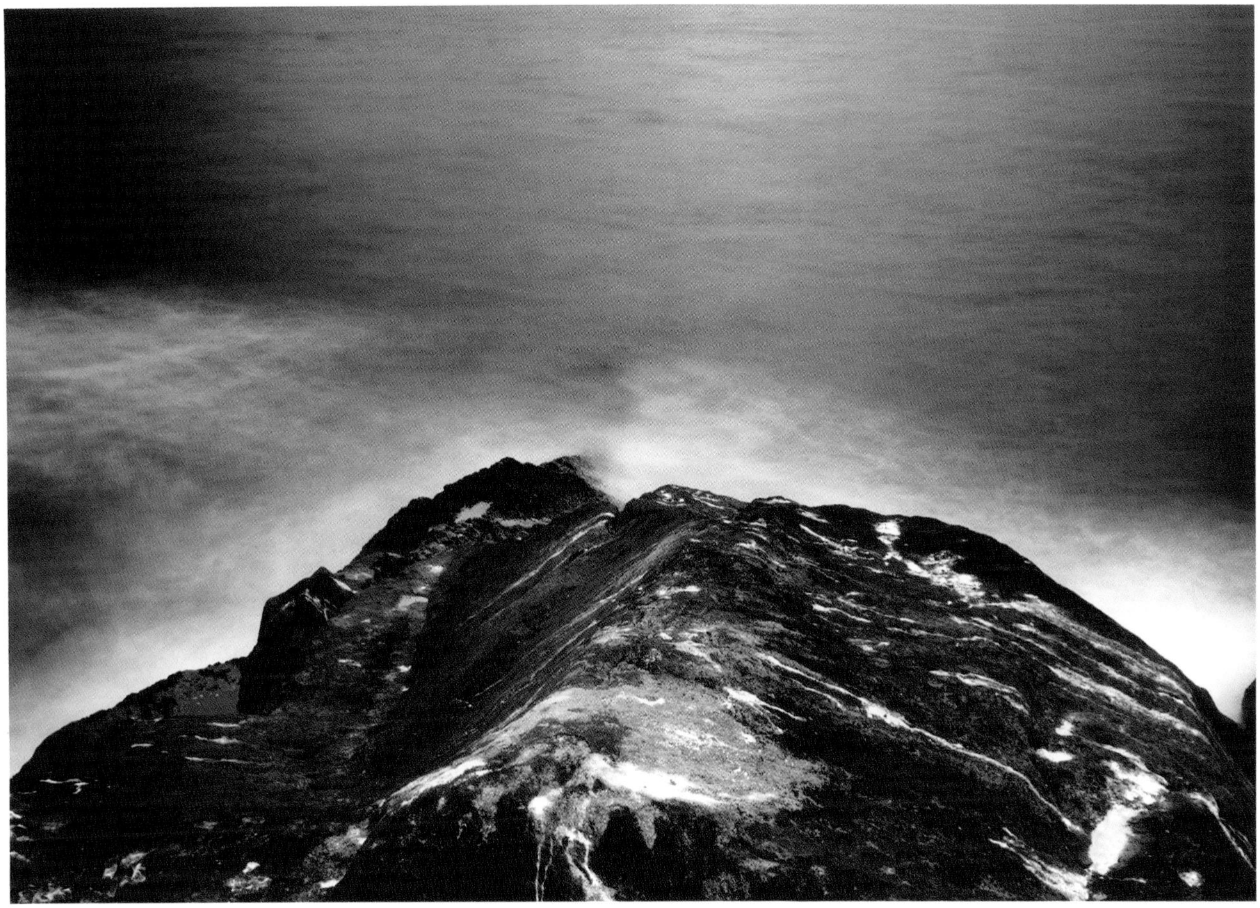

Furthest North – The Barents Sea – 71° 11′ 08″ Knivskjelodden, Norway, 2003–2004 The North-most point of Continental Europe 2003–2004

THOMAS JOSHUA COOPER (BORN 1946)
Silver gelatin print, 102 x 137 cm
Edition 3/3

Courtesy of Haunch of Venison, London

This photograph is part of Thomas Joshua Cooper's most ambitious project to date. Begun in 1990, 'The World's Edge – The Atlantic Basin Project' is Cooper's attempt to map all the terra firma extremities that surround the Atlantic Ocean. Armed with an eighteen ninety-eight wood and brass field camera and a tripod, Cooper travels to remote places, often retracing the tortuous steps of the heroic explorers of the past, and only takes a single shot at each location. In Cooper's photographs personal endeavour and self-discovery go hand in hand with pushing boundaries and geographical exploration. He often employs lengthy exposure times which lend his photographs an ethereal, meditative quality that belies the struggle involved in reaching each destination.

To date Cooper has completed the first part of his project, photographing the Western fringes of the Atlantic Ocean. This photograph was taken at Knivskjelodden in Norway, continental Europe's northernmost point. A narrow ridge with steep slopes situated on parallel 71°11′08″, Knivskjelodden can only be reached on foot by an eighteen kilometre return trip through grassland along a trail which becomes increasingly difficult to negotiate once it starts sloping towards the sea along smooth, wet rock.

From Knivskjelodden the view to the dramatic cliffs of North Cape across the bay is magnificent, but the nature of Cooper's project is such that he chose instead to photograph the point where Knivskjelodden's outlying rocks gently slope into the sea. Indeed, the landscape is quite anonymous and Cooper's characteristically extensive title is required in order to interpret it, but this does not detract from our viewing experience. Thanks to a long exposure, the mist rising from the sea dissolves the boundary between the icy rocky outcrop in the foreground and the calm sea in the background and the landscape is infused with an air of stillness. This, coupled with the exquisite tonal richness of the photograph, engenders a sense of awe similar in its effect to a quiet rendition of American Sublime painting. GB

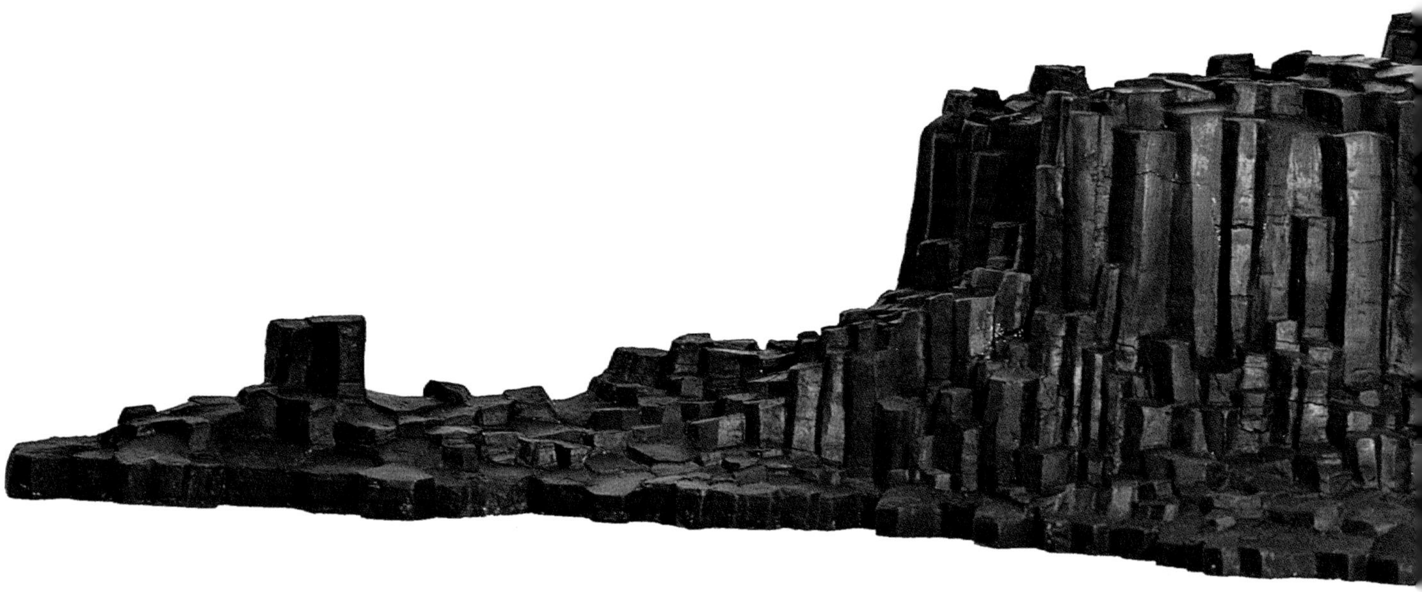

Basalt III (Horizon), 2004

TANIA KOVATS (BORN 1966)
Acrylic compound, polyflake, graphite, pigment, timber, 43 x 176 x 31 cm
Courtesy of the artist, London

Tania Kovats is an artist whose primary interest is landscape, and particularly landscapes where the workings of geology and the passing of time are most evident. She has said of her work: 'The processes and verbs of geology inform my work: eroding, shifting, erupting, compressing, solidifying, subsiding, tipping, and cooling. I look to either describe or use geological processes in the making of both my sculptures and my drawings … I see landscape as a series of incidents coming into being' (quoted in http://www.uwe.ac.uk/amd/acid/kovats.htm).

The geometric basalt columns that form the Giant's Causeway in County Antrim, northern Ireland, are one such landscape. A legend tells that the warrior giant Finn McCool, enamoured with a Scottish giantess from the Island of Staffa, built the causeway to bring her across the sea. Less romantic is the scientific explanation that movement of tectonic plates in the Tertiary Period, some sixty million years ago, caused enormous fissures through which basaltic lava erupted. Rapid cooling, probably due to the lava's contact with water, caused contractions and cracking which resulted in a mass of

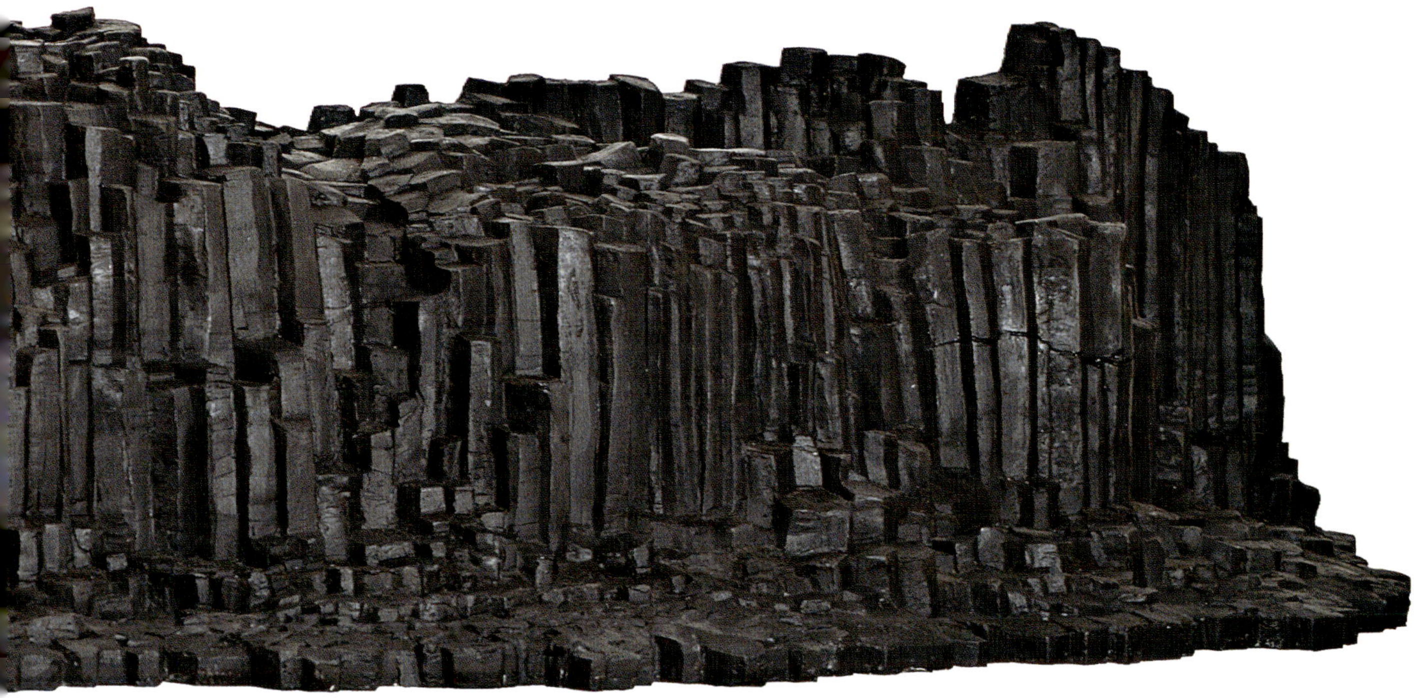

40,000 columns in strangely regular geometric shapes. Mostly hexagonal, the columns start under the sea and reach a height of approximately twelve metres. Kovats is interested in how geology cuts across boundaries – similar rock formations can be found in Fingal's Cave in Staffa and at the Devil's Postpile in California, which she had visited before undertaking the *Basalt* series.

With the wall-mounted *Basalt III (Horizon)* Kovats raises the columns of the Giant's Causeway from the ground and places them at eye-level to suggest the horizon. Playing with scale and positioning, she succeeds in turning an already implausible natural landscape into a floating fantasy island. Yet, just as the chaos of volcanic eruption was crystallised in the geometric order of the hexagonal columns, her act contributes to our understanding of this fantastic site, one of the most emblematic landscapes of the British Isles. GB

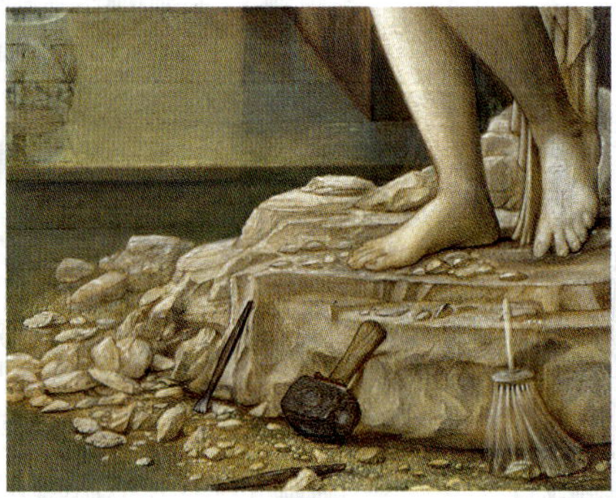

3 Metamorphosis

Go inside a stone
That would be my way.
Let somebody else become a dove
Or gnash with a tiger's tooth
I am happy to be stone.

CHARLES SIMIC (BORN 1938) *STONE*

ABOVE:
Sir Edward Coley Burne-Jones, *Pygmalion and the Image, 2, The Hand Refrains* (detail)
Birmingham Museums & Art Gallery

Stardust, 2003 ➤

GARY BREEZE (BORN 1966)
Bronze, diameter 16 cm
Courtesy of the artist

CONFERRING SYMBOLIC MEANINGS to stones is a practice as ancient as abstract thought and language itself. Every age and culture has been curious about the origins of their landscapes and speculated about them, sometimes through the creation of myths, by ascribing stories to particular outcrops and mountains or imbuing specific types of stones with particular meanings and properties, often coveting the rarest and most beautiful.

The medieval mind sought order and hierarchy, and alchemists created systematic lapidaries to record the symbolic associations of certain stones. Change and transformation have fascinated artists and makers before even Ovid's *Metamorphoses* provided a text. This chapter explores the power of rock and stone to change and be changed, whether by the human hand or the forces of nature. The change may be physical, reflecting the processes of changing earths into pigments, ores into metals, or rocks into sculptures – or it may be magical or symbolic.

Specific rocks, stones and precious metals have sometimes had different meanings in different cultures, but their importance is universal. Sometimes stones symbolize wealth, power and status through jewellery and regalia that is worn to be displayed. More privately they may provide individual protection, healing or prophecy through religious or mystical means. A stone has sometimes been thought to change whatever it touches, notably the life and status of its owner.

This sphere, made by the artist Gary Breeze, is composed of bronze letter forms that spell out the phrase 'In a sense human flesh is made of stardust.' Breeze demonstrates a contemporary awareness of the literal, physical and metamorphic processes at work in the making of the world. The sphere also delivers a poetic message of fundamental and universal truth that goes straight to the heart of this chapter. Almost everything in the universe, including ourselves, is made up of atoms that once burned brightly as fuel inside a star like our own sun, endlessly recycled in myriad forms over aeons. Countless millennia from now, all that is familiar to us will once more burn away brightly in future suns. We, as creative and industrious individuals, have been part of this process since prehistory, taking raw materials from the landscape and shaping, sculpting and grinding them to produce tools, colour, jewellery, sculptures and homes. As artists, however, and as humans capable of abstract thought, we also imbue these temporary forms with significance, symbolism, metaphor and meaning. We change the way the stone is viewed and esteemed.

Tin and copper ores have been excavated with difficulty from deep within the ground by determined miners, then pulverised, heated, melted, blended, forged and tested for at least the last 4,000 years. Bronze, a blend of these two metals and the technological mainstay of a culture lasting for thousands of years, is still the ultimate metal medium of sculptors and has been since antiquity.

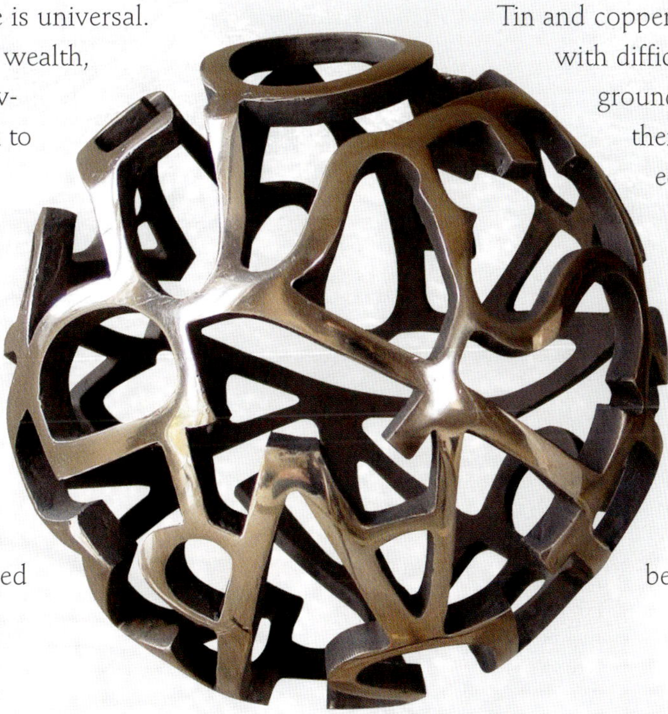

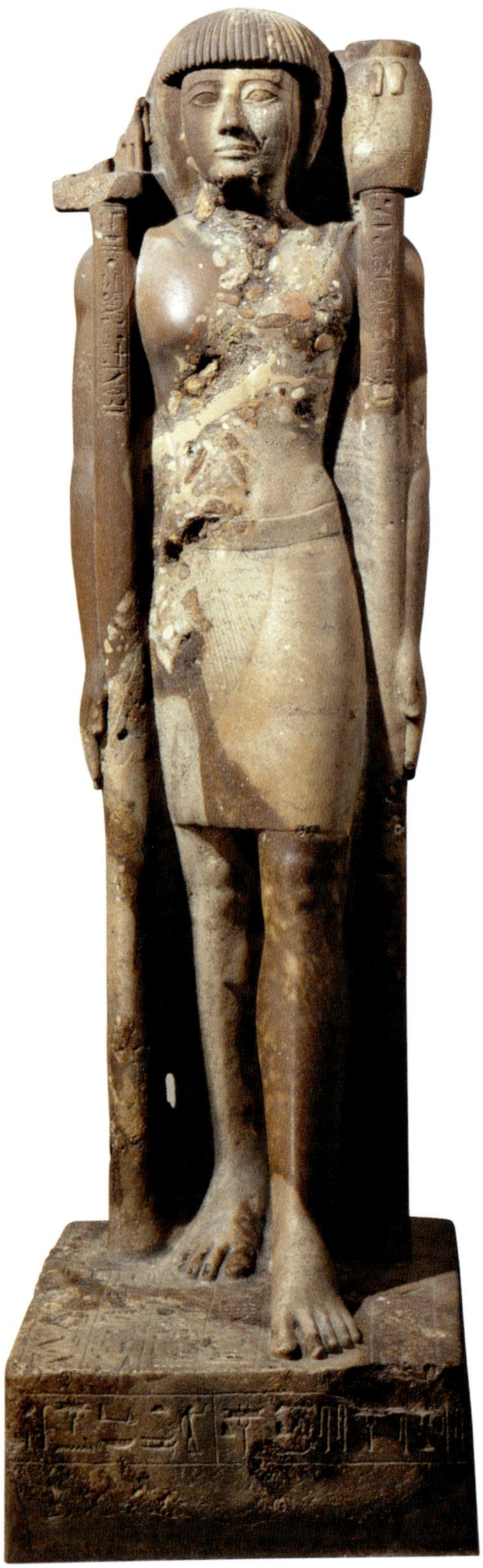

Sandstone conglomerate Statue of Khaemwaset, c. 1250 BC

19th Dynasty
From Asyut, Egypt, perhaps originally from Abydos
Sandstone, 138 x 43.1 x 55 cm

EA 947
The British Museum, London

King Ramesses II had several children by his many wives, the most famous of which is his fourth son Khaemwaset. He is remembered for his interest in preserving the history of Egypt and was the first person to organize the conservation of Egypt's stone monuments which had already stood for thousands of years.

Royalty were often deified, and statues were regarded as places where deities could manifest themselves after death. This statue shows Khaemwaset displaying his piety before Osiris, holding standards symbolic of the province of Abydos. The sculpting of this statue in sandstone containing a vein of pebbly conglomerate shows the incredible skill with which the ancient sculptors could transform even the most difficult materials. Why this particular block was deliberately chosen for sculpting is unclear, as large sandstone blocks without such awkward inclusions are in plentiful supply upstream in southern Egypt. However, the choice has produced a striking image. The conglomerate vein running up through the body to the chin is almost visceral, suggesting organs and body parts and transforms the statue, almost bringing it to life. The varied colours of the assorted quartz and sandstone pebbles, each with their own geological story to tell, also give the impression of brightly coloured garments or jewellery against the plainer background of the sandstone.

This complex rock was formed in a desert environment between one 146 million and sixty-five million years ago. The grains of sand were smoothed and polished by the wind before being bonded together by quartz, calcite, iron oxide and clays. However, the vein of rounded pebbles running through the statue is indicative of repeated, if occasional, water flow. This whole block must have been formed on its side in a wadi in the Egyptian desert in conditions not unlike those that prevail today. NL

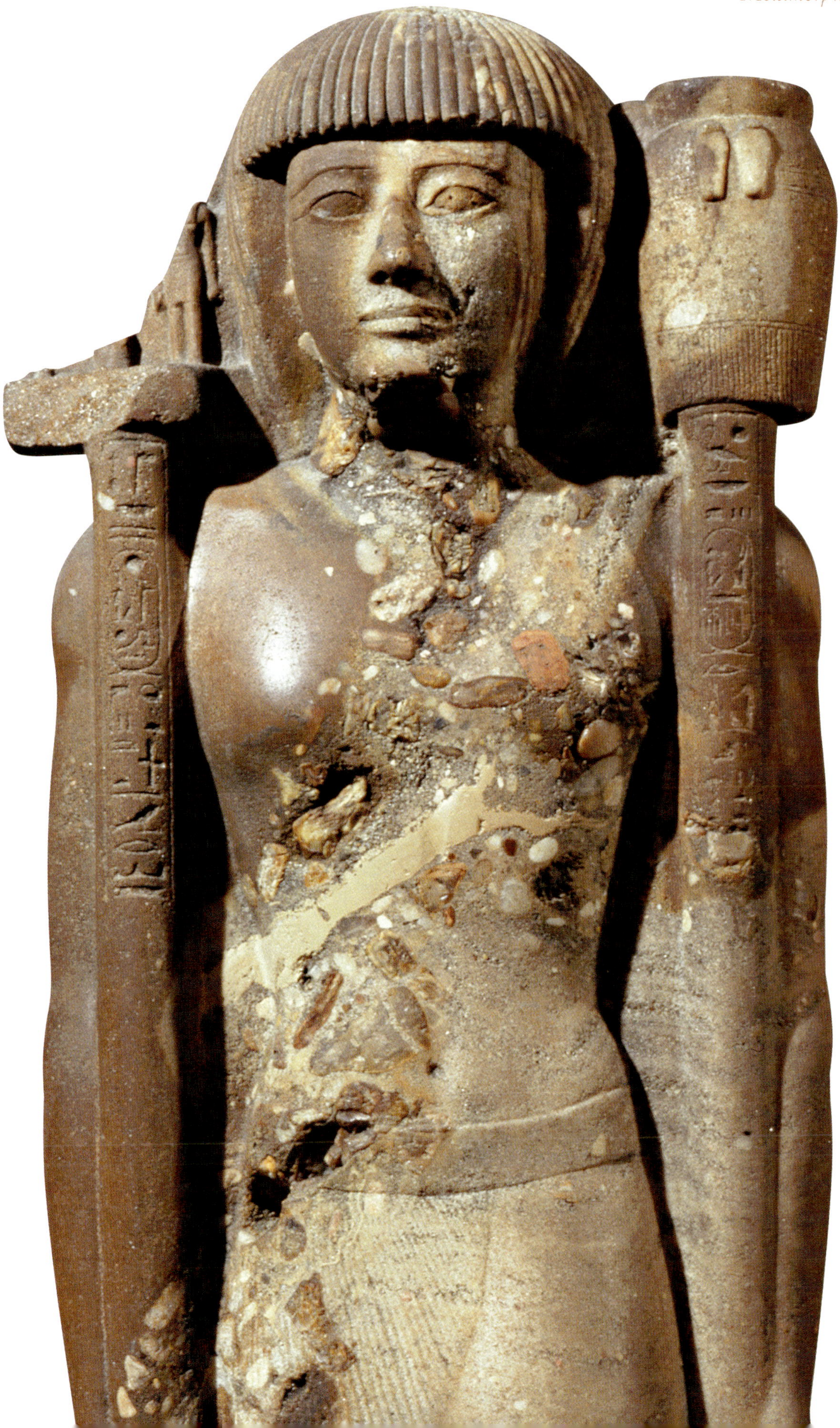

Serpentine Bowl

Medieval with 16th-century mounts
Germany
Serpentine, enamel and silver-gilt, diameter 25.4 cm
Dated 1521, with arms, probably of the Order of St John of Jerusalem
Victoria and Albert Museum, London

The use of this bowl is unknown. Its size suggests that it could have been intended for display more than for practical use, but the shape of the object is that of a drinking vessel. Silver or gilt mounts were often added to stone objects to increase their value and status, but in this case the use of serpentine is significant in itself.

Serpentine acquired its name from the snakeskin-like patterns which appear on its greenish surface. Traditionally, probably because of its appearance, it was thought to be a talisman against snakebites and by association was supposed to be effective against poison. This is somewhat ironic as the constituent materials of serpentine – the igneous minerals olivine and pyroxene – are identical to those in naturally occurring poisonous fibrous asbestos. Certain other hardstones, such as jasper, were believed to possess similarly protective powers and were also used in connection with food and drink. Although they were used because they were beautiful, expensive and therefore high-status materials, to know the extra dimension of meaning assigned to them adds to our understanding of why a specific stone has been used for a particular purpose.

In the case of this object, the stone bowl is older than its mount and would have been made at a time when belief in the stone's protective properties was the norm. By the sixteenth century, when its mounts were added, owners of the bowl would probably still have believed in its miraculous powers. By the mid-seventeenth century, however, when a London doctor, William Rowland, mentions the stone (*The Chymical Dispensatory*, London, 1669, 174), he considers that only the 'vulgar' believe that serpentine sweats in the presence of poison. His approach is dismissive of such superstition, but the fact that he mentioned it at all suggests that the belief was still current, and that old ideas died hard. FA

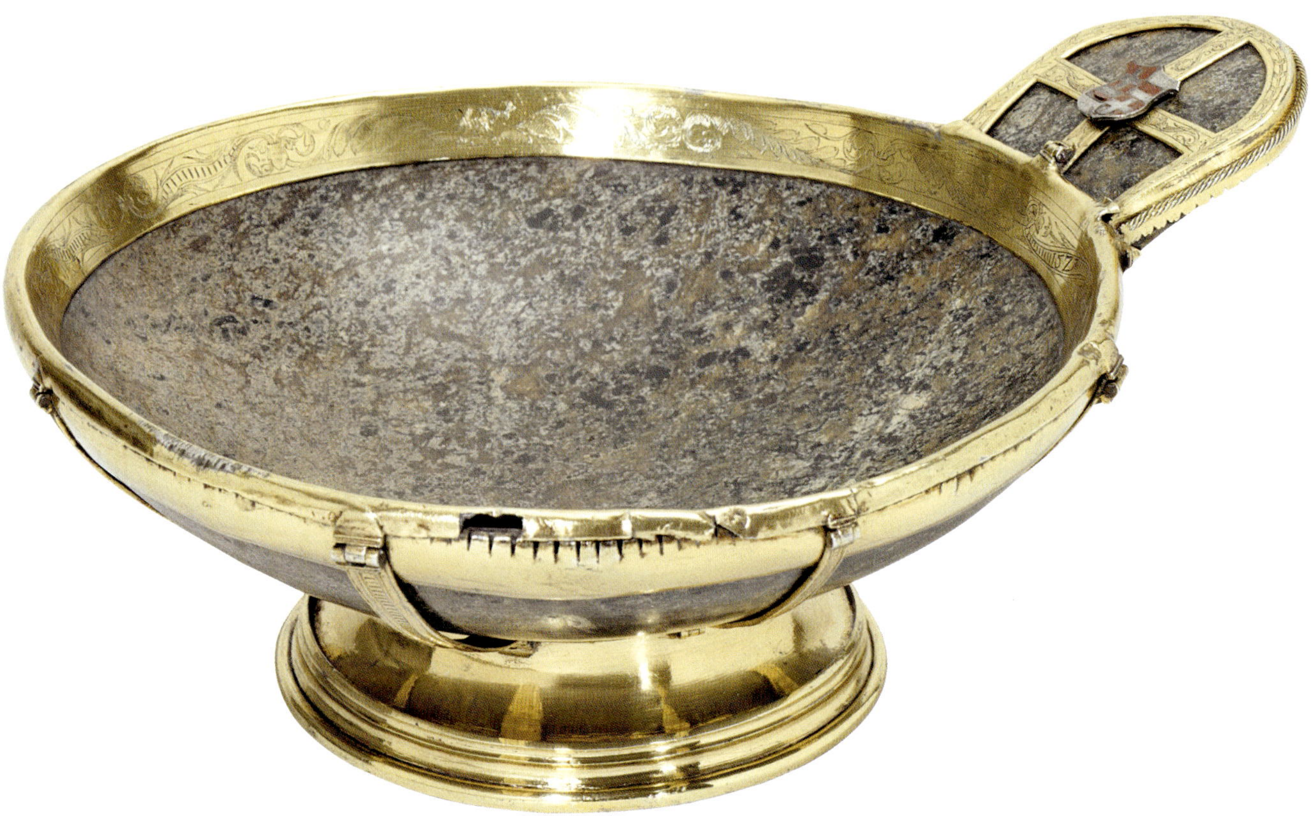

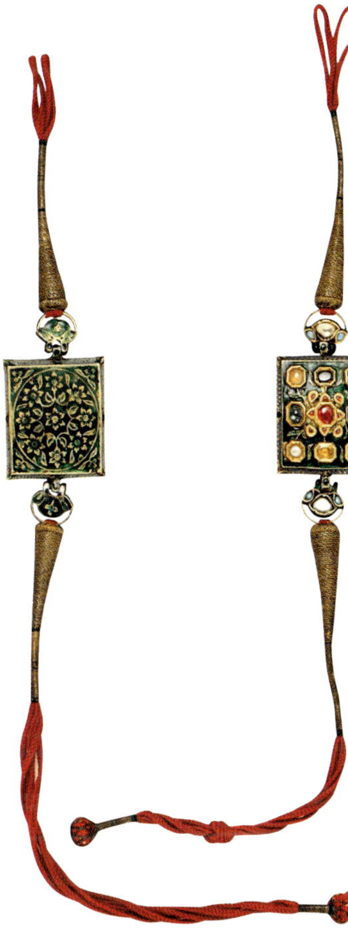

Pair of Navaratna gold Armlets enamelled with translucent green and pale opaque Turquoise and set with nine Stones and Diamonds, c. 1850

Delhi, India
Gold, enamel and gemstones, 6.3 x 3.1 cm
Victoria and Albert Museum, London

These armlets are set with the gemstones which appear in ancient Sanskrit texts as the most auspicious and important. They include five greater gems or *maharatnani* which are diamond, pearl, ruby, emerald and sapphire, and four lesser gems or *uparatnani* which comprise jacinth, topaz, cat's eye and coral. *Navaratna* means 'nine gems' in Sanskrit.

Navaratna had powerful talismanic value 2,000 years ago, and are still worn today. Each stone corresponds with one of the seven 'planets' known to antiquity (sun, moon, Mercury, Venus, Mars, Jupiter and Saturn) and the ascending and descending nodes of the moon, which are considered planets in Indian astrology. Wearing *navaratna* was traditionally undertaken with the advice of astrologers. This practice was considered to counter-balance any bad luck the heavens might bring, while attracting beneficial influences to the wearer.

There are some variations in the gemstones used in *navaratna* jewellery – the most important quality of the stones is their colour and so occasionally cheaper substitutes are made. Correspondences between gems and planets differ from those in Western countries. In India rubies represent the sun, the source of life. For this reason they are often found at the centre of a setting, encircled by gems representing the other planets. This is in contrast to Western traditions, where the sun is represented by yellow gems such as citrine and topaz.

Rubies, and other red gems such as garnet, spinel and jacinth (a name for red zircon) are particularly highly valued in Eastern cultures. Traditional writings contain many references to their significance. Hindu mythology describes the houses of the Gods as lit by glowing rubies, while two medieval Arab lapidaries, Al Tifashi and Al Biruni, testify to the importance of red stones in the Muslim world. The former asserts that rubies confer power, strength and courage (*Best Thoughts on the Best of Stones*, transl. Samar Najm Abul Huda, London, 1998, 98–99). Al Biruni praises jacinths, explaining that in the Koran the beauty of the virgin Houris of Paradise is described as resembling 'jacinth and coral-stone' (*The Book Most Comprehensive in Knowledge of Precious Stones*, transl. Hakim Mohamed Said, Islamabad 1989, 29). FA

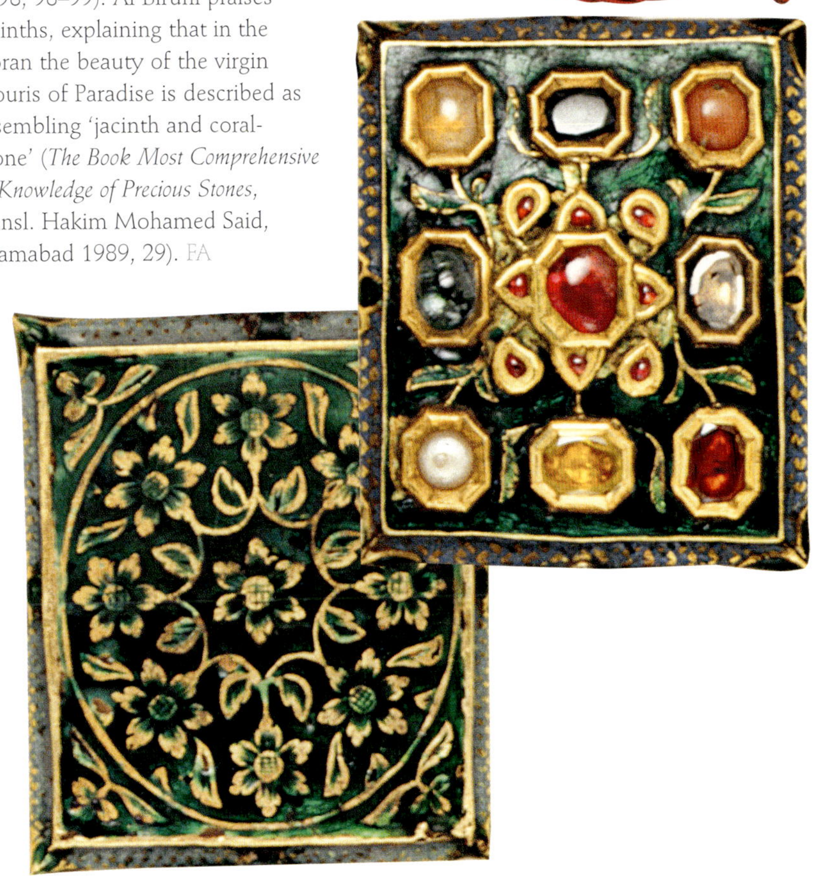

Falling Titan, 1786

THOMAS BANKS (1735–1805)
Marble, 83.8 x 90.2 cm
Signed and dated: *T. Banks Sculp . 1786*
Royal Academy of Arts, London

This extraordinary sculpture has always been admired for its dramatic impact, surprising scale and impressive physicality since Banks first presented it to the Royal Academy in London as his Diploma piece following his election as an Academician in 1786. It shows the fall of the giants, the rebel sons of Heaven and Earth who first piled Mount Osa on Pelion and then Mount Olympus on Mount Osa to reach Heaven in an attempt to dethrone Zeus. They were defeated by Heracles and buried beneath mountains and volcanoes.

This sculpture represents a clear manifestation of that impulse which sculptors since Michelangelo have expressed: the intellectual and emotional challenge of finding the form within the stone, rather than the more prosaic execution of a sculpting task. Banks began his working life as a stonemason and his daughter later recalled of this piece: 'I perfectly remember, on the occasion of that statue being worked, his saying in conversation that he conceived the subject to exist in the block of marble, *a priori*, and that it was called forth by the sculptor's hand.' This idea that the form already resides within the stone awaiting manifestation was first expressed by the art historian Giorgio Vasari in his description of Michelangelo at work.

Thomas Banks has chosen the perfect subject for his own claim to Michelangelo's mantle. He articulates a theme which was well known to travellers from Giulio Romano's virtuoso fresco decoration of the Room of the Falling Giants in the Palazzo del Té, Mantua. This was also a favourite subject with seventeenth-century artists such as Guido Reni and his followers (notably Bartolomeo Corialano, chiaroscuro woodcut, 1638) and Salvator Rosa (etching, 1663). Banks has chosen the whitest metamorphosed limestone from Carrara, Tuscany, favoured by sculptors including Michelangelo for the purity of its mineral content and the consequent lack of discolouration. Banks displays his virtuosity in contrasting the smooth skin of the principal figure with the rough-hewn rocks. AM

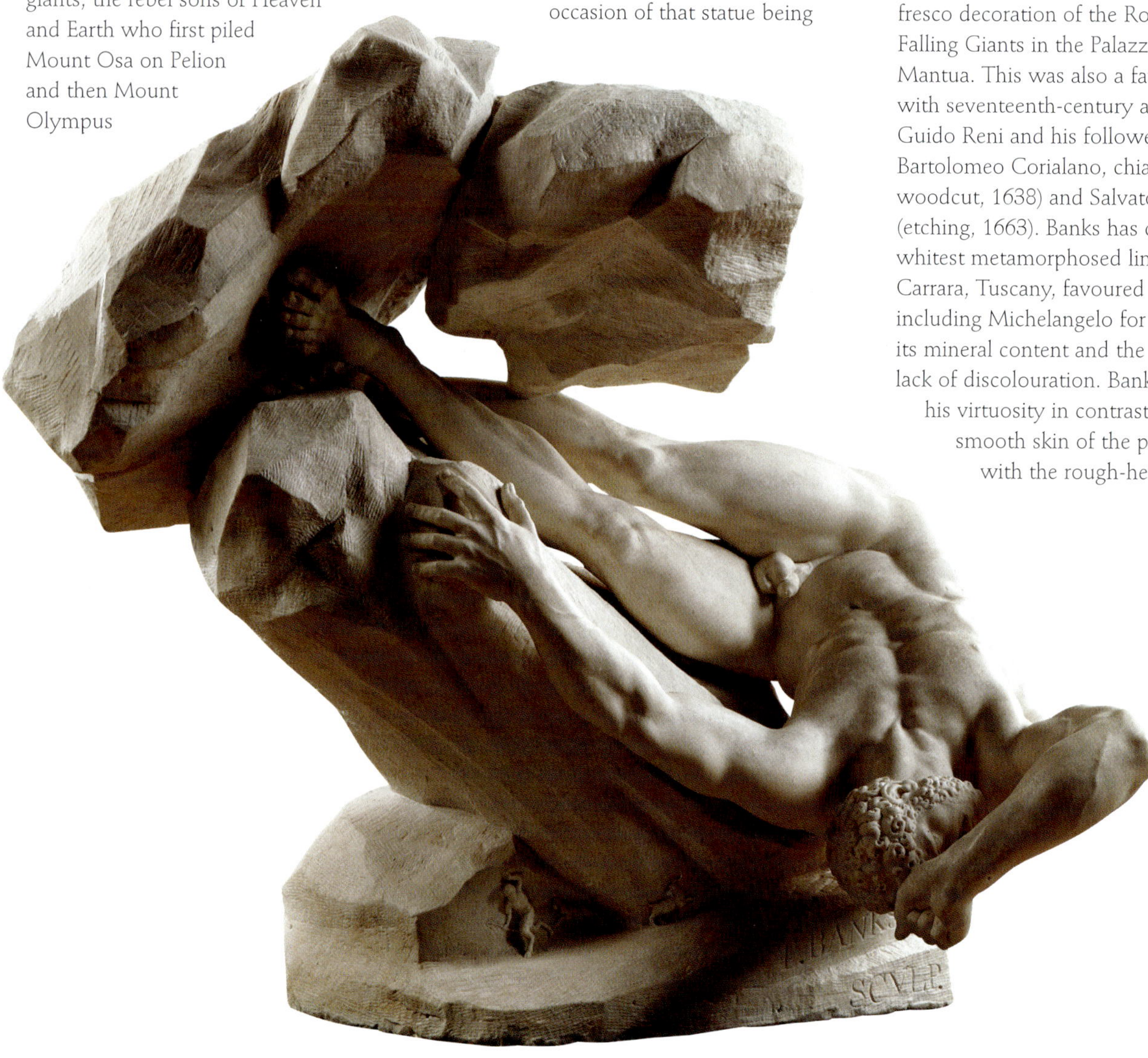

Pygmalion and the Image, 2, The Hand Refrains, 1878

SIR EDWARD COLEY BURNE-JONES
(1833–98)
Oil on canvas, 98.7 x 76.3 cm
Birmingham Museums & Art Gallery

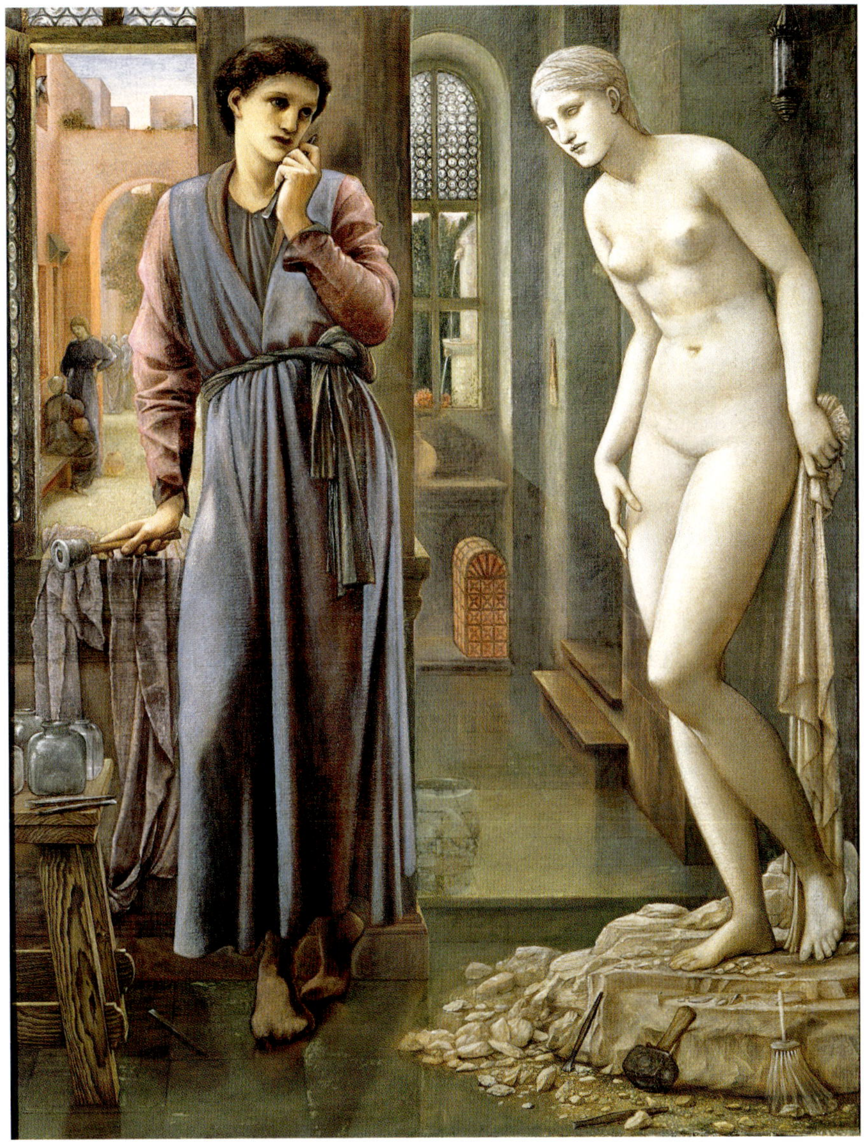

This painting represents one of the most celebrated moments from Ovid's tales (*Metamorphoses*, 10, fable 9), demonstrating visually the notion of transformation: in this case the sculpted figure literally turns to flesh. The original story tells how Pygmalion of Cyprus sculpted an image of a woman so beautiful that he fell in love with the statue. He prayed to Venus for help and the goddess made the image come alive, enabling the sculptor to wed his creation, Galatea. This is an idea which contrasts with the metamorphic tale of Medusa: one glance from the monster was enough to turn the onlooker to stone (Ovid, *Metamorphoses*, 4, v. 618).

In the case of Burne-Jones' image of Pygmalion with his life-size sculpture, the moment of metamorphosis is depicted by the artist to such a scale and smoothness that it is not possible for the figure to have been of any material other than stone. To emphasize the immediacy of the event, the sculptor still holds his polishing tool, while more tools and stone chippings lie at the feet of the 'awakening' figure. However, the original story as told by Ovid is of a statue made of ivory. Burne-Jones is not alone in having chosen to depict a statue whose scale is suggestive of stone, rather than of ivory. It has long been a part of the historiography of sculpture, since Giorgio Vasari first wrote of Michelangelo seeing the figure entrapped within a block of stone, to envision a sculptor releasing the imprisoned figure from the quarried stone block.

Pygmalion and the Image is one of two series of four paintings by Burne-Jones that tell Pygmalion's story. The power of his treatment of this subject derives in part from the personal nature of the subject matter. At the start of his work on the series in 1868 the artist was himself deeply in love with a young Greek woman, Maria Zambaco, and the first series was painted for her mother. Burne-Jones explores the difference between intellectual ideas of beauty, upon which an artist may apply their skill, with the reality of physical attraction which can overwhelm two lovers (*The Age of Rossetti, Burne-Jones & Watts Symbolism in Britain 1860-1910*, Tate, 1997, no. 38). AM

Queen Elizabeth II, 1953

CECIL BEATON (1904–80)
Semi-matt cibachrome print, 33.1 x 24.9 cm
National Portrait Gallery, London

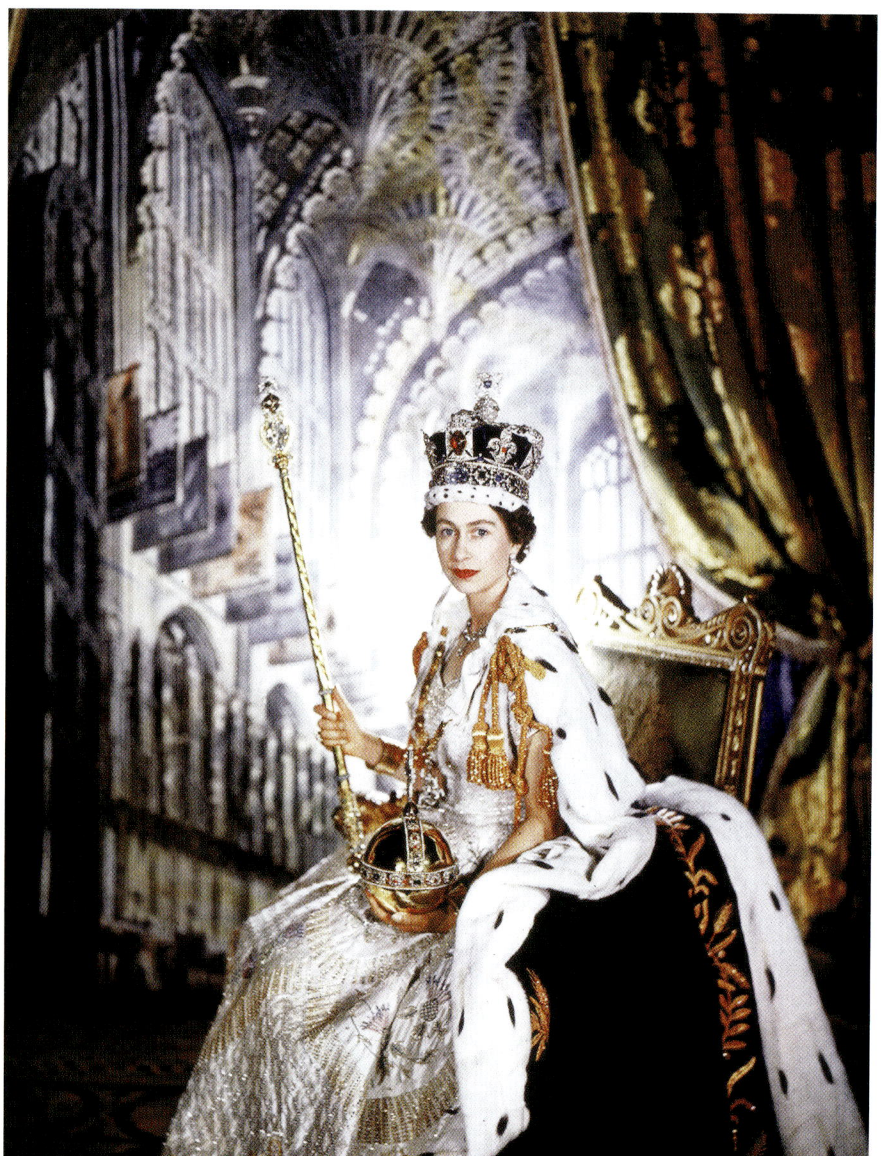

There could be no more direct expression of precious stones bestowing power and authority than this image of Elizabeth II in her coronation regalia. Precious stones and metals are the means by which this young woman is transformed from an ordinary mortal into a monarch. The identity of a state and visual representations of wealth, power, conquest and history are concentrated into this jewellery: she is metaphorically and literally weighed down with symbolism.

The Imperial State Crown is set with over 3,000 gems. Its principal jewels have histories and legends attached to them, the most complex of which is the 'Black Prince's Ruby'. This is in reality a spinel – a stone which resembles a ruby although it is not geologically related. It was given to Edward, the Black Prince, by a Spanish king who had killed its original owner to obtain it. The stone was also worn by Henry V at Agincourt and reputedly by Richard III at the Battle of Bosworth. The other jewels include sapphires which belonged to Charles II and Edward the Confessor, and pearls associated with Elizabeth I.

The largest stone is a diamond cut from the Cullinan diamond, the largest ever found. This was given to Edward VII and cut into several separate gems. One of these, 'The Star of Africa', adorns the royal sceptre.

The crown jewels are newer than most of the individual stones. In 1649 Oliver Cromwell ordered the gold to be melted down and the gemstones sold in a symbolic bid to destroy the trappings of kingship. Charles II bought back the jewels and had the regalia remade.
The crown has been reconstructed several times since but despite these alterations the crown jewels have become timeless visual expressions of national and personal power and status. The stones connect the Queen with past monarchs, making her the embodiment of a living symbol of sovereignty. FA

Untitled glass Sculpture #R212/B, 1988

COLIN REID (BORN 1953)
Glass, 48 x 15 cm
NWHCM : 1997.42 : D
Norwich Castle Museum & Art Gallery

This sculpture is made from cast glass. Known in ancient Egypt as 'the stone which flows', glass comprises a mixture of minerals. Silica and lime (both contained in sand) are combined with sodium or potassium. These earthy materials melted together at high temperature transform into a transparent, brittle substance which may be blown or moulded into forms practically inconceivable from the appearance of their original components. This process, though entirely manufactured, results in a metamorphosis so complete as to appear mysterious even when the technical procedures are known.

Glass has many unique qualities. In chemical terms, it is not a solid at all, but a super-cooled liquid. It is capable of continuing to flow when appearing to be in a solid state, and of returning gradually to its constituent parts. However, both these processes happen over centuries, too slowly to be visible to the naked eye.

Colin Reid's work embodies the transforming and infinitely variable nature of glass as an artistic material, exploring its qualities to the full. Although abstract in appearance, his glass sculptures are powerfully based upon natural forms and in particular upon aspects of rock and stone. He makes copies of rock formations and creates textures which may appear as solid as an iceberg or as volatile as boiling lava. Typically, he uses thick chunks of glass with alternately polished and sand-blasted surfaces which emphasize both the opaque and the translucent. They appear at once earthy and liquid, like the dual nature of glass itself, or indeed the planet as a whole. This sculpture calls to mind many natural phenomena: a ravine where the jagged edges have been worn and chiselled by time, a bolt of lightning, a fissure in the earth, or a slice of agate in which trails of coloured mineral impurities appear to float through and within the stone as if through water. FA

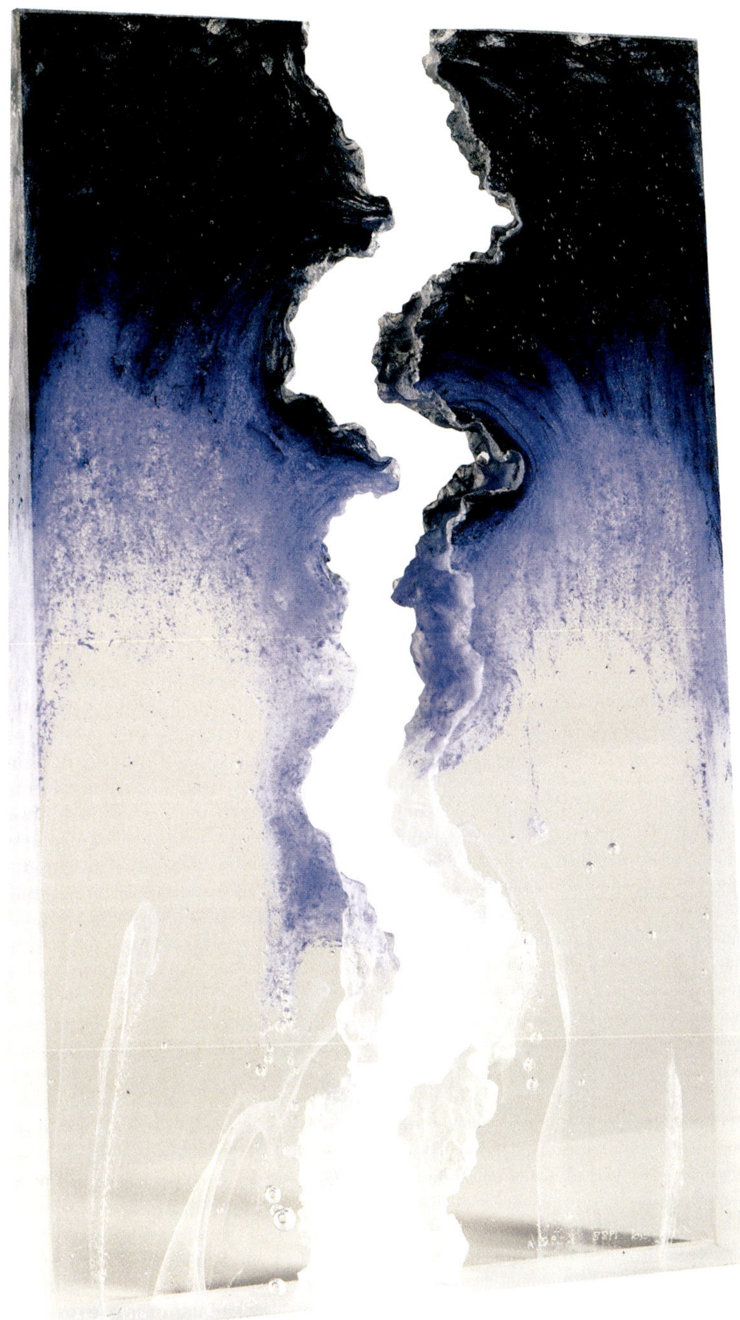

Full View of the Serra Pelada Gold Mine, Brazil, 1986

SEBASTIÃO SALGADO (BORN 1944)
Black and white photograph, 44.9 x 29.9 cm
Victoria and Albert Museum, London

Around 2,500 years ago, the Greek poet Pindar wrote, 'Gold is the child of Zeus, neither moth nor rust devoureth it but the mind of man is devoured by this supreme possession' (Pindar, *Fragments,* 222).

The attractive nature of gold, its resistance to corrosion and oxidation and its ready malleability are unique qualities among metals and go some way towards explaining why it has been highly prized since antiquity.

Until recently, the earliest gold artefacts were believed to have been made around 3000 BC by the Sumerians in what is now southern Iraq. In 1972, however, the earliest gold objects ever found, including bracelets and earrings, were accidentally discovered in Varna, Bulgaria. They are thought to date as far back as 4600 BC.

Gold was widely used in Ancient Egypt, Greece and Rome, but its use declined after the fall of the Roman Empire until Christopher Columbus discovered America in 1492. The 'conquistadores' of the sixteenth century arrived in the new continent to find a highly developed goldsmithing tradition. The Incas considered gold 'the sweat of the sun'. Looting and genocide quickly put an end to this tradition and soon the supply of American gold to Europe petered out. It was only with the Californian gold rush of 1848 that gold became available again in larger quantities. It is estimated that around 125,000 tonnes of gold have been mined in the last six thousand years and that ninety per cent of this has been produced since 1848 (World Gold Council website http://www.gold.org/discover/knowledge/aboutgold).

In 1980 the discovery of gold nuggets in the eastern Amazon in Brazil sparked the most spectacular gold rush in recent history. Among those who flocked to the goldmine that became known as 'Serra Pelada' ('Bald Mountain') were professional people such as lawyers and doctors. Most prospectors, however, were Brazil's agricultural poor who left their homes in the hope that gold would free their lives from destitution. At the beginning of the mine's exploitation, a tonne of gold was excavated manually per month. By 1985, over thirty-five tonnes of gold had been extracted without the use of any machinery. At the peak of the gold rush over 50,000 miners, monitored by military police, worked in the 200-metre deep pit, enduring abject living conditions in an atmosphere where humidity is never below eighty per cent.

Sebastião Salgado, an economist committed to third world development, turned to photography in 1973. Perhaps as a legacy of his former profession, his photographs tend to document the plight of the world's disenfranchised, and he has said of his work, 'You photograph with all your ideology' (Sebastião Salgado, *An Uncertain Grace*, London 2004, 147). His 1986 photographs of Serra Pelada are part of a project documenting manual labour that spanned several years and resulted in a book and exhibition called *Workers* in 1993. This photograph shows the gaping pit of the mine looking like a huge ant colony or a circle from Dante's Inferno. Swarms of miners in single file carry sacks of earth up the rockface on rickety ladders.
The sheer size of the pit renders them insignificant, anonymous, like so many insects carrying out a mechanical and seemingly endless task. The scene could not be further removed from the elegant jewellers' windows in which gold is eventually displayed. Salgado confronts us with the undesirable, shameful side of the remarkable transformation of gold from a simple ore in the earth to the ultimate status symbol. GB

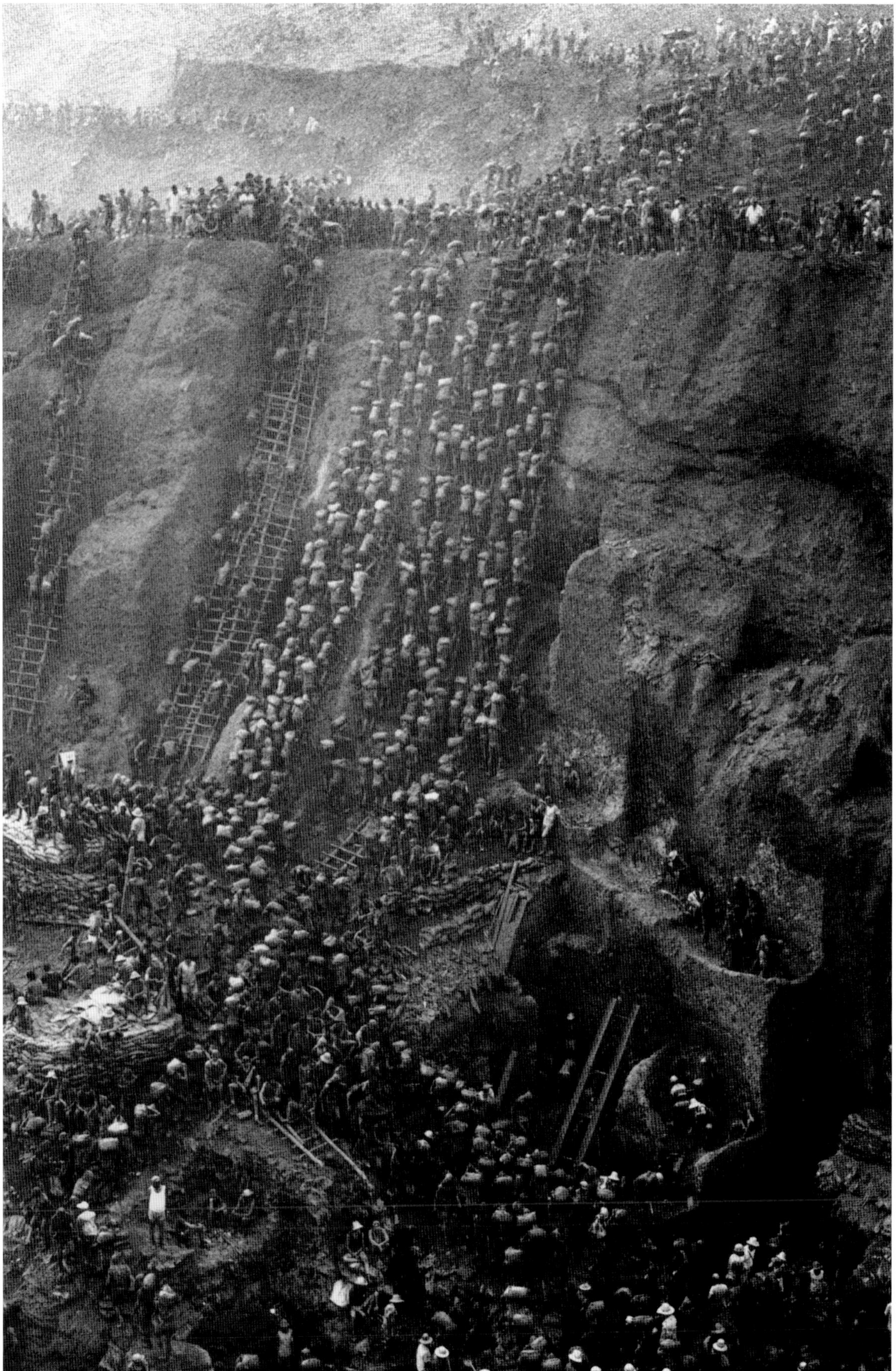

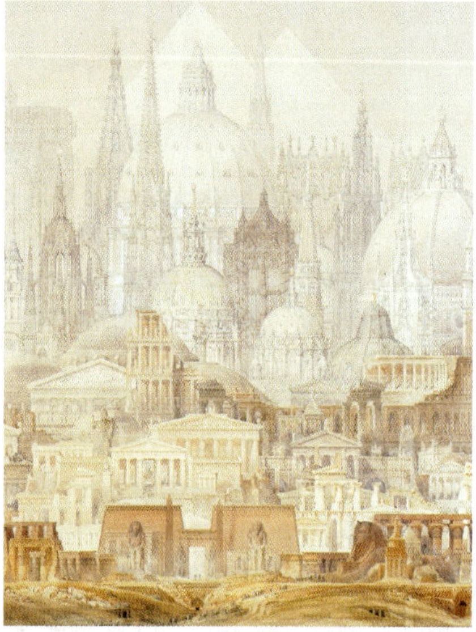

4 Studying the Rockface

There are no natural objects out of which more can be learned than out of stones. They seem to have been created especially to reward a patient observer ... For a stone, when it is examined, will be found a mountain in miniature

JOHN RUSKIN, *MODERN PAINTERS*, VOL. IV, P. 311

Study of a Block of Queensland Opal (detail) 1884 ➤

ALEXANDER MACDONALD (1839–1922)
Watercolour and bodycolour on paper
15.5 x 16 cm

Collection of the Guild of St George, Sheffield Galleries & Museums Trust

ABOVE:
C.R. Cockerell RA, *The Professor's Dream* (detail)
Royal Academy of Arts, London

THE DIRECT STUDY OF ROCKS has inspired artists since at least the Renaissance. The landscapes in the background of Renaissance religious paintings or portraiture are often uniquely attuned to the region in which the artist is working. Dürer's work was informed by his study of nature, including the rock formations at a quarry outside Nuremburg. More recently, painters and photographers, such as Jacqueline Hassink, have studied quarries and mines that have been cut by machine rather than eroded by time, bringing new perspectives upon the rockface.

As a young man, John Ruskin (1819–1900) – best known for his art criticism and championing of J.M.W. Turner – was initially inspired by geology. Ruskin was captivated by his first experience of the Alps at the age of fourteen. He studied the writings of the Alpine geologist Horace Benedicte de Saussure and his first professional publications were essays on the colour of the Rhine and the twisted strata of Mont Blanc for *The Magazine of Natural History*. He maintained this interest throughout his life, collecting geological specimens, publishing on geological matters and taking issue with post-Darwinian geologists such as the natural philosophe, John Tyndall.

In the fourth volume of *Modern Painters* Ruskin lamented that in his day no contemporary artist seemed interested in geology: 'it is only in ancient art that, generally speaking, we find any careful realization of Stones.' Ruskin is the prime example of the writer and artist who searches for the aesthetic motive behind the study of rocks and their representation in art, partly due to his belief that a divine order expressed itself even in the stones. Those most admired by Ruskin included artists such as J.M.W. Turner and John Brett.

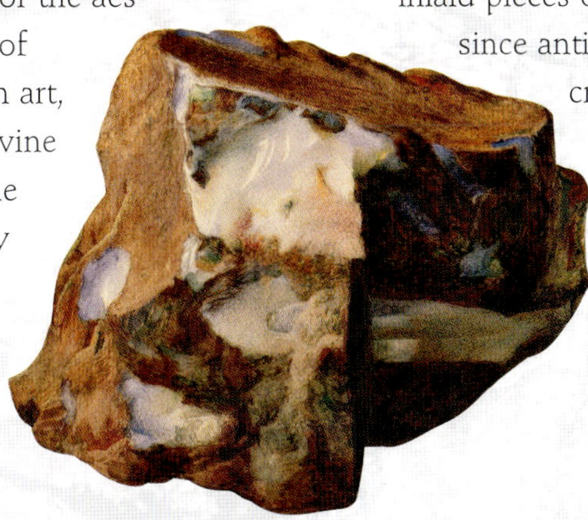

Accurate representations of geological specimens were in fact very much needed to aid comparison and research as the new science of geology gained a hold. Reproducing the colours and forms of geological specimens with meaningful accuracy was necessary to the publication of useful geological treatises, while also encouraging the intimate understanding of a specimen. Artists able to work accurately became sought after by collectors wishing to communicate their findings. This process stimulated a genre of beautiful and intricate studies that, whilst not intended as great works of art, nevertheless still provide us with some inspiring masterpieces of observation.

The block of Queensland opal in Alexander Macdonald's watercolour was described by Ruskin as 'the finest hitherto found, and for vivacity of scintillant colour, unsurpassable by any that ever can be found' (C. Morley, *John Ruskin; late work 1870-1890*, 1984, 95). and by another as an 'opal which possesses the deepest tones of blue, violet and green.... a noble subject to the lover of nature to depict, *if* only he can' (William White, *The Principles of Art as illustrated in the Ruskin Museum*, 1895, 519–20). In *The Elements of Drawing*, Ruskin assures students that if they can draw a stone 'rightly', 'everything within the reach of art is also within yours.'

Perhaps the most literal of art forms using stone are those works of art such as collectors' cabinets and collectors' tables that are made of *pietre dure* – inlaid pieces of shaped and polished stone. Made since antiquity, these were highly prized for the craftsmanship involved, the natural beauty of their materials and for the intellectual study they encouraged through comparing the individual pieces. The most practical and enduring use of stone for aesthetic purpose, meanwhile, is surely that of architecture.

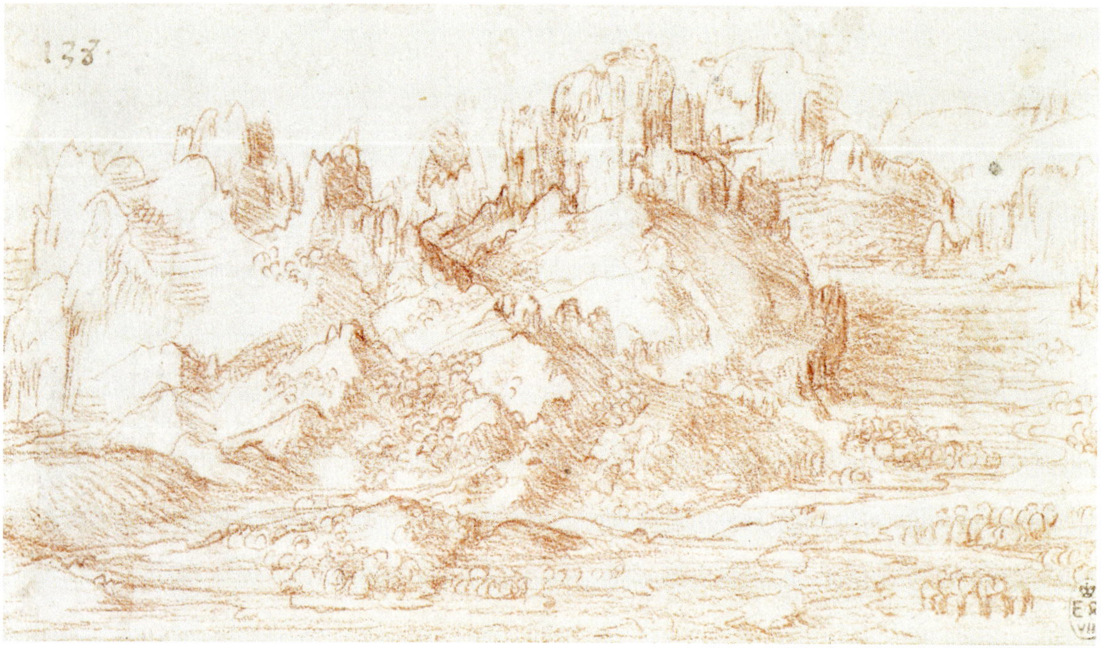

Mountains rising suddenly from the Plain, grassy and wooded below, rocky and precipitous above, c. 1500

LEONARDO DA VINCI (1452–1519)
Red chalk on white paper, 8.7 x 15.1 cm
The Royal Collection

Leonardo's fluid use of chalk here demonstrates a characteristic appreciation of the perspective of landscape as it recedes into the distance, the outlines flowing rhythmically into each other. Leonardo represents one of the earliest examples of an artist appreciating the forces of nature by bearing witness to an underlying structure. The mountains, particularly those around Carrara and also Venice, were the source of his understanding of forms and colours as seen in distant views. This small drawing is one of a series which demonstrates the study and understanding at the root of his landscape views in so many of his celebrated portraits, such as the *Mona Lisa* (Louvre, Paris). Leonardo's altarpieces of the Holy Family, notably *The Virgin of the Rocks* (National Gallery, London) and versions of *The Madonna of the Yarnwinder* (Private Collection), exhibit close study of rockfaces, providing one of the key means by which scholars may not only identify the actual landscape depicted, but also recognise the master's hand in paintings otherwise disputed as by his workshop (Carlo Starnazzi, 'The Landscape in the Madonna of the Yarnwinder', in *La 'Madonna dei fusi' di Leonardo da Vinci e il paesaggio del Valdarno Superiore*, Arezzo, Palazzo dei Priori, 1 July–15 November 2000, 37–64).

Leonardo's study of the rockface developed in the early years of the sixteenth century. An important group of his drawings of rock strata survive in the collection of Her Majesty the Queen, including studies in close detail as well as distant views. His writings also encompass both art and scientific enquiry, at one point expressing the idea that the 'anatomy' of the rockface is as real to us as that of the human body:

'We may say that the earth has a vegetative soul, in that its flesh is the soil; its bones are the array of the interconnected rocks from which the mountains are composed; its cartilage is the tufa stone; its blood is the veins of water; the lake of blood which lies within the heart is the oceanic sea; its breathing is the increase and decrease of blood in the pulses, and similarly in the earth is the flux and reflux of the sea, and the heat of the soul of the earth is in the fire which is infused throughout the earth, and the residence of its vegetative soul is in the fires, which in various places in the earth spout in baths and in mines of sulphur and volcanoes.'

RICHTER, J.P., *THE LITERARY WORKS OF LEONARDO DA VINCI*, 2, 1970, 1000

This is a deeply personal response to the structures of the world, as much informed by an understanding of geology as of the human body. AM

A Selection of Corals, patterned Stones, Asbestos, Fossils, Ammonite and Hard Stones, c. 1600–50

ANONYMOUS ITALIAN
Watercolour and bodycolour over black chalk, 39.4 x 25.5 cm
From the Paper Museum of Cassiano dal Pozzo
The Royal Collection

Cassiano dal Pozzo (1588–1657) was one of the most important art patrons in seventeenth-century Italy. A friend of Galileo, he was admired for his learning in the fields of natural history and antiquities and he played an active part in the first scientific society in Europe, the *Accademia dei Lincei*, to which he was elected in 1622.

Cassiano conceived the ambitious project of employing artists to make copies of all surviving examples of Roman antiquity. These works were classified thematically in his 'Paper Museum', to record as complete a picture as possible of ancient civilisation. At the same time he commissioned a comparable number of natural history drawings, including geological specimens, which were similarly classified. These were consulted by scholars and dilettanti throughout Europe. Cassiano dal Pozzo's 'Paper Museum' came to represent the finest imperative to acquire knowledge in the joint fields of art and science, using artists as distinguished as Pietro Testa and Pietro da Cortona. Most of the collection passed from the Dal Pozzo family to Pope Clement XI and his nephew Cardinal Albani, before being bought by King George III in 1762.

This series of drawings direct from nature is by an anonymous artist who demonstrates a facility beyond that of a copyist. The sheet shows a variety of corals and stones of different types as a single group of twenty-five studies. The paintings are not ordered numerically, but according to a visual design. Among the stones are no. 8, asbestos; no. 30, operculum, or *Umbelicus Veneris*, a gold-bearing rock; no.31, a dark red crystal prism; no. 19, a 'Judaic Stone' found in Palestine and valued for its curative qualities; no. 53, a jasper mounted as an amulet, and an emerald and a piece of sodalite, both numbered 54 (*The Paper Museum of Cassiano dal Pozzo (1588–1657)*, British Museum, 1993, no.133; Scott, A. and Freedberg, D., *The Paper Museum of Cassiano dal Pozzo, Series B, Part Three, Fossil Woods and other Geological Specimens*, Belgium, 2000). AM

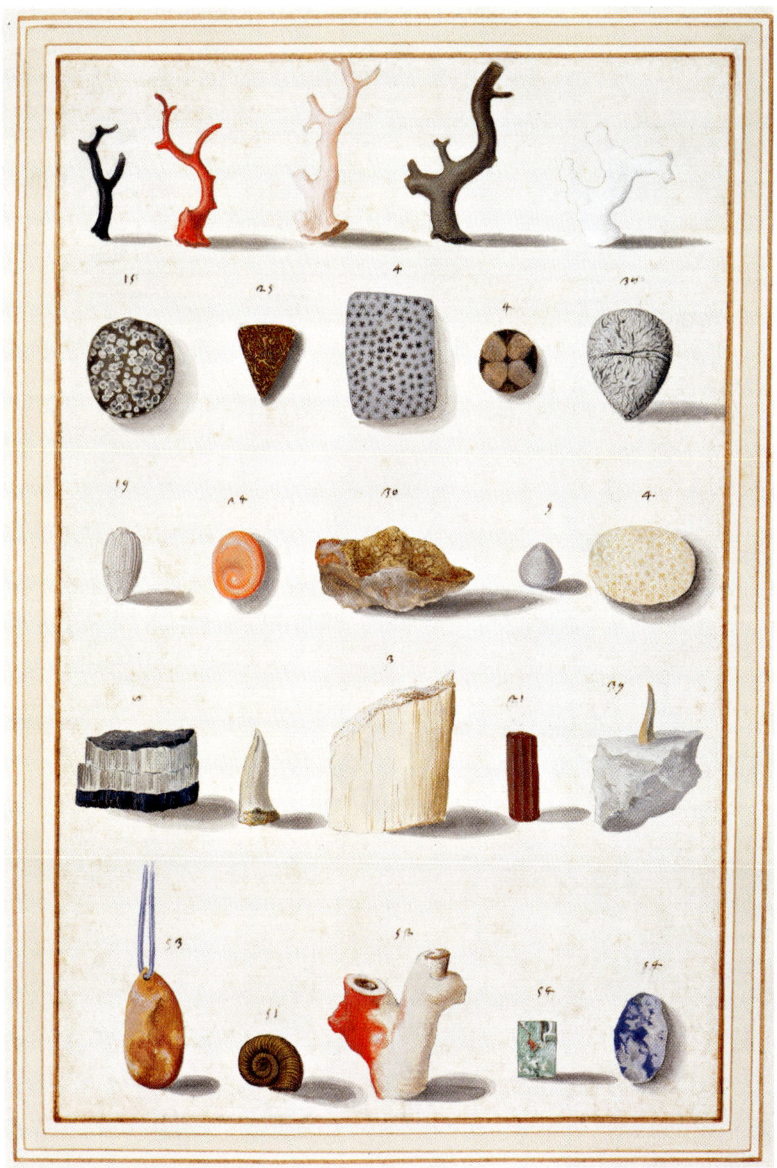

Collector's Cabinet, c.1620

PRAGUE, CASTRUCCI WORKSHOP, PROBABLY COSIMO THE ELDER
Pietre dure, ebonised and gilded wood, 48.5 x 48.6 x 25.4 cm
The Gilbert Collection, London

This cabinet was made for the Holy Roman Emperor Rudolph II and would have housed small and precious objects. Rudolph was the leading art patron of his day, and made his court at Prague a centre for artists and craftsmen from all over Europe. The Castrucci workshop was set up with Florentine craftsmen to provide works of art in *pietre dure* ('hard stones'), of which Rudolph was one of the first major collectors outside Italy.

Pietre dure involves a skilled and painstaking technique of making pictures or patterns from cut and shaped marble and semi-precious stones. Each stone is chosen so that its natural qualities contribute to the picture as a whole. *Pietre dure* artwork has been practised since antiquity but became a particular speciality of Florence during the sixteenth century, reflecting the wealth and culture of Renaissance Italy. Artefacts made in *pietre dure* were very highly prized, both for the level of craftsmanship required and for the luxurious nature of the materials. In this piece the colours of the stones in each panel are subtly harmonized so that the overall effect is as naturalistic as possible. The stones used are local to Prague, and are softer in colour than those native to Florence.

Pietre dure panels were most often incorporated into pieces of furniture. Collectors' cabinets like this one were particularly suitable for work in *pietre dure*. The magnificence of the piece reflects the status of the precious objects such cabinets were designed to house as well as, in this case, the status and taste of its royal owner. The wide range of stones used also makes the cabinet a collection in itself. Emperor Rudolph is known to have been interested in the sciences as well as in the arts, and stones used in this way may be seen to have served a dual purpose. In addition to housing precious objects, the cabinet may be used both for aesthetic appreciation and intellectual study. FA

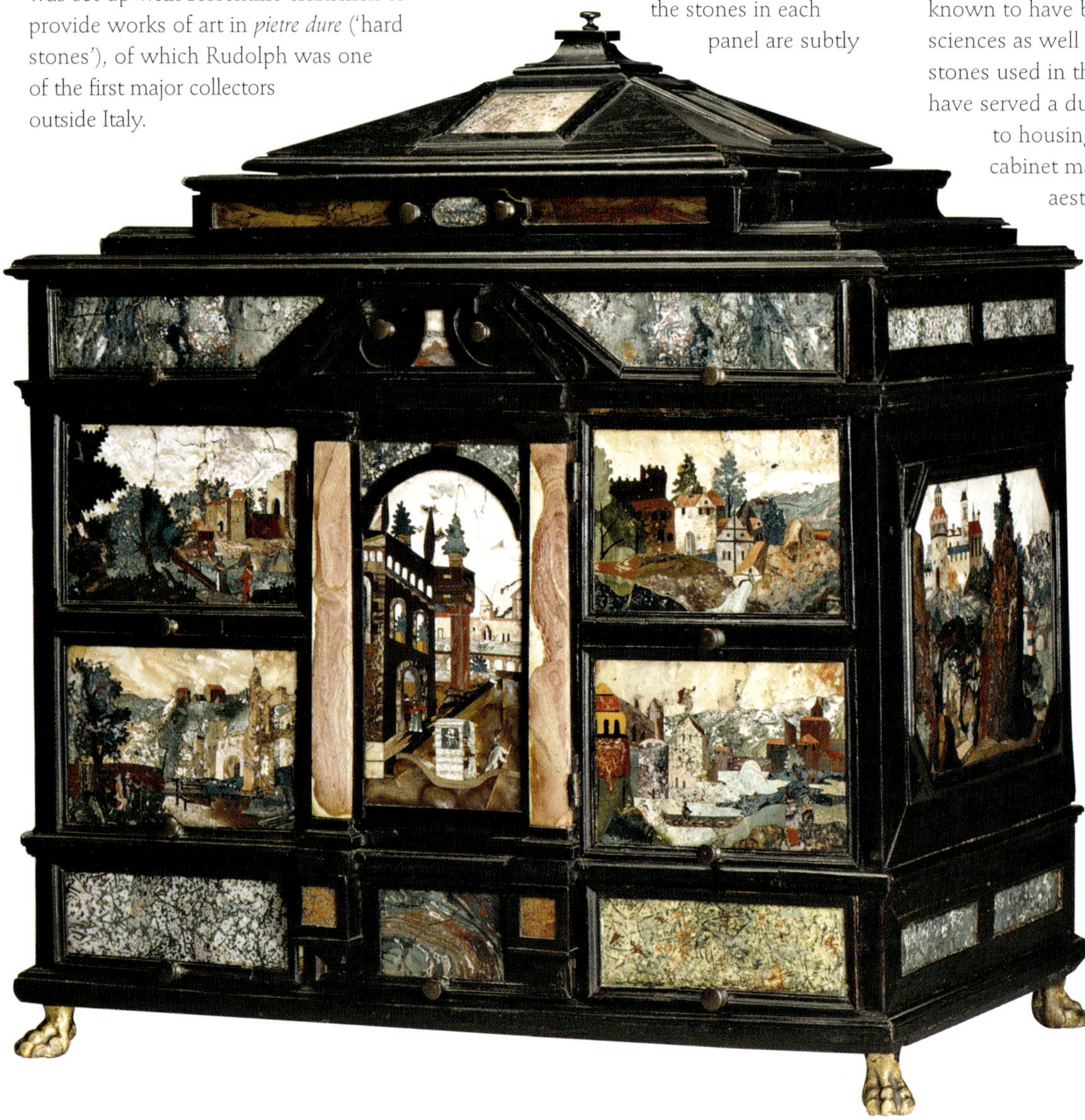

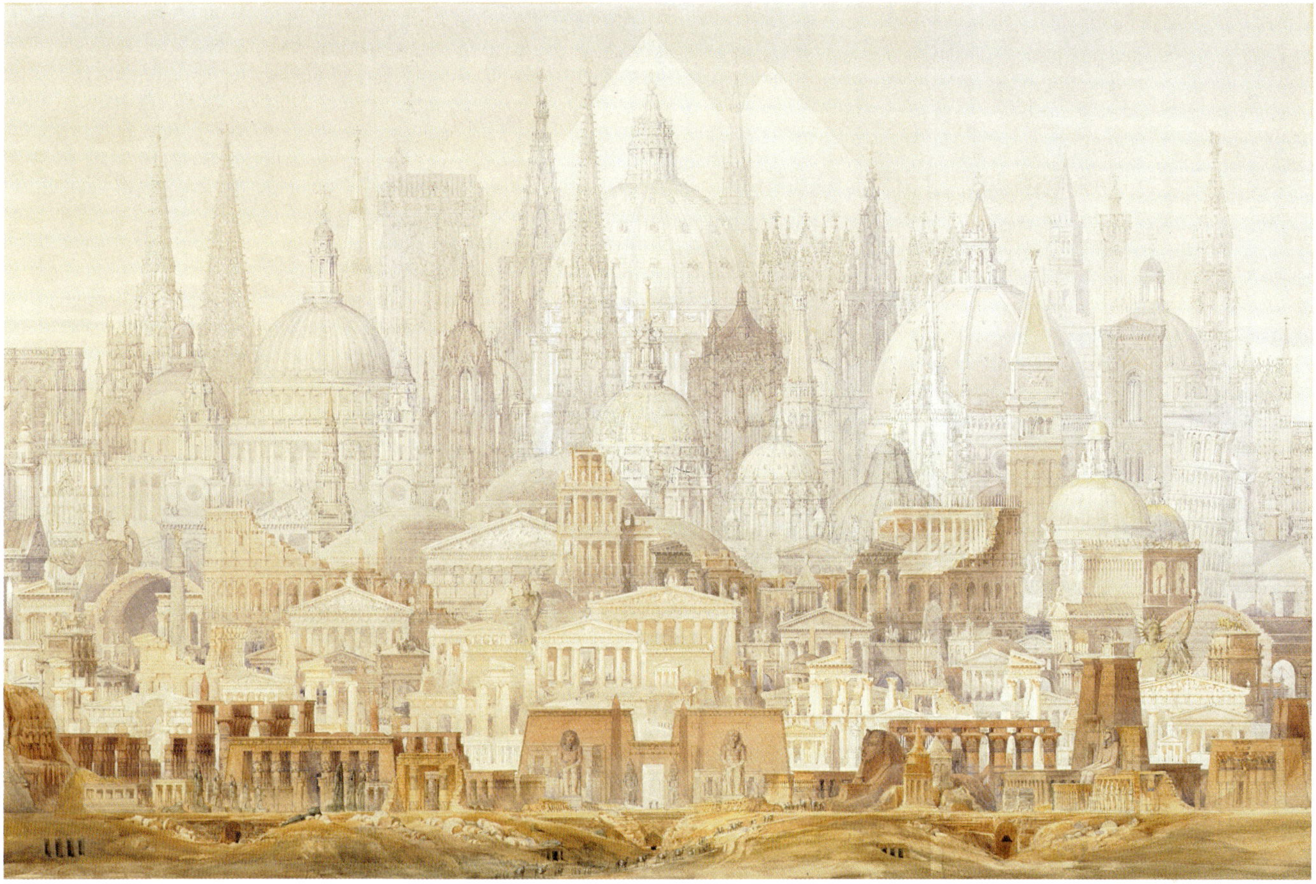

The Professor's Dream, 1848

C.R. COCKERELL RA (1788–1863)
Pencil, pen and ink and watercolour, 112.2 x 171.1 cm
Royal Academy of Arts, London

This astonishing and summative work is an image without precedent in the history of the representation of building with stone. Cockerell provides a comparison of images of iconic buildings which are all drawn to the same scale. The buildings constitute a timeline of architectural achievement literally in the shadow of the great pyramids of Egypt, a paean of praise to the architectural endeavour of humankind since the Egyptians created their built environment. It is at one level a 'pattern book', but also an imaginative recreation of buildings as exemplars of architectural achievement as in a vision.

The dreamlike quality of Cockerell's composition lies in the way celebrated buildings are gathered together not simply for the sake of comparison, but in a manner which helps to explain the evolution of Western architectural styles since ancient times. Buildings are presented in timeline configurations, in terraces heaped one above the other, where the achievements of one era literally stand as the foundation for the next. The oldest foundation is the earth itself, with the entrance to the Great Pyramid of Cheops at Giza at its centre. In Cockerell's time this was still the tallest building in existence and the silhouette of Cheops appears in the distance, flanked by the pyramids of Khafre and Menkaure. The world's most famous architectural achievements crowd beneath these venerable shadows.

The extraordinary nature of the scale used to make this dream a reality lies in the essential relationship between the human body and the scale of all architecture. Although there is a cacophony of domes and pillars, spires and entablatures, we are reminded of the essential human scale through the presence of a number of the most celebrated colossal statues of antiquity. They provide the measure by which we may judge the reality of the dream. Cockerell makes manifest his own study and teaching of architectural practice at a time when stone was about to be superseded as the sole foundation for all building. AM

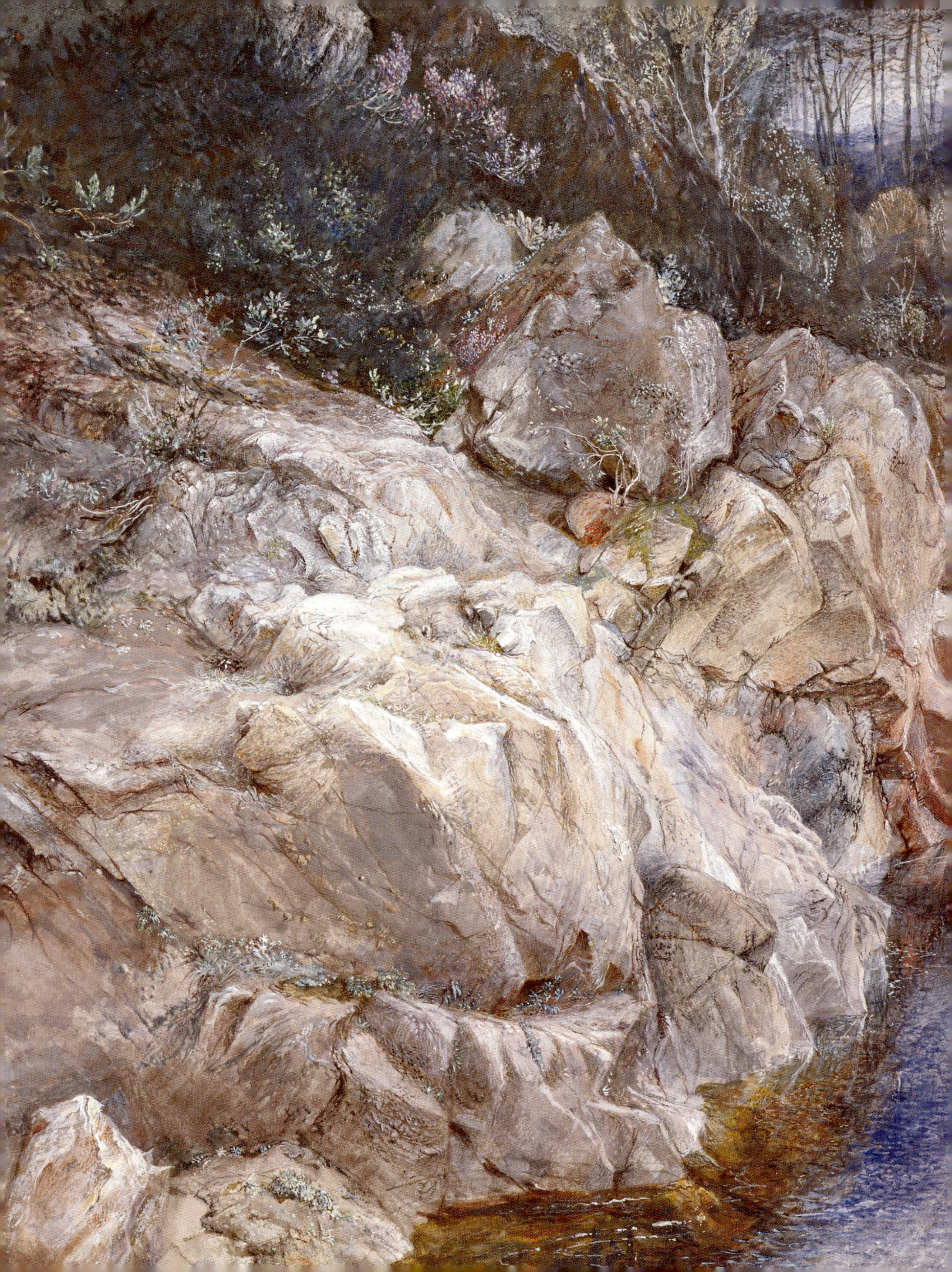

In the Pass of Killiecrankie, 1857

JOHN RUSKIN (1819–1900)
Pencil, ink, watercolour and bodycolour; 28.7 x 24.7 cm
Inscribed and dated on old backing board *In the pass of Killiecrankie / J.R. 1857*
The Syndics of the Fitzwilliam Museum, Cambridge

Killiecrankie is renowned in Scotland and beyond both for its history and for its spectacular scenery. Situated three miles north of Pitlochry in Perthshire, it was the scene of the Battle of Killiecrankie, the first Jacobite uprising in 1689 when Bonnie Dundee defeated the forces of William of Orange. For a mile, the rushing River Garry flows through the steep wooded gorge, cutting through beds of Dalradian metasedimentary rocks formed under great heat and pressure 850 million years ago. It forms part of the natural corridor through the Grampians linking the Scottish Highlands and the Lowlands. As a fine example of ancient Scottish mixed woodland with rare flora and fauna, it has been designated a Site of Special Scientific Interest and is owned by the National Trust for Scotland.

Ruskin had an abiding interest in geological subjects, and declared Scotland 'one magnificent mineralogical specimen' (E.T. Cook, eds.: *Works*, xxxvi, 373). In 1857 he 'sulkily' consented to accompany his parents there on a holiday: 'Papa and mamma, wistfully watching the effect on my mind, show their Scotland to me.' (*Præterita*) They stopped near Killiecrankie at the end of August, and for a week he spent six hours a day meticulously working on this drawing. His first study of the area, also filled with closely observed geological detail, was made on a previous Scottish holiday in 1853 when Millais began painting his famous portrait of Ruskin standing by a mountain stream. Ruskin made his own monochrome study (*Gneiss Rock at Glenfinlas* 1853, Ashmolean Museum, Oxford), presumably to aid Millais in painting the background. He believed that the character of a locality could only be conveyed by close scrutiny of the rock formations and the vegetation adhering to them.

The intensely worked *In the Pass of Killiecrankie* is in strong colour, the mossy rocks virtually filling the page, with every lichen, moss, crevice and contour depicted with a Pre-Raphaelite degree of finish. Ruskin seems to have been especially proud of the work, exhibiting it twice in his lifetime. NW

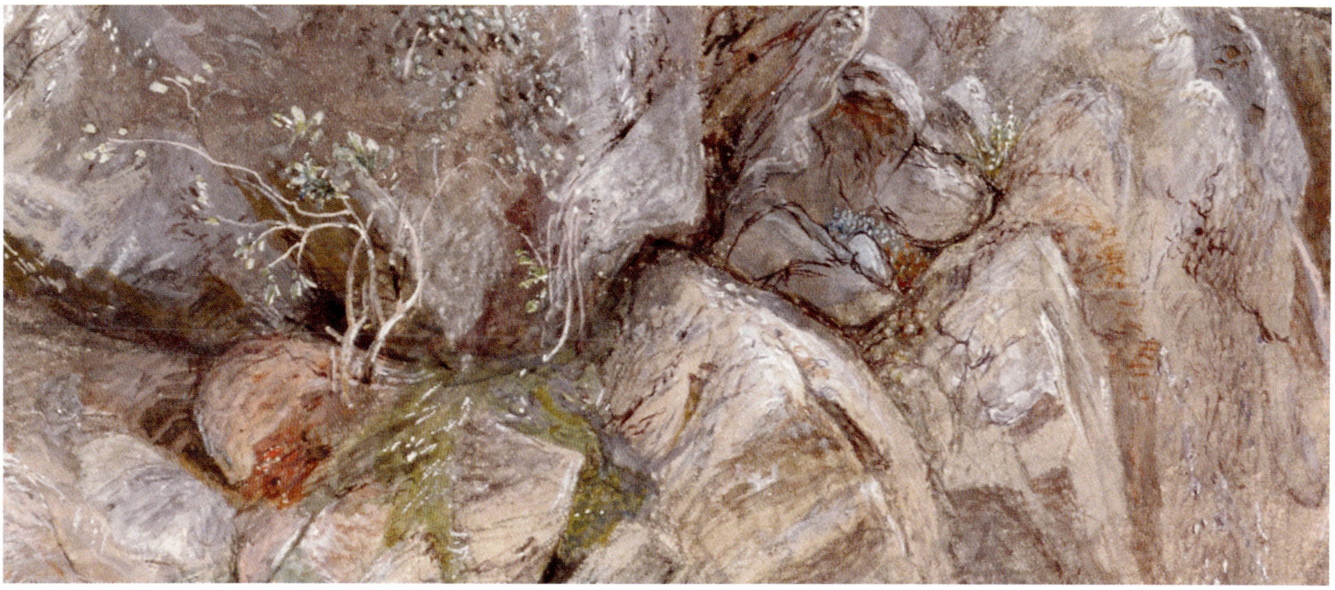

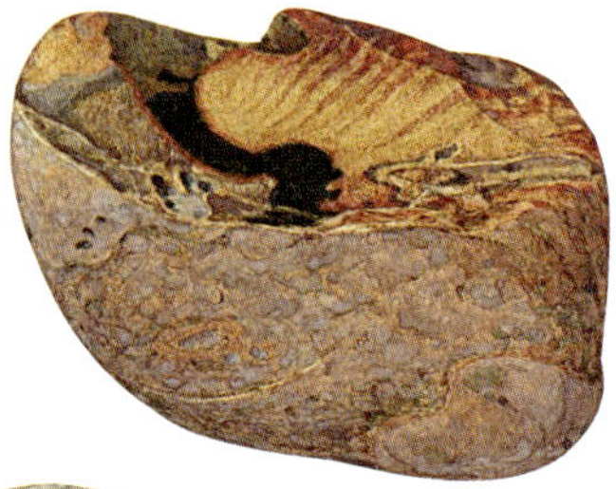

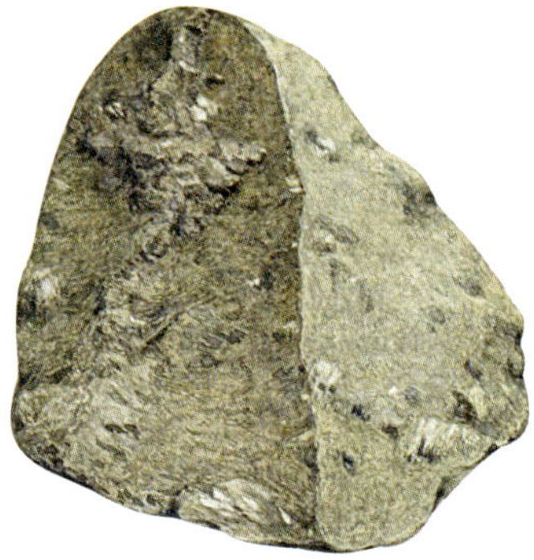

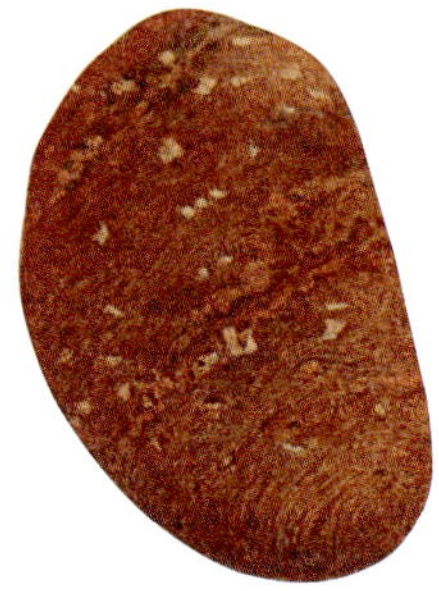

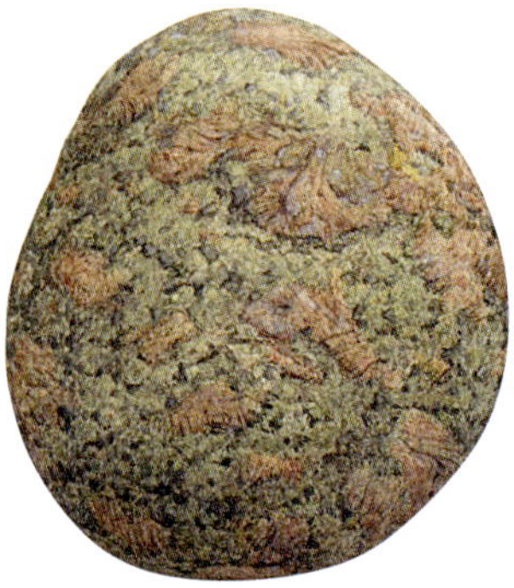

Pebbles found on British Beaches

John Fullwood (1854–1931)
Watercolour on paper, each 14 x 8.5 cm

Courtesy of the Trustees of the Natural History Museum, London

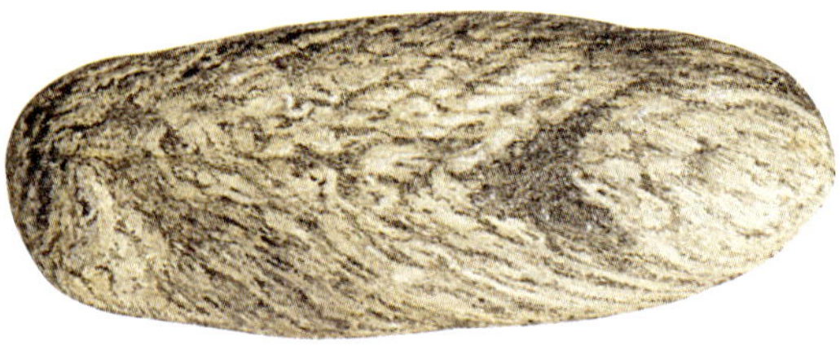

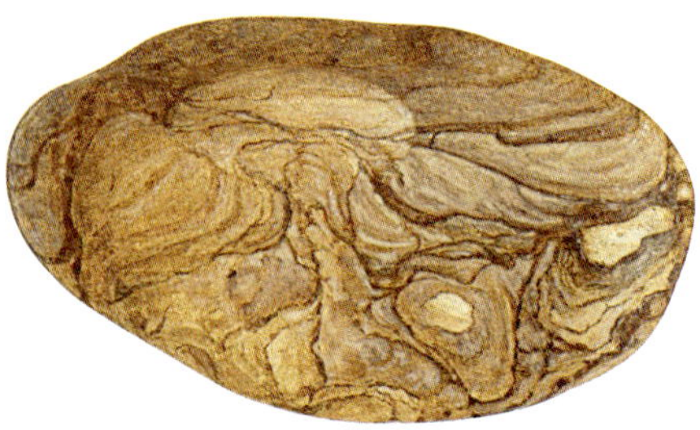

John Fullwood FRSA, RBA, FSA was one of the most celebrated landscape painters of his day and a well-known copperplate etcher and illustrator of architecture. He studied in London, Paris, Berlin and Birmingham and exhibited with both the Royal Academy and the Royal Society of British Artists on numerous occasions.

His study of geology is less well known. He liked to draw and paint the pebbles he found on beaches around Britain as a hobby. He made dozens of these extraordinary and beautifully executed watercolours. At a time when photography was still in its infancy and coloured photographic reproductions merely a dream, such painstakingly detailed and accurate representations of geological specimens were needed to enable practitioners of the relatively new science of geology to undertake their studies and research. Producing accurate illustrations of minerals in their natural colours was, and still is, notoriously difficult. Fullwood clearly understood the scientific and artistic imperative that one of the best ways to study and understand an object is to draw it with total accuracy.

Scientific study can also open the door to more personal reflections. An extract from Fullwood's obituary shows us a surprisingly philosophical and spiritual aspect of his scientific endeavour: 'As a hobby, Mr Fullwood studied Geology, and was fond of collecting stones from the beaches round our coasts and painting pictures of them. He knew the history of each one. Some he would have to cut open so that he could paint the intricate pattern revealed within. Some of these pictures resemble landscape in miniature with mountains, rushing streams, and purple skies.' NL

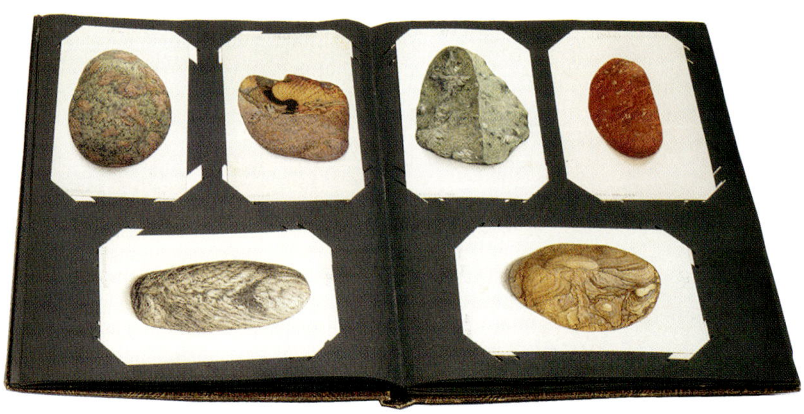

Ring, 1963

DESMOND CLEN-MURPHY (BORN 1924)
Silver and rose quartz, 4.1 x 2.2 x diameter 2.3 cm

Ring, 1963

DESMOND CLEN-MURPHY (BORN 1924)
Silver-gilt and amethyst, 3.8 x 2.4 x diameter 1.9 cm

Ring, 1964

DESMOND CLEN-MURPHY (BORN 1924)
Gold, silver, smoky quartz and iron glance 3.8 x 2.8 cm

Collection of the Worshipful Company of Goldsmiths

These three rings were made in the 1960s. Their simple stark lines, innovative settings and angularity place them stylistically within the Modern Movement. Jewellery of the 1960s, like applied art in other media, was experimental and forward-looking and often broke away from established conventions. Semi-precious stones, like these here, were popular and were used in innovative ways with unusual materials.

These three stones are amethyst, rose quartz and smoky quartz, all variations of the same mineral. One of the most variable crystals, the colour of quartz is greatly affected by traces of other minerals found within it. The romantically named rose quartz contains impurities of manganese or titanium, while amethyst gets its purple colour either from iron or manganese. Smoky quartz acquires its shades of brown or black when irradiated. Some quartz is naturally subjected to radiation when in the earth, although as this stone is popular for jewellery, it is now often irradiated artificially.

These rings are of artistic interest for the prominence of the stones. The artist has focused closely on the gems, allowing their natural forms to shape the appearance of the pieces, with the metalwork settings taking a secondary, supporting role. He has seen these stones as works of art in their own right, and has brought out their three-dimensional qualities to create works which resemble space-age architecture or futuristic abstract sculptures. The emphasis on the rough gemstones also creates an ancient, almost primitive feel to these rings, a combination of timelessness with ultra modernity. The shape of the stones has in each case been wrought by natural processes rather than by artifice, however, and reminds the viewer and wearer that nature is often considered the greatest artist of all. FA

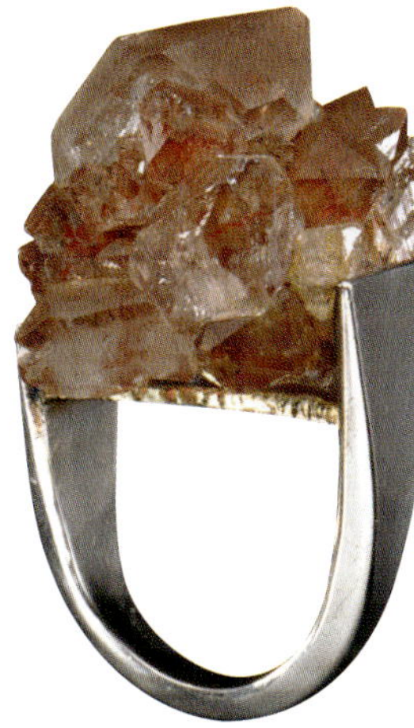

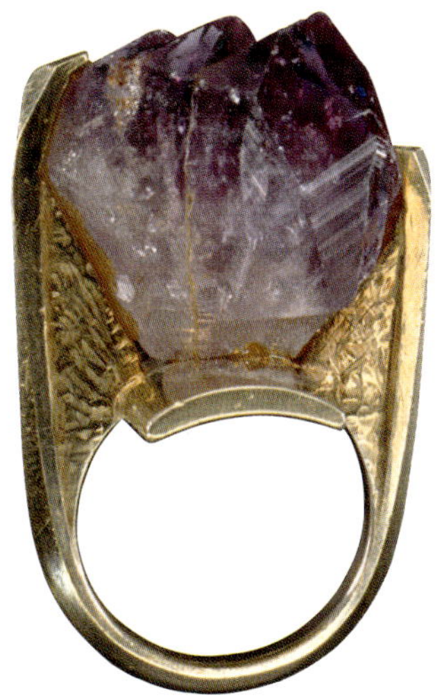

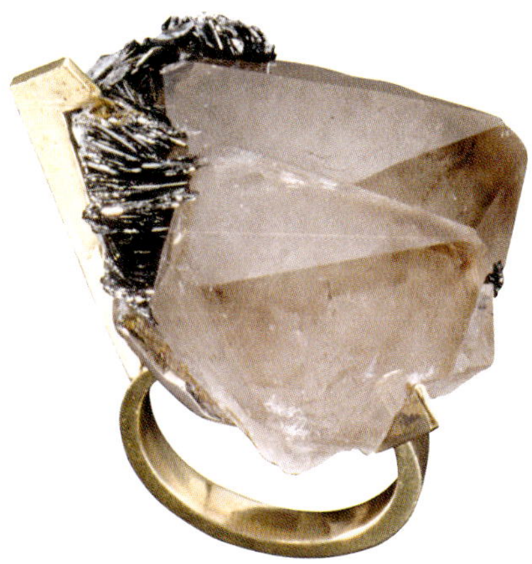

Mother and Child, 1936

HENRY MOORE (1898–1986)
Ancaster stone, height 51 cm
British Council Collection

Henry Moore first carved a mother and child in 1922 and returned to the subject throughout his career. Here the subject has been realized in Ancaster Stone, a type of oolitic limestone from Lincolnshire that has been quarried as a sculptural material since the Roman period. Moore favoured the surface interest and 'earthy' qualities of stones such as Ancaster, which contrasted with the purity of traditional stones such as white Italian marble. He was not interested in turning stone into flesh, but rather revealing the values and qualities intrinsic to stone.

The figures are represented through careful reference to the undulating forms of the limestone. The result is an almost abstract rendering of the subject that demonstrates the importance that Moore placed on understanding and directly engaging with his chosen material. As Moore himself described in 1934: 'Every material has its own individual qualities. It is only when a sculptor works direct, when there is an active relationship with his material, that the material can take its part in the shaping of an idea' (Henry Moore in Herbert Read (ed.) *Unit 1: The Modern Movement in English Architecture, Painting and Sculpture*, London, 1934, 29).

Mother and Child demonstrates Moore's growing interest in abstraction and surrealism, and in particular the biomorphism of artists such as Jean Arp. During the 1930s he explored shapes and forms that appear to be made as much by the creative processes of nature as by artistic intervention. By aligning his work with nature, with rocks and pebbles eroded by the action of wind and water, Moore strove to create elemental forms that had a universal emotional significance.

In *Mother and Child* the merging of the figures' bodies into a single form creates a psychological portrait of the relationship between mother and child that extends beyond formal considerations. The work operates as a poignant expression of the child's physical and emotional dependence on the mother, giving 'plastic expression to the child's point of view, or way of feeling' (P. Fuller, *Henry Moore: An English Romantic* in S. Compton (ed.), *Henry Moore*, Royal Academy of Arts, London 1988, 41). NT

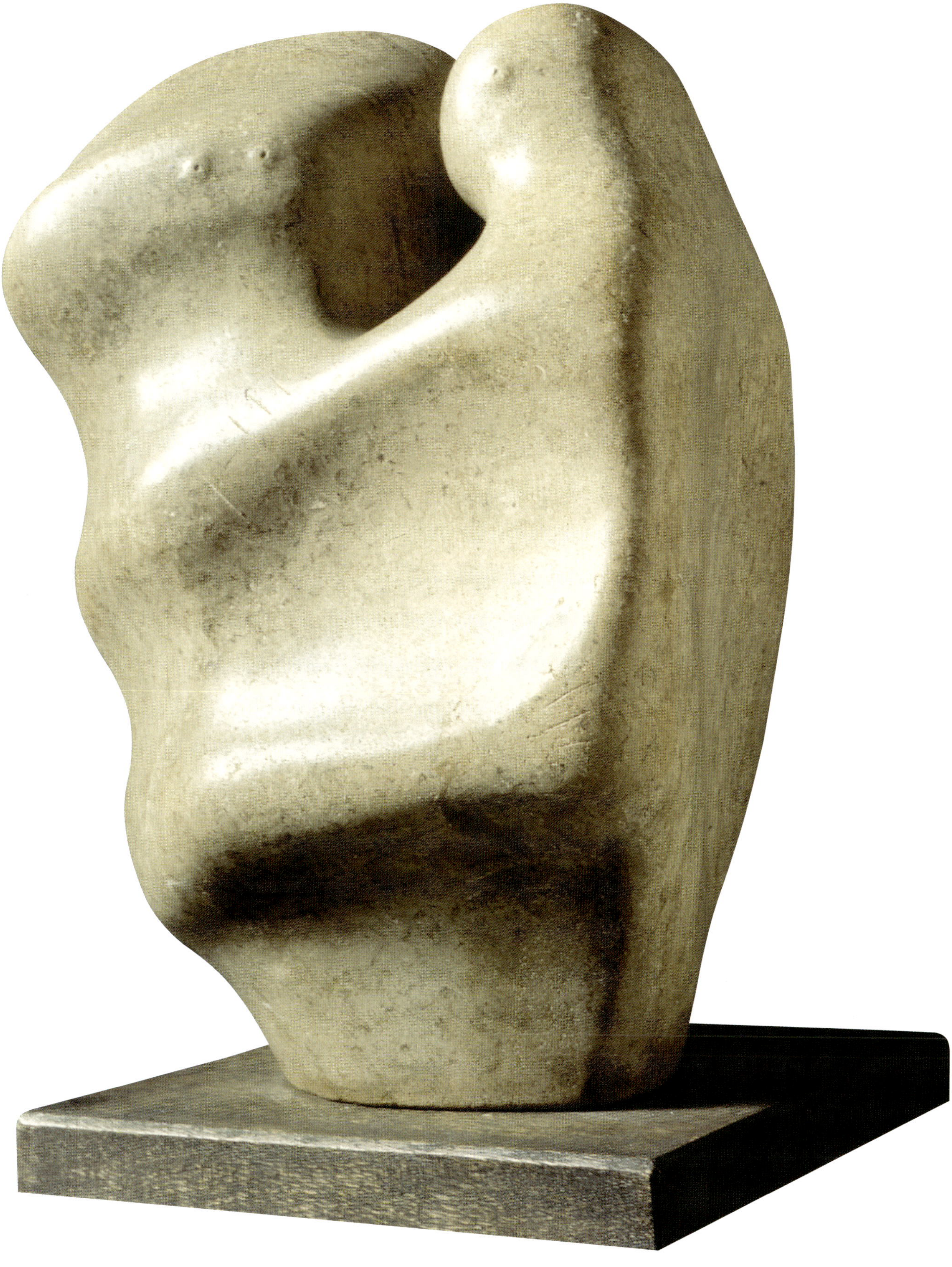

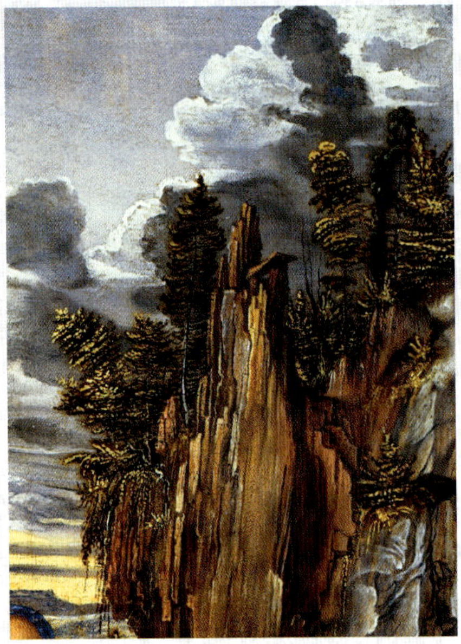

5 Prayer and Meditation

To see a world in a grain of sand…

WILLIAM BLAKE, *AUGURIES OF INNOCENCE*, C. 1800

ABOVE:
Albrecht Dürer, *Saint Jerome* (detail)
National Gallery, London. Bought with the assistance of the Heritage Lottery Fund, the National Art Collections Fund and the J. Paul Getty Jr through the American Friends of the National Gallery, 1996

Lingbi meditative Rock with wooden Stand carved with Lingzhi Fungus ➤

Qing Dynasty, 19th century
Stone and wood, height 48.9 cm

OA 1992.7-8.1
The British Museum, London

SINCE THE EARLIEST TIMES certain rocks and stones have been appropriated as the abode of Gods and were therefore sacred. The Mother Goddess of Asia Minor, Cybele, was worshipped in the form of a meteoric stone, which in 204 BC was brought to Rome to be placed in a temple on the Palatine. The stone at Bethel, or the House of God, in Canaan was used by the Hebrew patriarch Jacob as a pillow, which he anointed. The Christian faith has traditionally used rock as a symbolic aid to prayer and belief. Biblical texts tell us of St Peter as Christ's rock and in Genesis 28:22 Moses declares: 'And this stone which I have set for a pillar, shall be God's house.' Moses also strikes a rock to bring the spiritual refreshment of water (Exodus 17, 1–7) while the Ten Commandments were written on tablets of stone, symbolizing their fundamental longevity.

Rocks feature as a popular motif in Chinese art, symbolizing long life, friendship and the stability and calm of the Taoist paradise. Natural 'lingbi' rocks are used for meditation, to contemplate one's place in the world: cracks and holes in these natural rocks are considered to provide glimpses of constellations beyond in the mind's eye. In parts of China sacred stones are used to invoke rain or to encourage the conception of a male child.

The placing of rocks in meaningful arrangements goes back at least 5,000 years. Zen philosophy teaches that we can experience the large in the small, the universal in the personal and that in a grain of sand we may glimpse the meaning of the world. For centuries Japanese Zen masters have cultivated gardens of harmoniously arranged rocks and raked gravel to create landscapes for peaceful contemplation which have been called 'gardens of the mind'. More formal arrangements of stones on a larger scale include great architecture such as the cathedrals of Europe. Other places of worship and ceremony, including henge monuments, also provide suitably inspiring sites at which to pray, meditate and seek sanctuary.

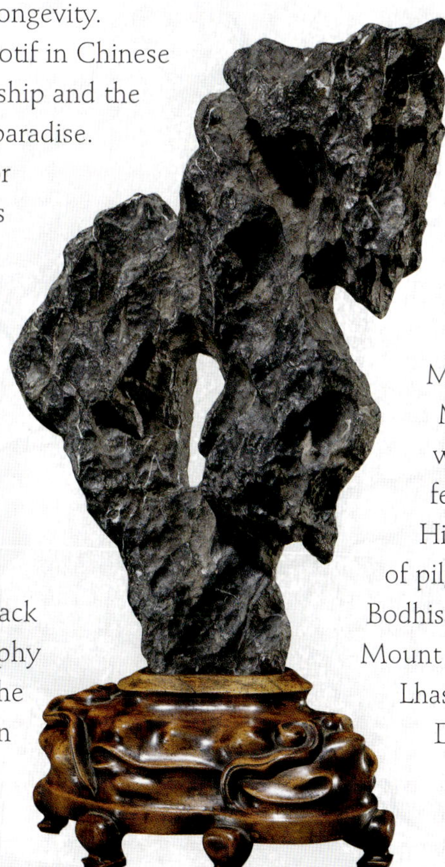

Mountains too have provided artists with a spiritual source of imagery and symbolism. Throughout the ancient world sacred mountains such as Mounts Olympus, Fuji and Everest have provided the link between heaven and earth, and have been the dwelling places of Gods and Goddesses. The Egyptians, Babylonians and Assyrians believed that a sacred mountain in their own country was at the centre of the world. For the ancient Greeks this place was marked by the stone monument in the temple of Apollo at Delphi. The principal Mesopotamian Mother-Goddess was called Lady of the Mountain (Ninhursag) because mountains were the source of water and therefore fertility. In India, Mount Kailasa in the Himalaya is the home of Shiva, and a centre of pilgrimage. For Buddhists, the home of the Bodhisattva Avalokiteshvara, was the mythical Mount Potala, the name also given to the hill at Lhasa in Tibet on which the palace of the Dalai Lama stands (Hall 1994, 104–6). AM

St Clement striking the Rock, c. 1500

BERNARDINO FUNGAI (1460–1516)
Oil on linen on wood, 43.1 x 65 cm
York Museums Trust (York Art Gallery)

Little is known of the Sienese painter Fungai beyond his work on the monochrome frescoes of the cathedral at Siena and a dated altarpiece of 1512 in a Sienese church, but he may also have specialized in handling expensive mineral pigments. In 1494 he was commissioned to decorate ceremonial banners with gold and azure, and five years later he gilded the cathedral's organ case. His work was essentially decorative and his paintings of the life of St Clement have an expressive charm, despite the horror of the story they tell.

Pope Clement I was the fourth Pope, whose martyrdom is told in two panels from a reredos, of which *St Clement Striking the Rock* is one. The second panel shows how he was subsequently thrown into the sea with an anchor tied around his neck. This story goes on to say that the sea flowed back a mile or so to reveal the body of the saint resting in a beautiful marble shrine.

St Clement was ordered to his death by the Roman Emperor Trajan because of the success of his proselytising. Sent to work in the hard limestone marble quarries of the Crimea, he performed a miracle by saving some 2,000 Christians who were also working in the quarry. He struck a rock with his mattock from which a spring subsequently burst forth, enabling the Christians to drink and survive. This story, like that of Moses striking the rock (Exodus 17, 1–7), reminds us how the Christian belief embraces stories of martyrdom and saintliness associated with stones, in the simplest devotional sense. In their striking of rocks, both Moses and St Clement bring forth water, a metaphor for the spiritual refreshment that nourishes the Christian Church.

Clement and the prophet Moses both prefigure Christ, who was to die on the rock of Golgotha. For the Christian faith, stones have developed as metaphors for both steadfastness and spiritual nourishment, just as St Peter was Christ's 'rock' (see p. 69). AM

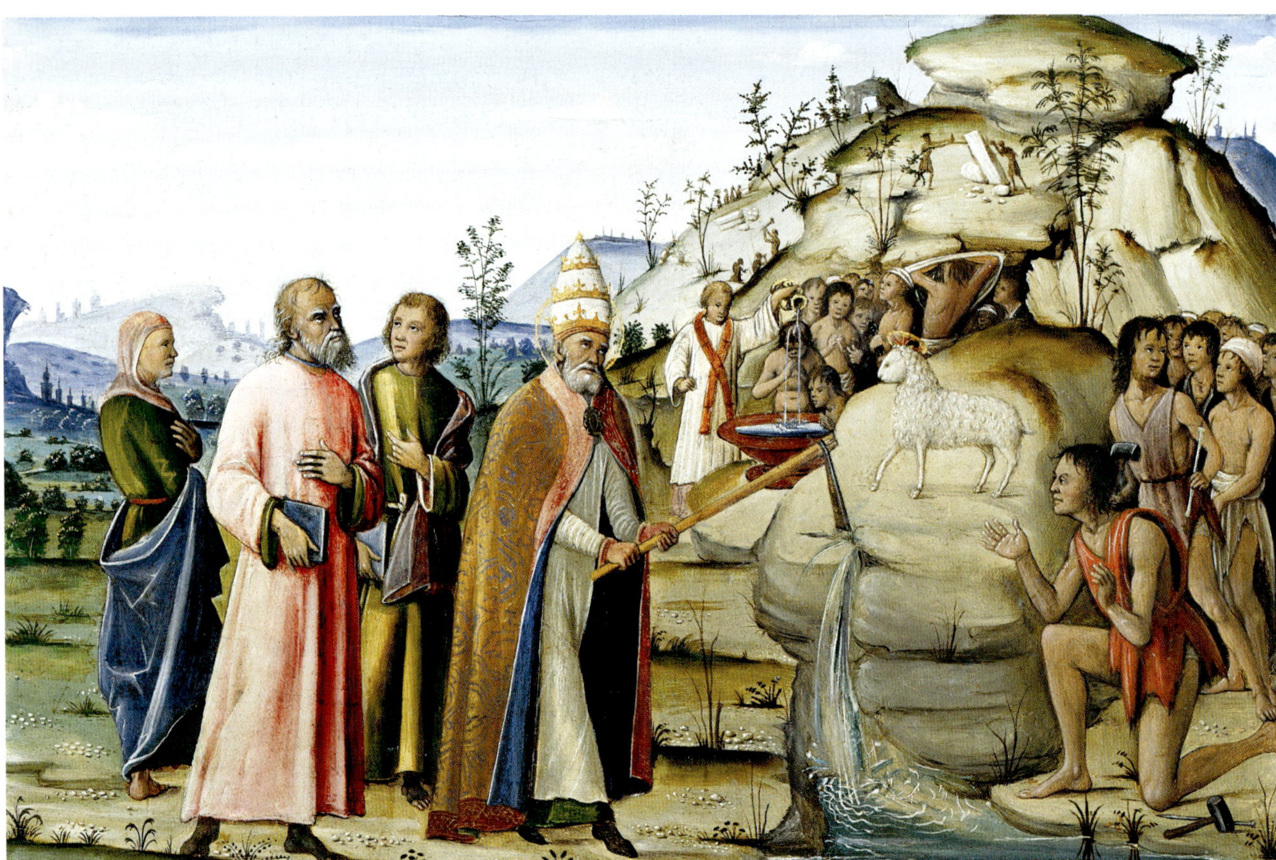

Saint Jerome, c. 1496

ALBRECHT DÜRER (1471–1528)
Oil on wood, 23.1 x 17.4 cm

National Gallery, London. Bought with the assistance of the Heritage Lottery Fund, the National Art Collections Fund and Mr J. Paul Getty Jr through the American Friends of the National Gallery, 1996

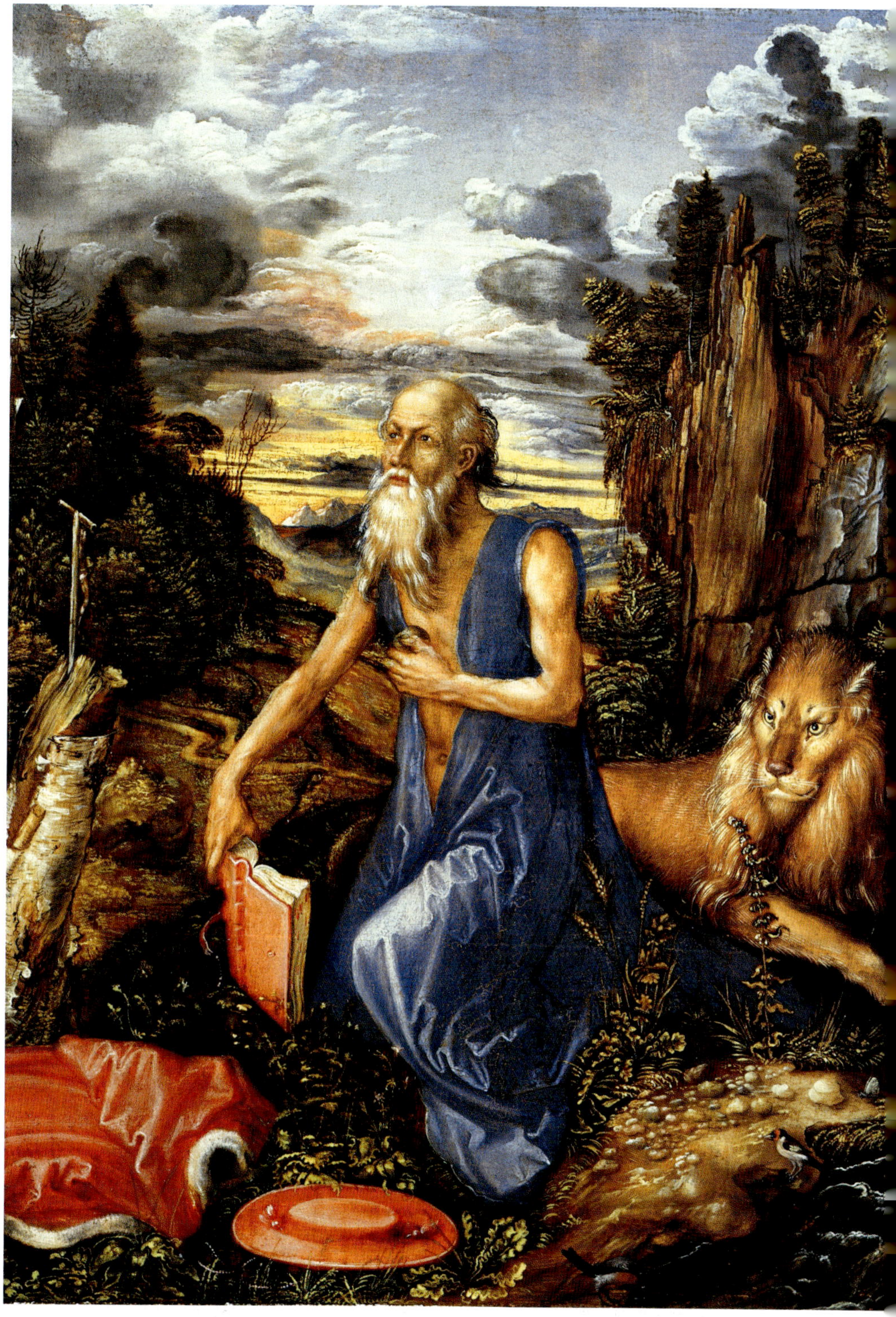

This jewel-like devotional painting shows St Jerome, one of the most learned Fathers of the Church, at prayer. He holds in his right hand the Bible, which he translated into the Latin 'Vulgate' version, still the official Bible of the Roman Catholic Church. Born in Dalmatia, he died in 405 AD, having forsaken his comfortable family background for a contemplative life. The wilderness in which he is sometimes depicted in Renaissance painting is often a rocky setting to emphasize the austerity of his existence. The saint's biography was translated by Dürer's friend, Lazarus Spengler, in 1514, and the artist's numerous printed images of him suggest a real engagement with Jerome as a subject. An etching also shows him as a penitent in the wilderness, as does a closely related engraving considered to date from around 1496.

The painting dates from early in Dürer's career. Although inspired most probably by the example of Giovanni Bellini, he also made drawings of a quarry outside Nuremberg (notably those in Musée Bonnat, Bayonne and the British Museum), using them as the direct source for his rocky setting. These drawings emphasize how Dürer incorporates a precise study of a rockface while creating an isolated wilderness, clearly enabling him to articulate the rock forms with absolute realism. The penitent saint holds a stone with which to chastise himself and to deaden his flesh to temptation, while the attendant lion and discarded cardinal's mantle and hat relate to his past life. The pink and lemon sunset sky behind the Saint has an added cosmological resonance as the panel bears the image of a comet, or heavenly body, in a night sky on the reverse (see p. 6). Dürer had previously painted a fiery explosion over a landscape on the reverse of his painting of *Christ as the Man of Sorrows* (c. 1493; Kunsthalle, Karlsruhe) and there is a clear sense that the panel has a developed meaning for the artist. Dürer is almost certainly referring the devotee to the Saint's meditations in his painting of the comet. AM

Portable Altar, c. 1200

From Hildesheim, Germany
Stone, copper, ivory, gold, rock crystal, 35.4 x 25.1 cm
M&ME 1902.6-25.1
The British Museum, London

This altar combines various techniques of metalwork, stone and ivory carving and miniature painting. It is also a reliquary. The slab on the reverse is interspersed with strips of gilded copper which bear the names of forty saints. It also conceals a cavity where relics of these saints are kept. Relics were greatly revered in the medieval Catholic church, making this a highly valued and precious devotional object which would have accompanied its owner while travelling. Inscriptions indicate that the original patron was Theodoric, Abbot of Hildesheim from 1182–1204.

The importance of the altar's function is reflected in the richness of the materials used and the complexity of its construction. The marble, once thought to be porphyry but more likely to be a type of Purbeck marble, gives the piece a sombre appearance. It is significant to note that this stone forms the focal point of the altar – the engravings, paintings and the carvings of the Crucifixion and the Virgin frame the stone at the centre. It is possible that this central position and the dark reddish purple colour of the stone resembling blood enabled the stone to be used as a meditation aid, encouraging its owner's gaze to be drawn and his mind to focus inwards on the blood of Christ and the martyrs. Four of the earliest martyrs, Peter, Andrew, Stephen and Laurence, are engraved into the altar's gilded surface.

Marble is not the only significant use of stone in this altar. The miniatures on vellum are held in place under rock crystal. This is a translucent variety of quartz, prized since ancient times. It possessed a clarity which early glass did not, and this was often equated with purity. For this reason, in the Christian tradition it was considered particularly appropriate for reliquaries. Relics inside this altar include hair, textiles and semi-precious stones associated with St Christopher, patron saint of travellers.
FA

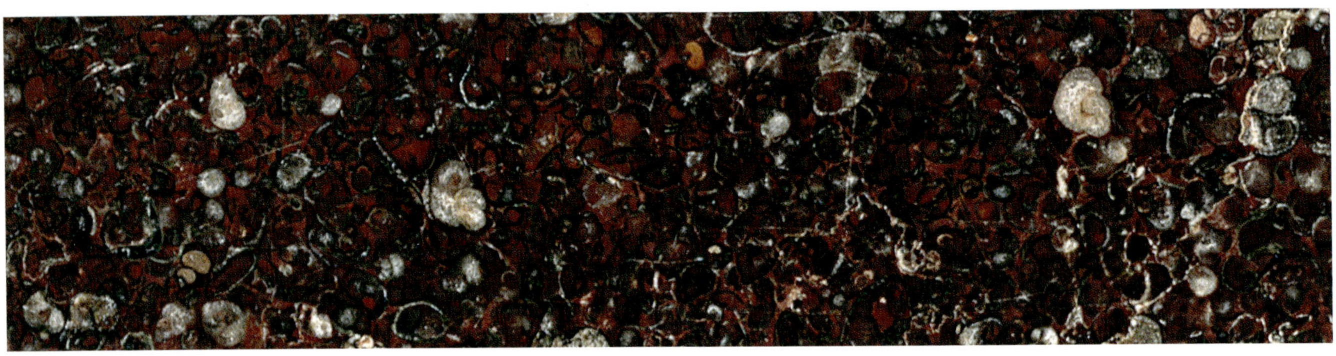

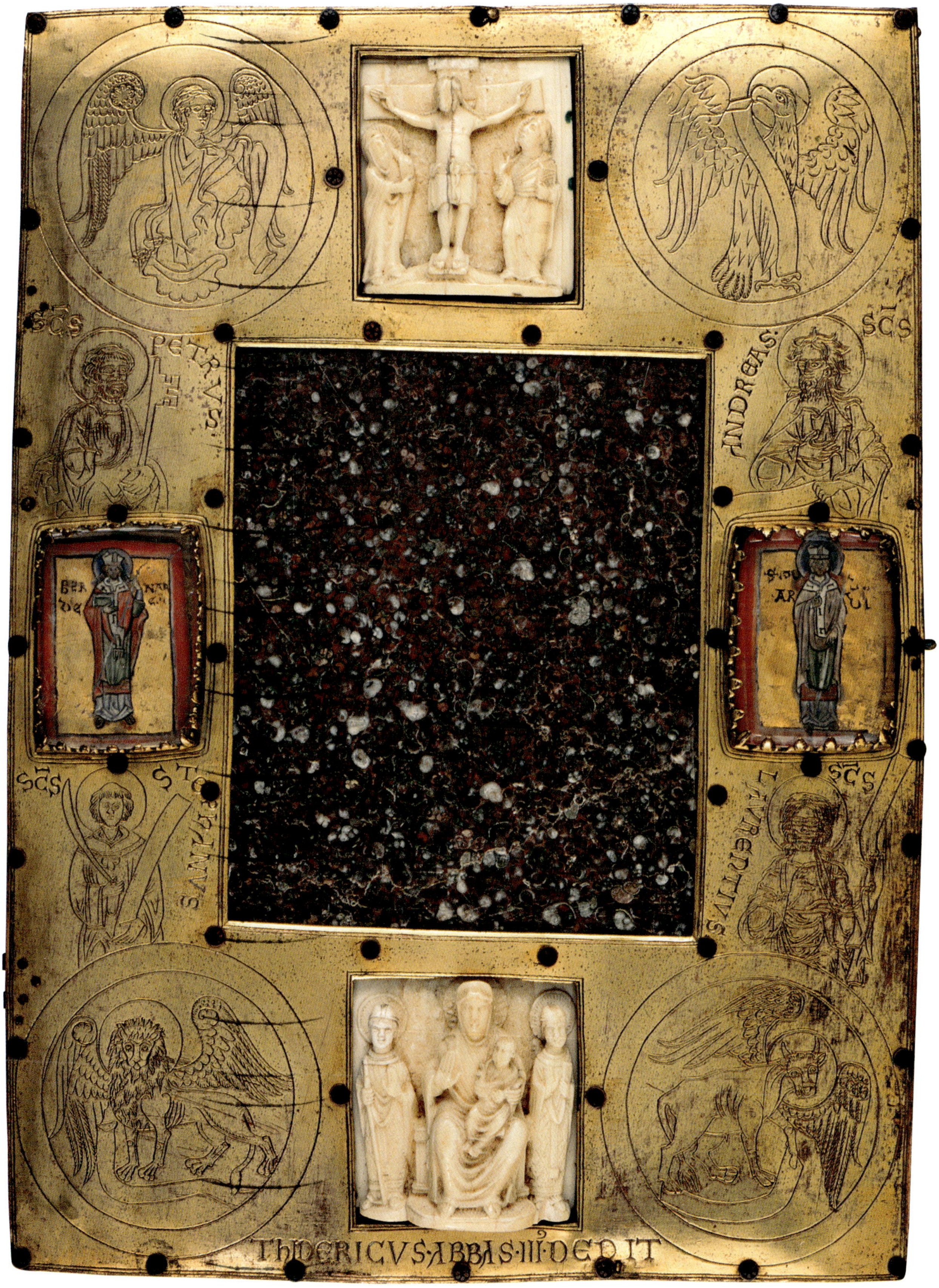
PETRVS
ANDREAS
LAVRENTIVS
ThDERICVS·ABBAS·III·DEDIT

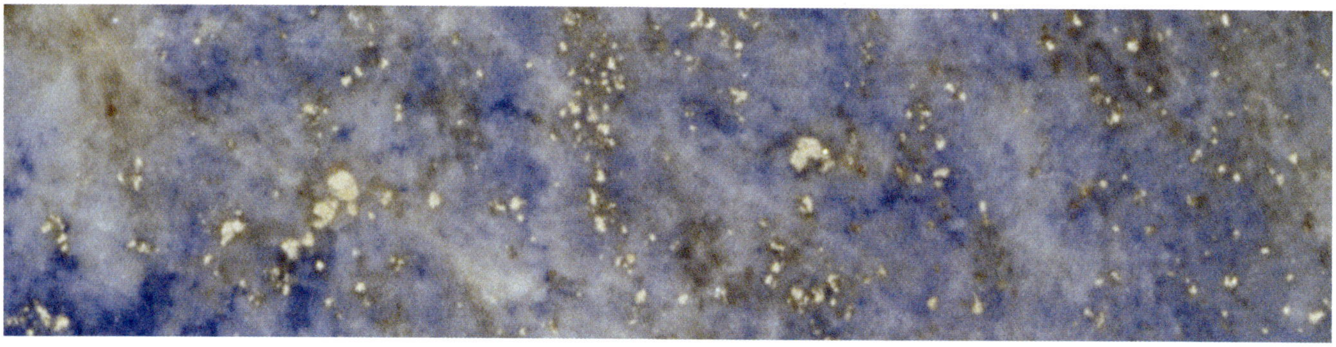

Pax, c. 1500–50

ATTRIBUTED TO VALERIO BELLI
(1468–probably 1546)
Silver-gilt and ormolu with lapis lazuli,
21.2 x 11.2 cm

Victoria and Albert Museum, London

The religious purpose and high status of this pax are emphasized by the use of lapis lazuli to represent the heavens. This stone was prized from ancient times for its beauty and rarity. The best-quality stone is of a deep blue and contains specks of iron pyrites which sparkle like gold. The paler coloured stone, as seen on this pax, is considered slightly less desirable, although here it is artistically highly appropriate and has clearly been chosen deliberately to resemble the sky. Lapis is mined almost exclusively in Afghanistan and, reflecting its popularity, was one of the first precious stones ever to be imitated in glass.

When ground to powder and mixed with a binding medium lapis was used by the ancient Egyptians both as paint and for eye make-up. It was also the source of the most highly valued blue pigment in European art – ultramarine. The term lapis lazuli comes from the Arabic word for blue, and the meaning of ultramarine (literally 'across the sea') reflects its exotic origins. Other available blue pigments were inferior in quality and colour: ultramarine was the richest and most vivid blue known until a synthetic equivalent was manufactured in the nineteenth century. It was very expensive to make and thus kept for the most important pictures, or to emphasize the most prominent subject within a picture. To commission or own a painting containing a large quantity of ultramarine was a status symbol and a conspicuous sign of wealth. In religious paintings it was traditionally used for the Virgin Mary's robe, reflecting the reverence accorded to her by the Catholic Church.

Here lapis lazuli adds an extra element of status to the Nativity scene depicted on this pax, which was designed to be handed round during Mass and kissed by the congregation as a sign of peace. The slabs of stone, combined with the classical backdrop to this Nativity scene and the imposing architectural and mythological influences of its surround, exemplify the monumental grandeur of Italian Renaissance decoration. Motifs were frequently borrowed from Greek and Roman classical sources, even for overtly Christian sacred objects.

In the ancient world lapis was sometimes thought of as interchangeable with sapphire. Because of their colour both stones were connected with the sky and with the heavens and were therefore considered particularly suitable for religious objects. FA

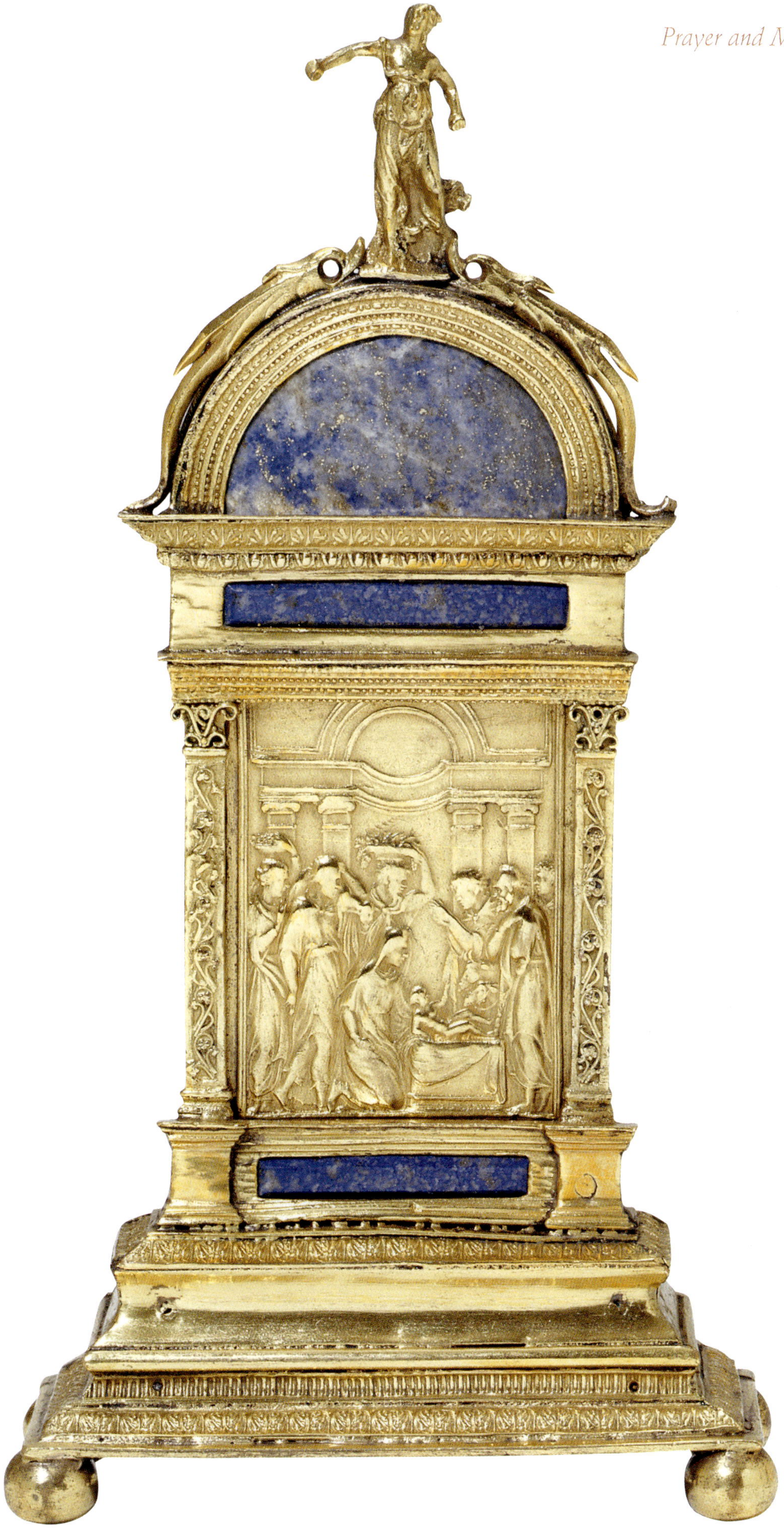

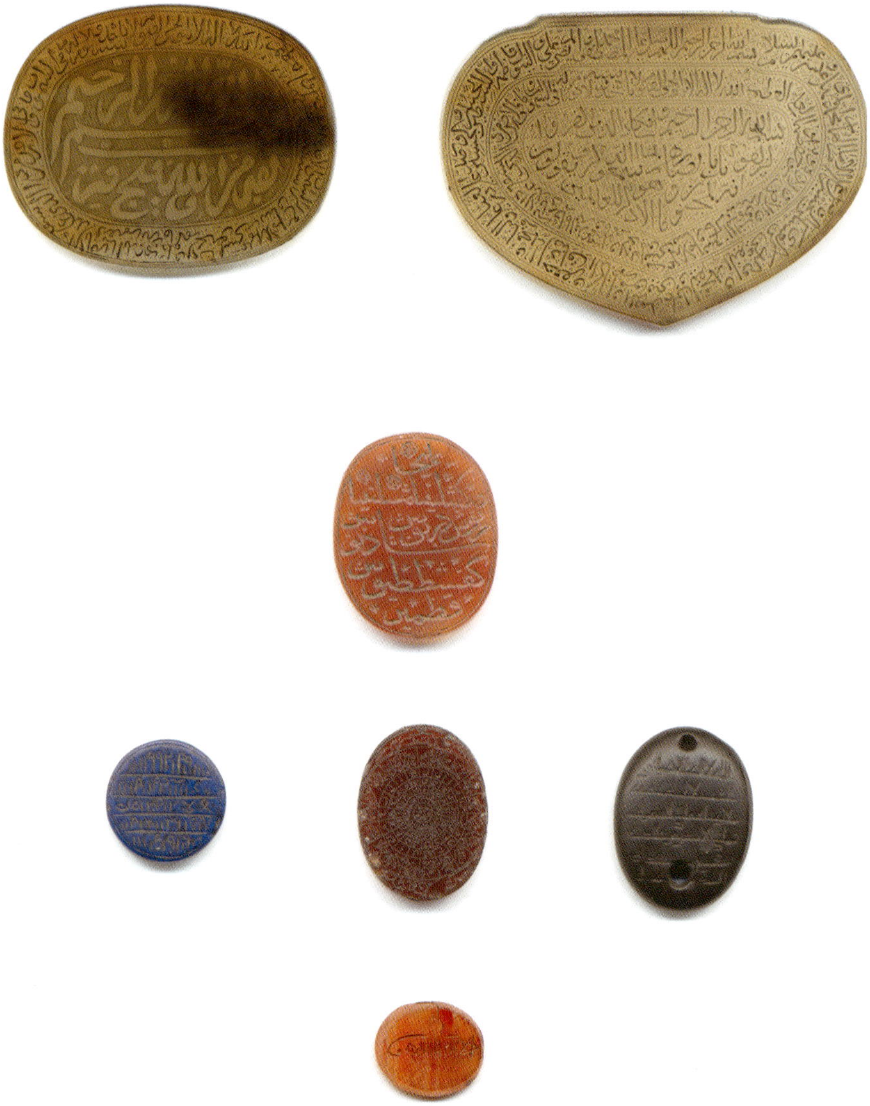

Amulets

Dates unknown
Lapis lazuli, carnelian, limestone, quartz
OA+14278; OA 1883.10-31.19; OA+13499; OA Marsden 9; OA Sloane 4; OA 1878.12-20.68, Christy Collection; OA 1866.12-29.101
The British Museum, London

These amulets are mostly made of semi-precious stones variously inscribed with verses from the Koran and auspicious or magical words and signs. Of the stones used here lapis lazuli was especially valued for its rarity, quartz (rock crystal) was considered to confer good fortune, while carnelian was said to have been the favourite amuletic stone of Muhammad.

They are all engraved in positive rather than negative, and so are intended to be read rather than be used as seals, which in other ways they closely resemble. There is an overlap in meaning and intention between seals and amulets in the Islamic world. Seals probably derived from amulets and often contained similar inscriptions. They were generally protective of their owners' property and their persons (For further discussion see Porter, 2004, 135–49 and Collon, ed. 1997, passim).

When does a prayer become a spell? Traditionally, Islam did not condemn magic out of hand. Acceptable magicians were those who worked for and with Allah, not against Him. For all kinds of magic and divination, however, according to the medieval writer Ibn al-Nadin, seals ('designs on stones, stringed beads and signet stones') were all important tools. (Porter 2004, 142).

On these amulets, the magical mingles with the sacred. Some Koran quotations are included for specific purposes – such as the 'Victory verse' which was intended to be carried into battle. Key religious words and phrases appear, such as *bismillah* ('In the Name of God') – the opening words of the Koran. Other amulets comprise arcane combinations of numbers and letters or the so-called 'Seven Magical Signs', which were considered strongly protective and are meant to refer to the greatest name of God.

In all these examples it is not just the significance of the inscriptions, but also that of the stones upon which they are carved, that imbue them with talismanic power. FA

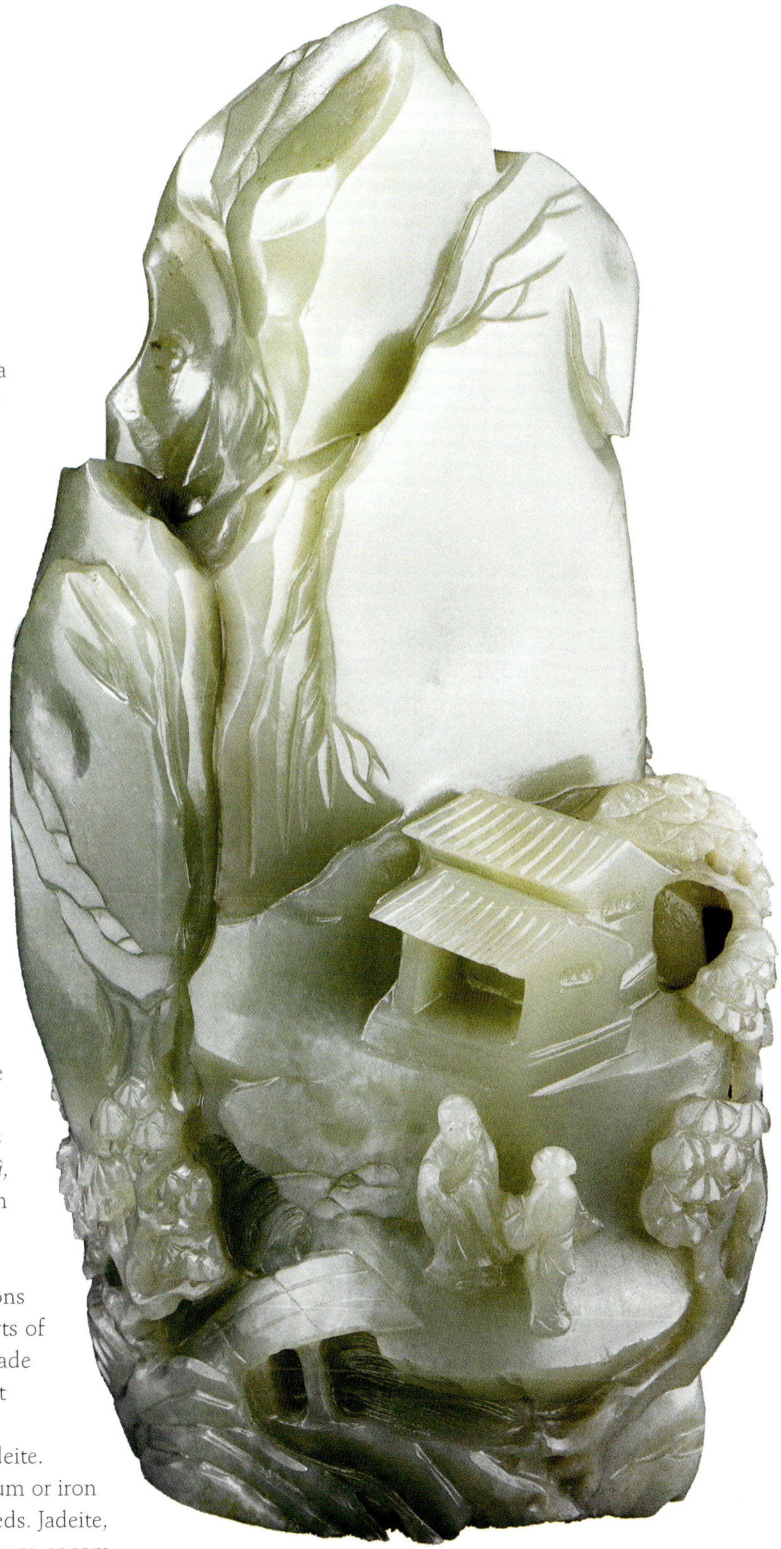

Jade Mountain (Scholar's Rock)

Qing dynasty, 18th century
From China
Jade, height 15.5 cm
OA 1930.12-17.10
The British Museum, London.

This finely carved scene in jade depicts sages and boys in a garden beside a mountain and stream, echoing the ancient tradition of monumental landscapes in Chinese painting. Recognizing and contemplating 'the large in the small' is a philosophical tradition reaching back thousands of years. Reproduction of the world in miniature is a recurring theme in Chinese art, and representations of mountains in particular signified escape from China's highly ordered, bureaucratic society to the natural world. In Taoist thought, the mountains were also the home of the immortals, and so symbolized paradise and the attainment of everlasting life.

Such artworks would be placed on a scholar's desk to stimulate contemplation. They could also be made of turquoise, bronze, porcelain or carved bamboo root. Naturally shaped roots, rocks, gourds and other such objects were similarly symbolic. However, jade has always been the material most highly prized by the Chinese, even above silver and gold:

'The beauty of jade is revealed in its five virtues: its lustre produces a feeling of warmth, or the virtue of humaneness; its translucence enables one to comprehend its inner markings, revealing the virtue of morality; its tone when struck reverberates; and its purity penetrates far, which is the virtue of courage; sharp and austere, it injures no-one, which demonstrates its purity' (From *Shuōwén Jiězì*, the first Chinese character dictionary, compiled by Xǔ Shèn about 100 AD).

From ancient times, this extremely tough translucent stone has been worked into ornaments, ceremonial weapons and ritual objects. Recent archaeological finds in many parts of China have revealed not only the antiquity of the skill of jade carving, but also the extraordinary levels of development it achieved at a very early date.

The English word 'jade' refers to both nephrite and jadeite. Pure nephrite is white but the presence of copper, chromium or iron creates colours ranging from green-greys to yellows and reds. Jadeite, which was rarely used in China before the eighteenth century, encompasses an even wider variety of colours than nephrite. NL

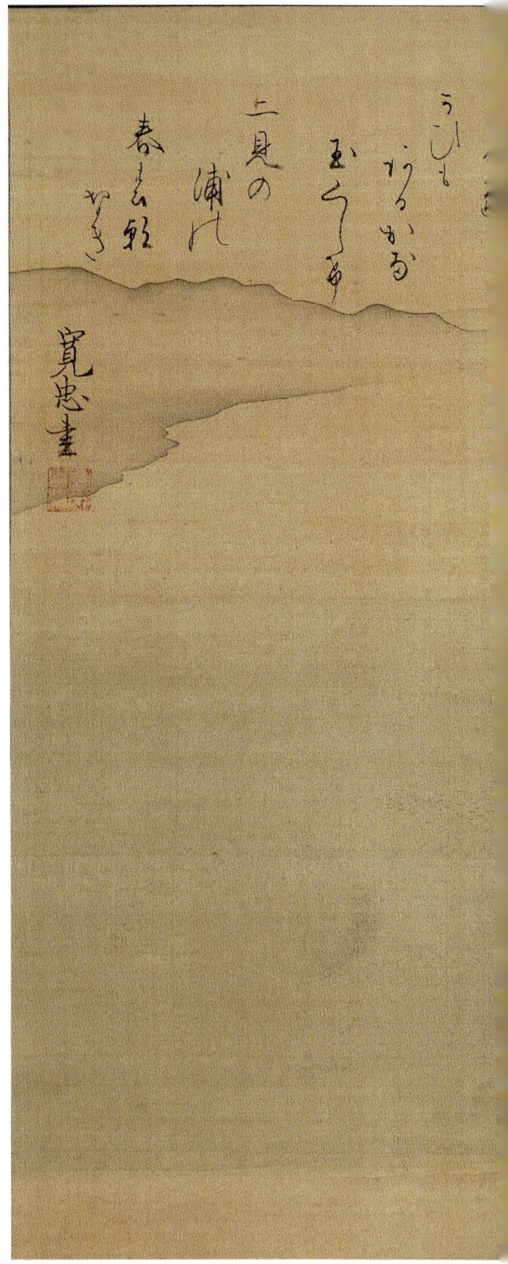

Futaminoura Bay with a distant View of Mount Fuji c. 1811

YOKOYAMA KAZAN (1781/84–1837)
Hanging scroll: ink and colour on silk, 43.4 x 70.9 cm
Signed: Kazan sha
Seal: Isshō
Inscription signature: Hirotada sho
Inscription seal: 'Seal of Hirotada'
JP ADD 798 (1984.6-11.01)
The British Museum, London.

This view across Ise Bay shows the *Meoto-iwa*, or 'wedded rocks', at Futaminoura. The two rocks, considered to be male and female, are named Izanagi and Izanami and represent the primal couple in Japanese traditional history. According to Shintö legend, it is from this couple that all the Japanese islands originate. The rocks are joined in matrimony by a sacred rope and in the distance the red sun is rising behind the ever present silhouette of Mount Fuji. Some of the tiny figures shown on the beach are prostrated in worship before the sacred rocks, Fuji being in view behind the rocks in the distance. The wedded rocks are in the vicinity of the shrine at Ise and thanksgiving pilgrimages to this shrine attracted great crowds of worshippers: the last in the Edo period, in 1830, is said to have attracted 2,280,000 devotees in just one month. An eclectic mix of faith systems, including Zen and Shintö, remains a significant part of Japanese culture today.

The inscription is a *waka* poem by the high-ranking courtier Fujinami Hirotada (1759–1824), while the box in which the scroll is stored also bears an inscription by Hirotada (Clark, T., *100 Views of Mount Fuji*, London, 2001, 31). The inscription records when some pilgrims preparing to worship the rising sun saw Mount Fuji illuminated with unusual clarity, despite its great distance.

Fuji became the centre of a cult-following in the seventeenth century and this deepened the symbolic influence of the mountain in the Japanese mind. A key figure in the development of the Fuji cult was Jikigyō Miroku (1671–1733), an oil merchant from Edo. While climbing the mountain he had visions of the Buddha most associated with Fuji according to Shintö, Sengen Daibosatsu. In 1733 Jikigyō Miroku duly undertook a death-fast at Eboshi Rock near the seventh of the ten stage ascent of Fuji.
AM

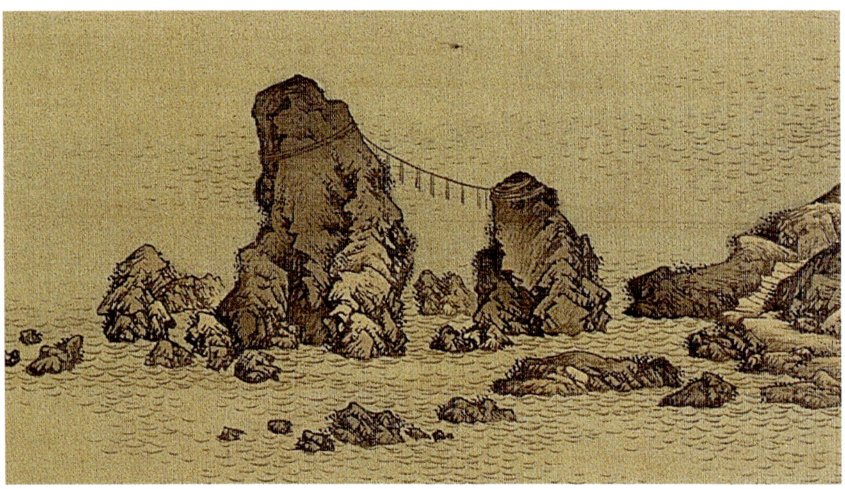

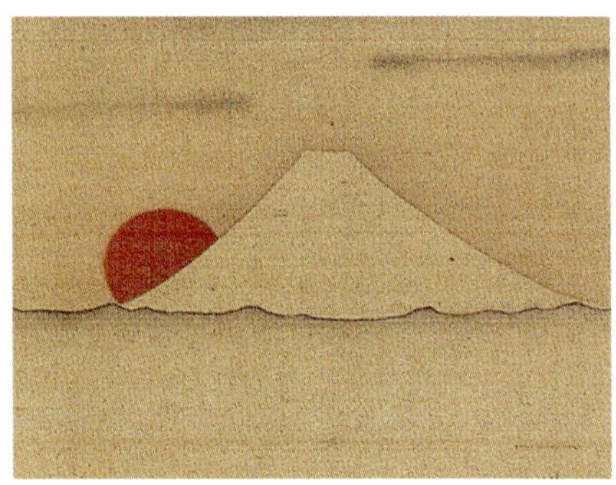

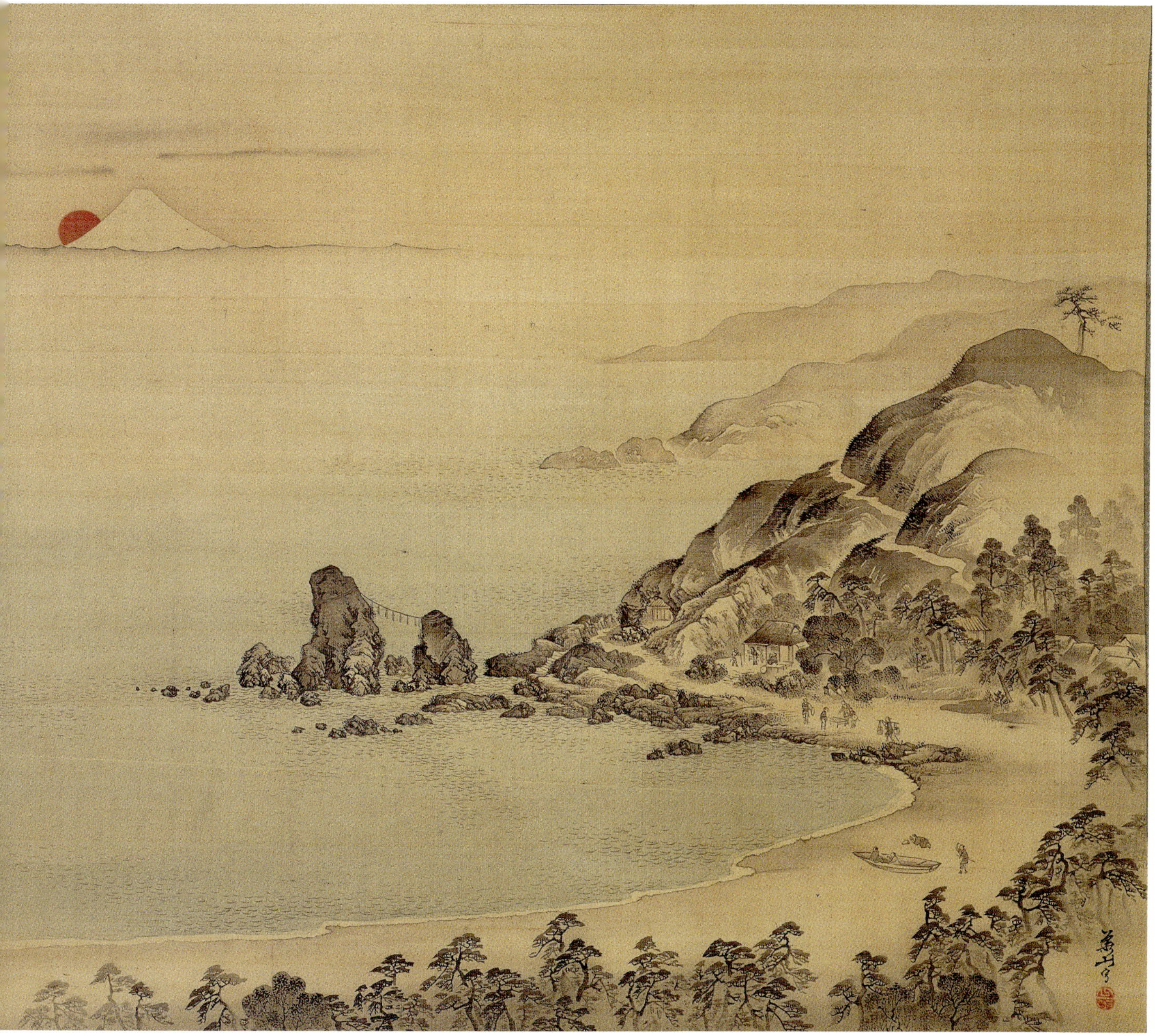

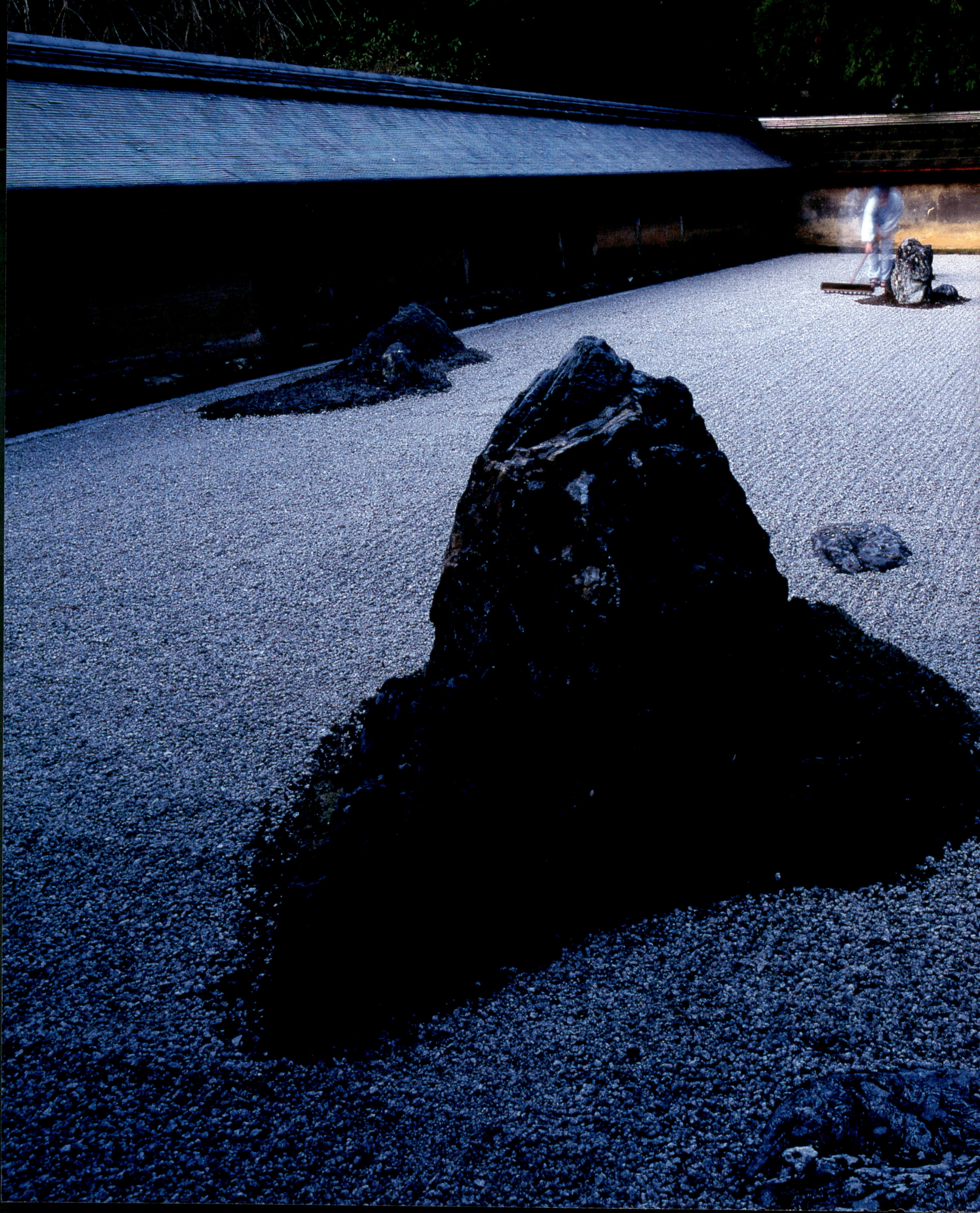

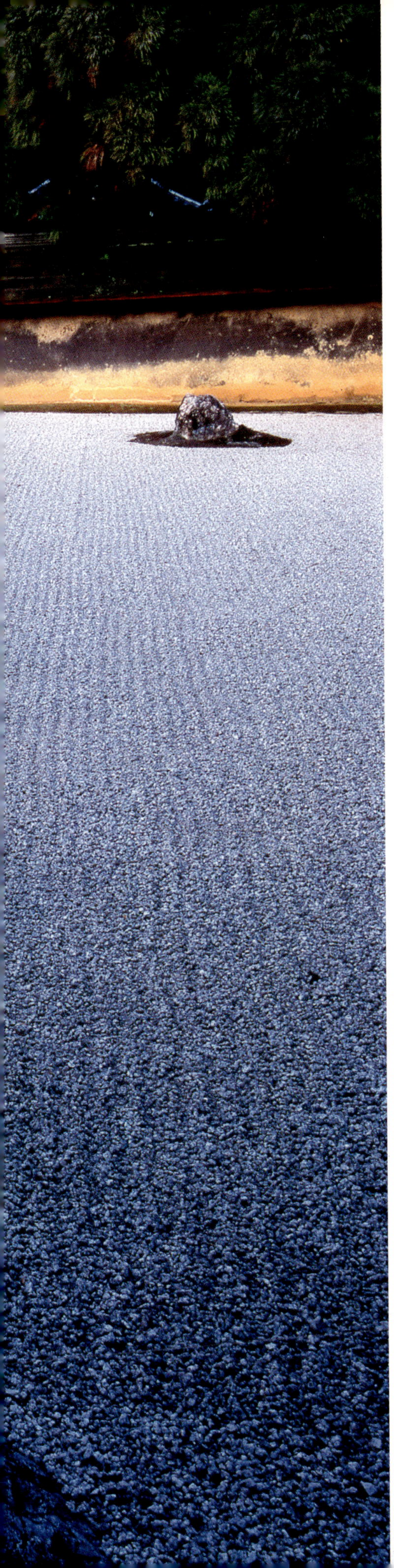

Ryōan-ji 2, 1992

TADAYUKI NAITOH (BORN 1941)
Photograph, crystal print, 22 x 22 cm
Courtesy of the artist

The meditative landscapes of Japanese gardens owe their origins to a concept of landscape gardening brought from China in the seventh century. The rock gardens represent an aesthetic response to both faith and nature, encouraging an appreciation of the universal within the particular. Tadayuki Naitoh seeks to capture, through the contemporary medium of photography, the rhythm and quietude that is communicated through the abstract designs originally conceived to harmonize with the seasons by Buddhist monks. The single upright stone may be seen to signify the steadfast strength of the Buddha. Tadayuki Naitoh bathes his image in an ethereal light, increasing the other-worldly sense of the Zen Master's design.

The *karesansui,* or rock garden, at Ryōan-ji (Temple of the Peaceful Dragon) in Kyoto is associated with the Zen Master Soami and dates from the late fifteenth century. Thirty metres wide by ten metres, the garden contains fifteen rocks arranged in such a manner that only fourteen can be seen at once, from whichever angle the garden is viewed. Only when you attain spiritual enlightenment as a result of deep Zen meditation can you see the last invisible stone with your mind's eye. The fifteen stones are arranged in an uneven configuration, placed over a flat, gravelled rectangular area bordered by a low wall. A sense of vast emptiness is created by the relatively small scale of the rocks amidst the meticulously raked white *shirakawa* sand, which may be contemplated from the edge of the Abbot's house. The encouragement to meditate upon the abstract qualities of harmony, to increase understanding of the universe as a whole, is the essence of Zen philosophy. The meditation produces a sense of 'no-mind', a much-valued state of awareness.

Rocks in Japanese thinking represent a complex heritage of Shintö as well as Zen Buddhist ideas. An auspicious quality of rocks within the Zen tradition is that powerful dragon gods were thought to hatch from stones, while in Shintö worship white sand is considered holy.
AM

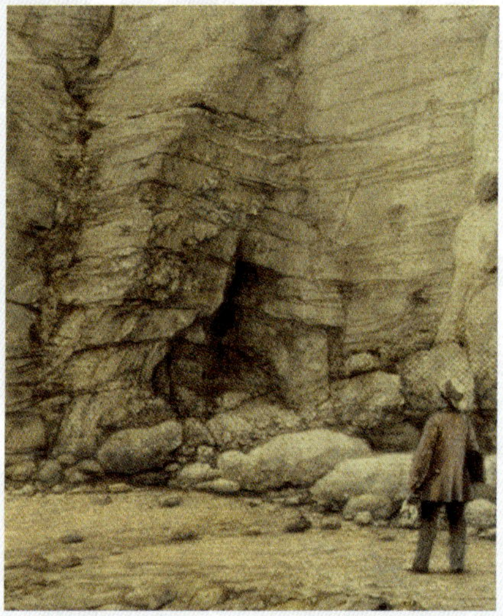

6 Memory, Myth and Meaning

Menhir:

A tall (hir) upright monumental stone (men), of varying antiquity found in parts of Europe, and in Africa and Asia

SHORTER OXFORD ENGLISH DICTIONARY

ABOVE:
William Dyce, *Pegwell Bay, Kent – A Recollection of October 5th 1858* (detail)
Tate, London. Purchased 1894

Standing Stone inscribed with Ogham Letters ➤
Erected and engraved 5th or 6th century AD
Deelish, Aghabullogue, Cork, Ireland
Fine-grained red sandstone, about 380 million years old, height 95 cm
M&ME 1884.06-09.1
The British Museum, London

TO WANDER AMONG LANDSCAPES in the presence of monumental stones evokes memory, provokes myth and invites meaning. Sometimes the positioning of the stones is natural, making manifest their geological origins. Occasionally the stones have been deliberately positioned and may be carved, sculpted or engraved, providing evidence of humankind's immediate and personal interaction with the environment. They can evoke the memory of ancient civilizations – perhaps Neolithic, or those of Greece or Rome.

Erecting engraved stones as memorials to loved ones now lost is a worldwide instinct that deliberately counterpoints the brevity and frailty of human life with the strength and durability of stone to symbolize our love, memory and human spirit. Churchyards directly chart family achievement and loss. The standing stone pictured here, a fine-grained red sandstone that formed in marine waters about 380 million years ago, was found in 1826 in the boundary ditch of an old burial ground of Deelish township, County Cork, Ireland. It was probably set upright and engraved sometime around the fifth or sixth century AD. The lines carved on to the edges of the stone are an early coded form of the Irish language known as Ogham script, used occasionally on boundary markers, burial stones and ceremonial monuments by the ancient bards, druids and elite of Ireland, Cornwall and Wales. Usually recording simple genealogical statements including the names of parents and tribes, the script consists of short or long lines arranged to cut across a vertical base line, such as the edges of this stone.

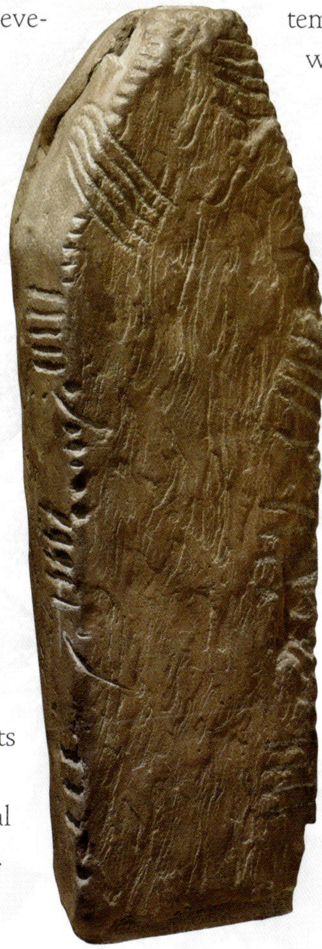

Here the script is engraved on both sides of the stone but because the lower half of the stone is missing the inscription is incomplete. This makes it problematic to interpret but it appears to read '...lot, of the tribe of Coribiri". 'Lot' probably relates to the name 'Cobalot', and the Coribiri are a known tribe of Leinster and in this instance the inscription is presumably commemorative of a particular individual.

At other times the rocks and stones we see are natural and uncarved, yet seem to be arranged by some unseen hand, providing us with stories, legends and creation myths. Ancient and modern artists have felt the need to respond to these landscapes, and their responses call to our attention the natural formations of our surroundings from which we may too easily be divorced by modern life, encouraging us to contemplate the passage of time and our place in the world. The use of stone as a metaphor reaches its peak in masonic symbolism, where stonemasons' customs and tools are used to give allegorical instruction in moral and spiritual values, to guide the apprentice to become the perfectly shaped stone to take their place in the Temple of God.

Stones need not be monumental, however, to be associated with personal memory, myth or meaning. Carved and polished jet, a form of fossilized wood, was worn as jewellery in Victorian times to symbolize mourning for a loved one. Precious and semi-precious stones continue to be worn to show off their worth and beauty and are universally regarded as status symbols. They can also have more subtle meanings and powers, symbolizing chastity or purity, detecting poisons or infidelity or simply providing protection and good fortune.

Lovers' Brooch

13th century
England
Gold, sapphires, rubies and enamel, diameter 3.8 cm
M&ME AF 2683
The British Museum, London

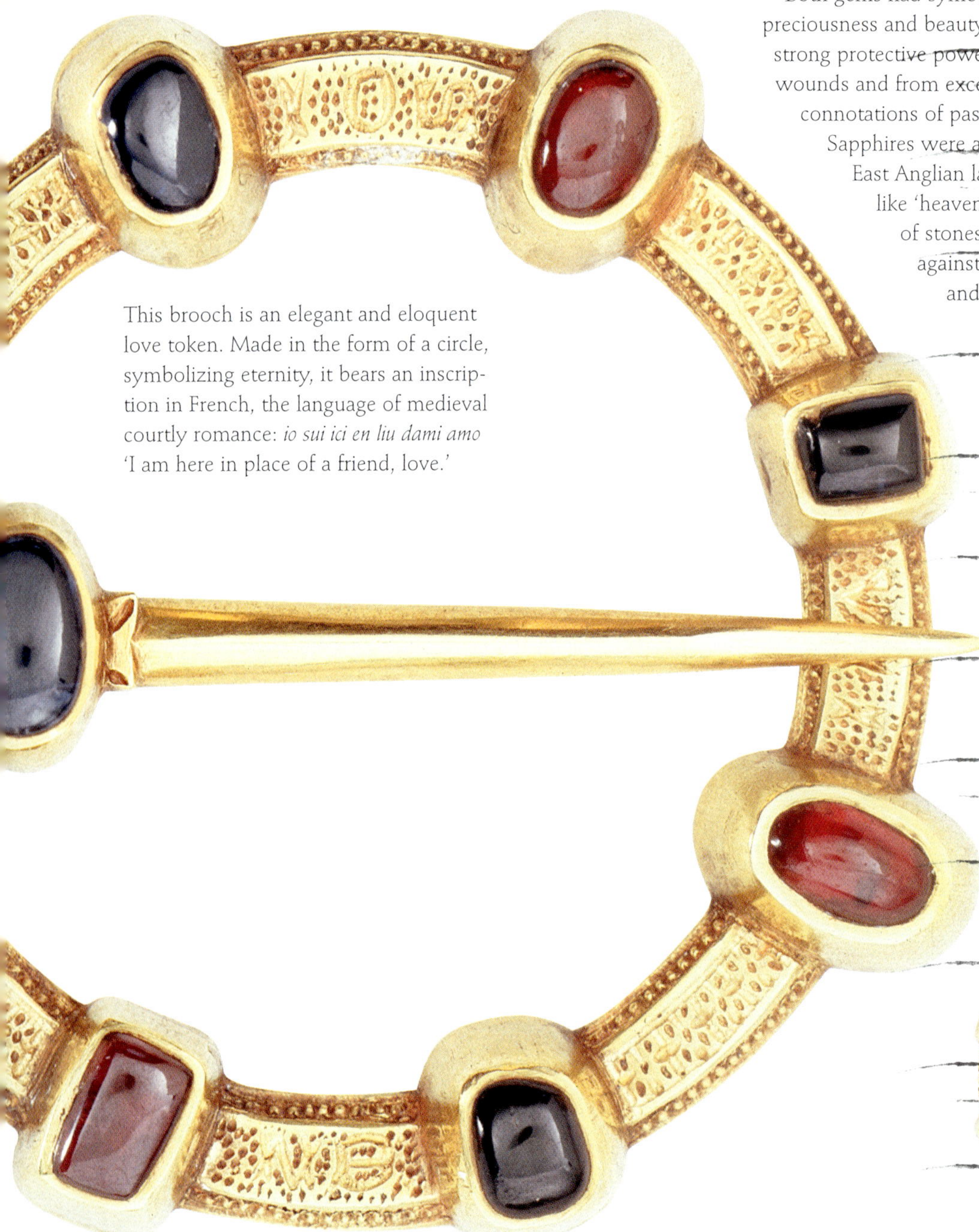

This brooch is an elegant and eloquent love token. Made in the form of a circle, symbolizing eternity, it bears an inscription in French, the language of medieval courtly romance: *io sui ici en liu dami amo* 'I am here in place of a friend, love.'

The gems with which the brooch is set were the most valuable and highly regarded gemstones available at the time. It is customary today to think of diamonds as the most prestigious of stones, and therefore those most appropriate for a lover's gift, but they were not available in the Western world until more than a century after this brooch was made. The Italians were the first to import diamonds from the East, but until this point rubies and sapphires – imported from India, Burma and Sri Lanka – were the most valued stones in Western jewellery.

Both gems had symbolic meanings beyond their simple preciousness and beauty. Rubies were supposed to have had strong protective powers, preserving their owner from plague, wounds and from excessive lust, although the stone also has connotations of passionate love suggested by its colour. Sapphires were also protective, described by the medieval East Anglian lapidary Bartholomaeus Anglicus as being like 'heaven on a clear day'. To him it was the 'best of stones, fit for the fingers of kings.' It protected against strife and poison, comforted the body and cheered the heart (*De Proprietatibus Rerum*, c. 1240, translated John Trevisa, Oxford 1975, 834 ff). Its blue colour was also considered to symbolize chastity and purity because of its connections with the sky and – by association – with heaven. As a consequence it was a favourite, along with amethyst, for ecclesiastical jewellery.

The giver of this brooch is saying many things through the language of stones. He is declaring his love, hoping to keep his lover safe and exhorting her to be true to him. FA

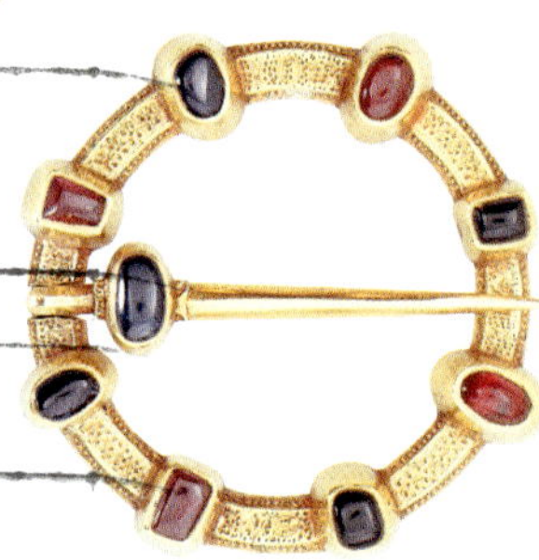

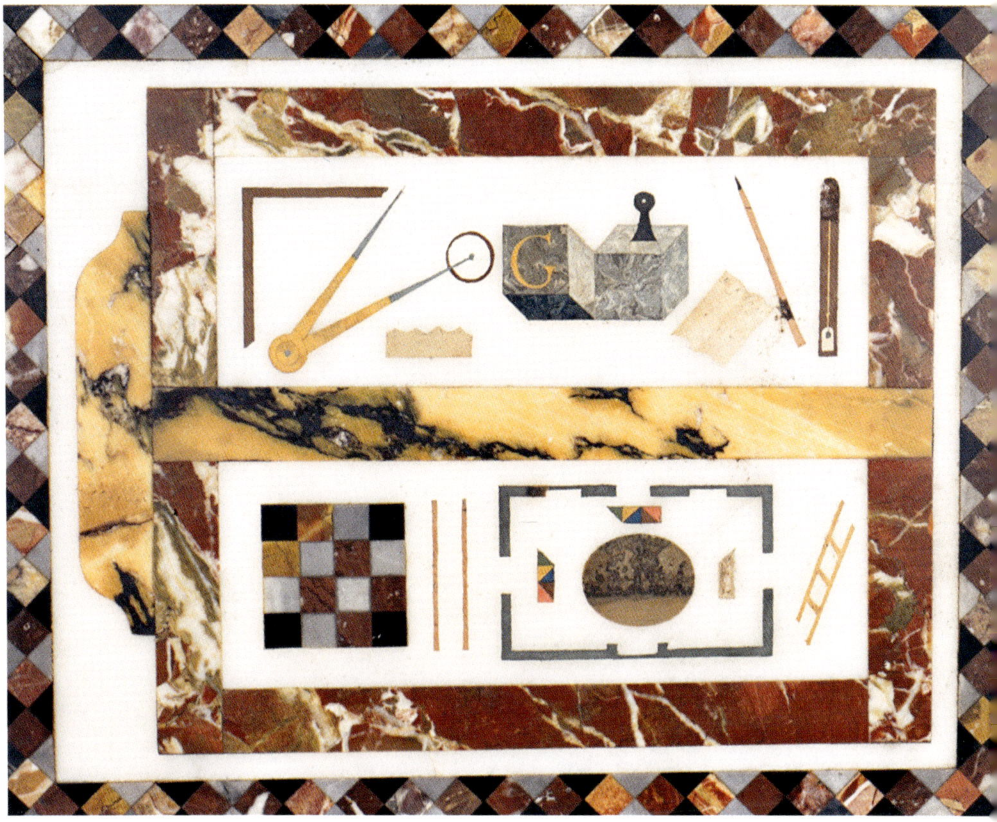

Master's Tracing Board

English, late 1700s
Marble, 18.4 x 23.1 cm

The Library and Museum of Freemasonry, London

A key aspect of the centrality of stone in human history is the art of building with stone. Stonemasons have developed their art since earliest times, working to principles which have developed buildings as expressions of humankind's place in the world. Freemasonry is a society of individuals concerned with moral and spiritual values whose members are taught its precepts by a series of ritual dramas, which follow ancient forms, and use stonemasons' customs and tools as allegorical guides.

Each tool represents a moral capacity which the mason has to apply in daily life. The level, here shown in yellow-veined marble dividing the image in two, represents judgement and equality. Reading the top half, from left to right, the square and compasses are probably the most recognizable symbol of freemasonry. The square is critical in good building practice and for freemasons symbolizes the importance of maintaining a balance between justice and mercy. Compasses are used by stonemasons to determine limits and proportions representing the idea of keeping matters in balance.

The point within a circle (shown at the tip of the compasses) represents an individual brother and the circle the boundary line of his duty to his God and his fellow men. Below the point is a rough stone or ashlar with an adjacent smooth worked stone inscribed with the letter G, which stands for God: stone in its rough and unpolished state is emblematic of mankind in his natural condition – ignorant, uncultivated, even vicious. Once humankind is educated and able to control his passions, leading a pure life, 'he is then represented by the Perfect Ashlar, which, under the skillful hands of the workmen, has been smoothed and squared, and fitted for its place in the building' (Albert G Mackey, *A Lexicon of Freemasonry*, 8th edition, undated).

The maul is used to level worked stone, while the open book represents the Volume of Sacred Law – the Bible or appropriate religious book open during Masonic lodge meetings. It is not entirely clear what the next symbol represents. In other Masonic boards it is simply a wooden stick or wand but here it appears to be a skirret, used to draw arcs and circles with a line attached to a pin at one end (here shown wound round), and a marker such as a pencil or chalk at the other. In freemasonry the skirret conveys the idea of laws, traditions and fundamental principles. The final tool is a plumb rule, used to mark perpendiculars, in freemasonry a symbol of rectitude.

The lower register of symbols (left to right) displays first a mosaic pavement, which represents the traditional flooring of the Temple of Solomon. The two parallel lines (shown to the right) represent Moses and Solomon. Next is a building plan of Solomon's Temple. The final tool is Jacob's ladder which features in the first degree of freemasonry (Thanks go to Diane Clements for advice concerning the symbols). AM

Stonehenge, c.1825–28

JOSEPH MALLORD WILLIAM TURNER
(1775–1851)
Watercolour, 27.9 x 40.4 cm
Salisbury and South Wiltshire Museum

Stonehenge is one of the world's greatest prehistoric monuments and for 5,000 years has been a constant source of wonder and speculation. Originally a circle of timbers, it was rebuilt in stone around 2500 BC. In an amazing feat, about eighty volcanic bluestones – each weighing up to four tonnes – were dragged and floated by river 245 miles from the Prescelli Mountains in north Wales to Salisbury Plain and erected. After a period of abandonment, in around 2300 BC an even bigger Stonehenge was begun. The bluestones were rearranged and giant grey sandstones (Sarsens) were transported from Marlborough Downs, twenty miles away – even though these weighed up to fifty tonnes each.

Countless artists have been drawn to Stonehenge and it has evoked a variety of strong responses. Familiar all around the world, it provides a striking iconic image resonant with myths and has been represented in just about every medium. By the time artists such as Turner and Constable sketched Stonehenge, several of the stones had fallen or were leaning at precarious angles. At the beginning of the twentieth century work began to straighten and reset the stones until at last by 1964 Stonehenge, although ruined, stood as it was erected by prehistoric man on the alignment of the rising of the midsummer sun.

Sketchbooks in Tate Britain show that Turner sketched Stonehenge in c. 1799–1802 and again in 1811, and he probably returned to these sketches in about 1825 when he was commissioned to provide subjects to be engraved for *Picturesque Views in England and Wales* (published in 1829 and engraved by Robert Wallis). Amidst the dramatic ruins, Turner has intensified the drama by showing white lightning streaking through a mass of billowing storm clouds and illuminating the centre of the ancient circle of stones. Surrounding the scene are death and destruction, with the shepherd and sheep struck by lightning and the dog baying by its master's side. NW

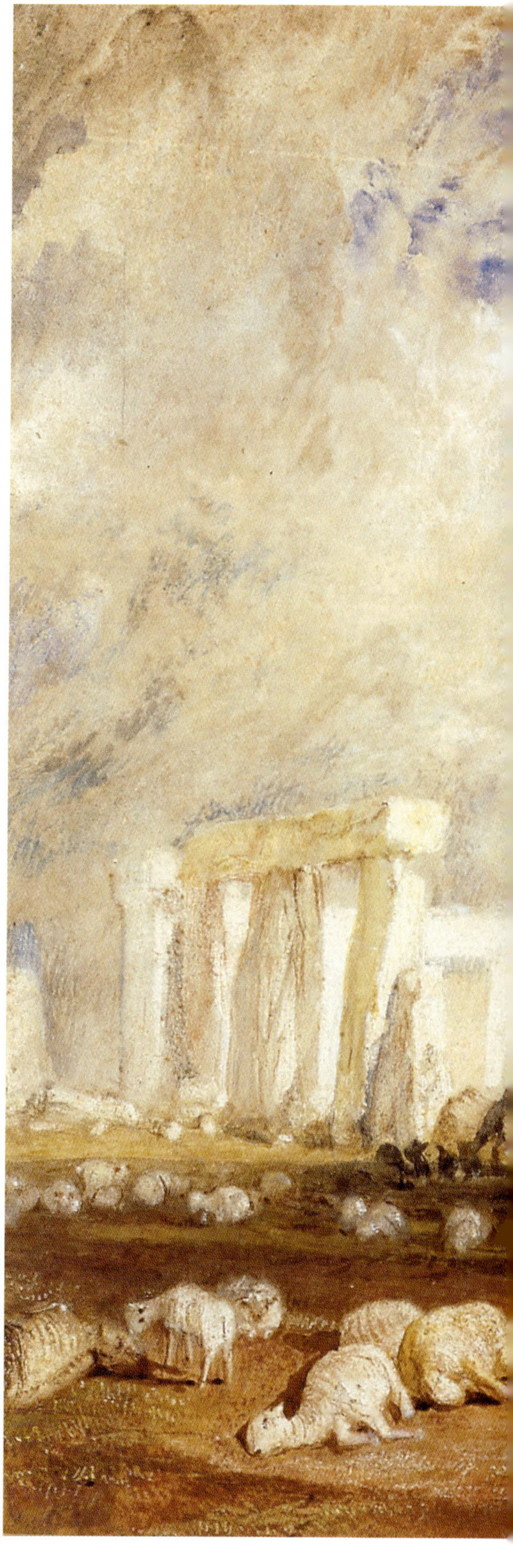

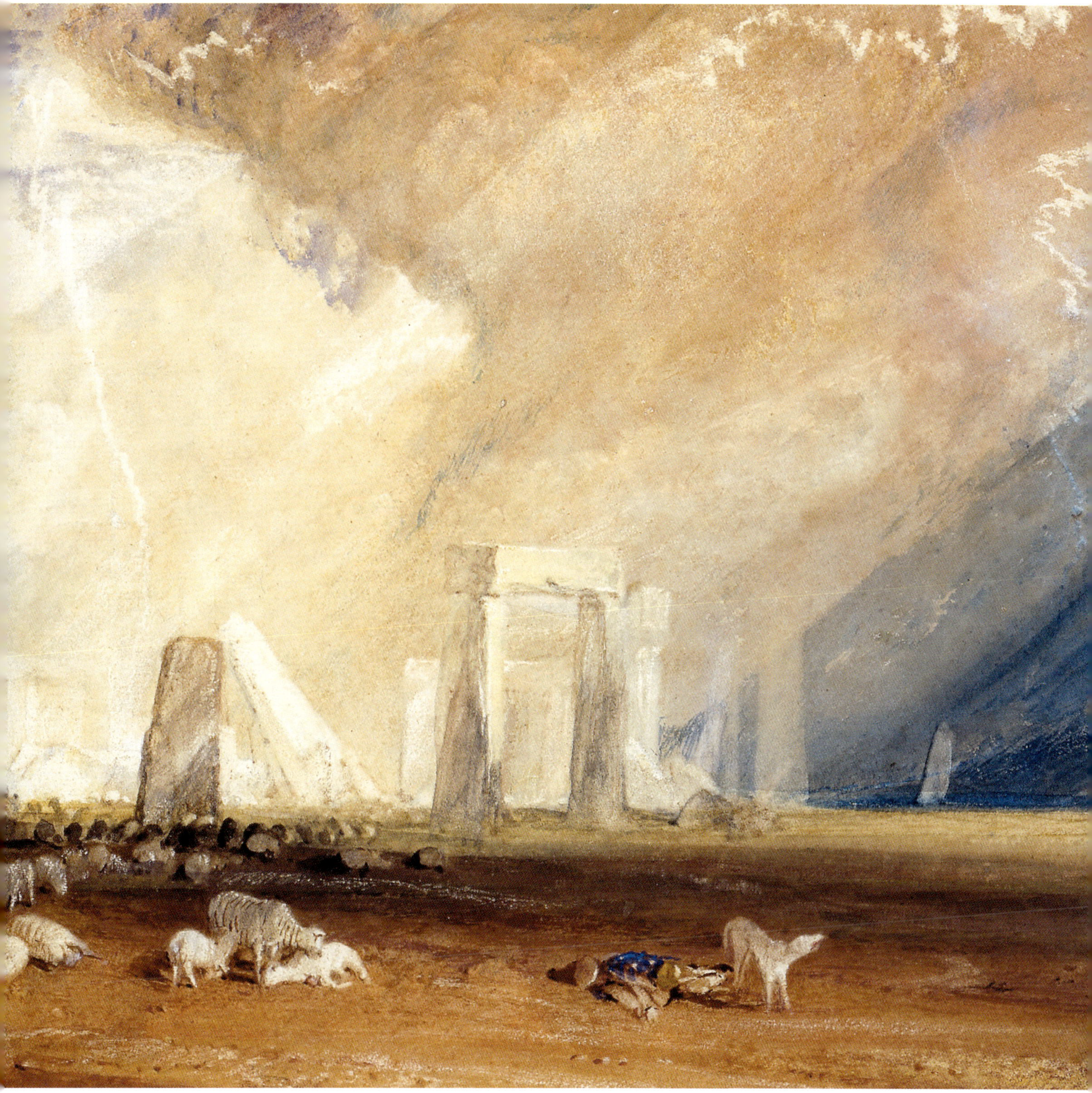

Pegwell Bay, Kent – A Recollection of October 5th 1858, c. 1858–60

WILLIAM DYCE (1806–64)
Oil on canvas, 63.5 x 88.9 cm
Tate, London. Purchased 1894

William Dyce's achievements as an artist relate to his ability to create Pre-Raphaelite effects derived from direct study, while also at times achieving a poetic sense of mood and atmosphere. In the autumn of 1858 William Dyce visited with his family the popular holiday resort of Pegwell Bay on the east coast of Kent, where he made a watercolour (Aberdeen Art Gallery and Museum) on which this painting is based. Dyce's intrinsic interest in geology shines through this image, together with a melancholy atmosphere as the members of his family are shown each isolated in contemplation of the rock pools and – in his own case – of the rockface itself. Dyce depicts himself at the edge of the painting in the right middle distance observing not only the cliff face, but also the track of a comet.

The title of the painting – exhibited at the Royal Academy in 1860 – reveals not only that the painting is based upon a recollection after the visit, but the specific time when Donati's comet was passing. According to the *Illustrated London News* (22 October 1858, 380), this comet was thought to be the largest and brightest ever seen when viewed on the night of 5 October. Dyce was almost certainly aware of the current debates about comets, as to whether they were the results of planetary catastrophe or simply drifting bodies that indicated the evolution of the solar system.

Dyce here creates an iconic image by contrasting heavenly and human affairs and timescales. He balances the literal geology of the site, the independent concentration of the beachcombers and his own scrutiny of the striations of time within a larger concept of time and space. We are invited to engage in the brevity of the moment and even recollection, when compared to geological time. Dyce pursues a strictly geological approach to his subject which, although the product of direct study, also acquires resonance and meaning enhanced by advances in scientific debate and his skills as an artist (*Pre-Raphaelite Vision Truth to Nature*, Tate, London, 2004, 188). AM

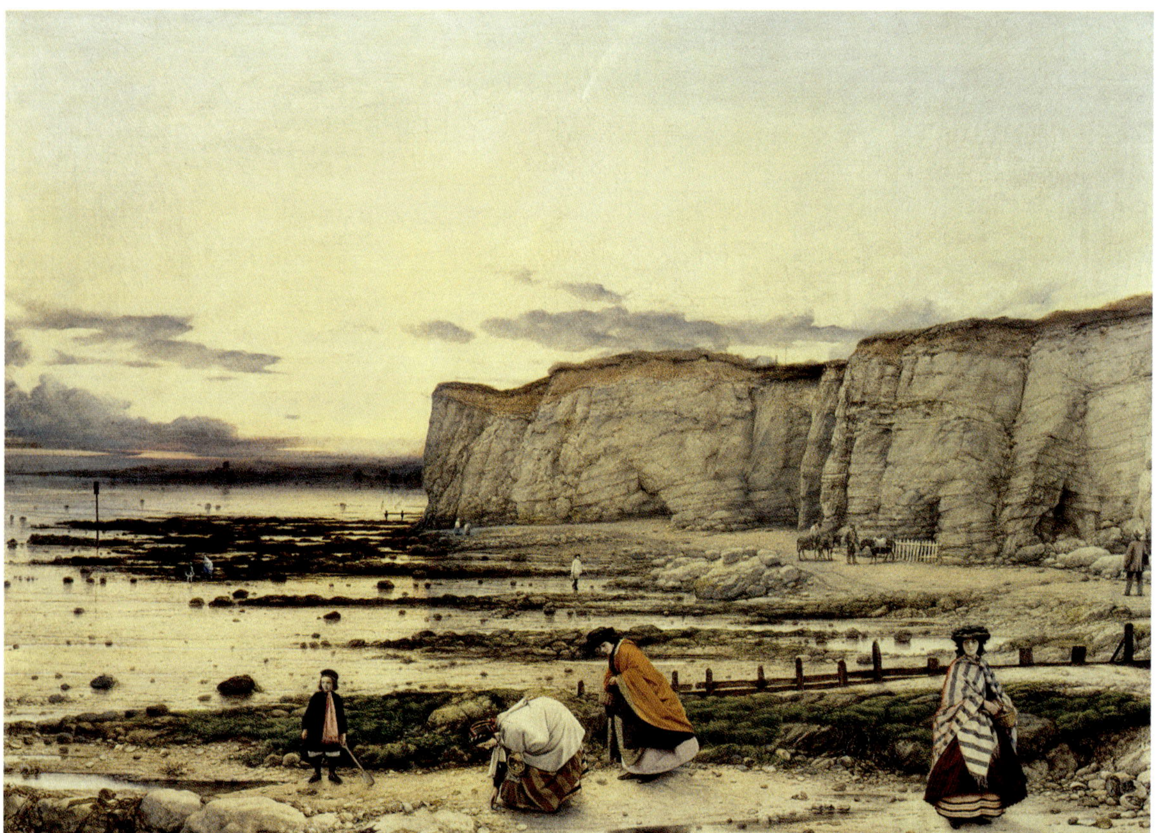

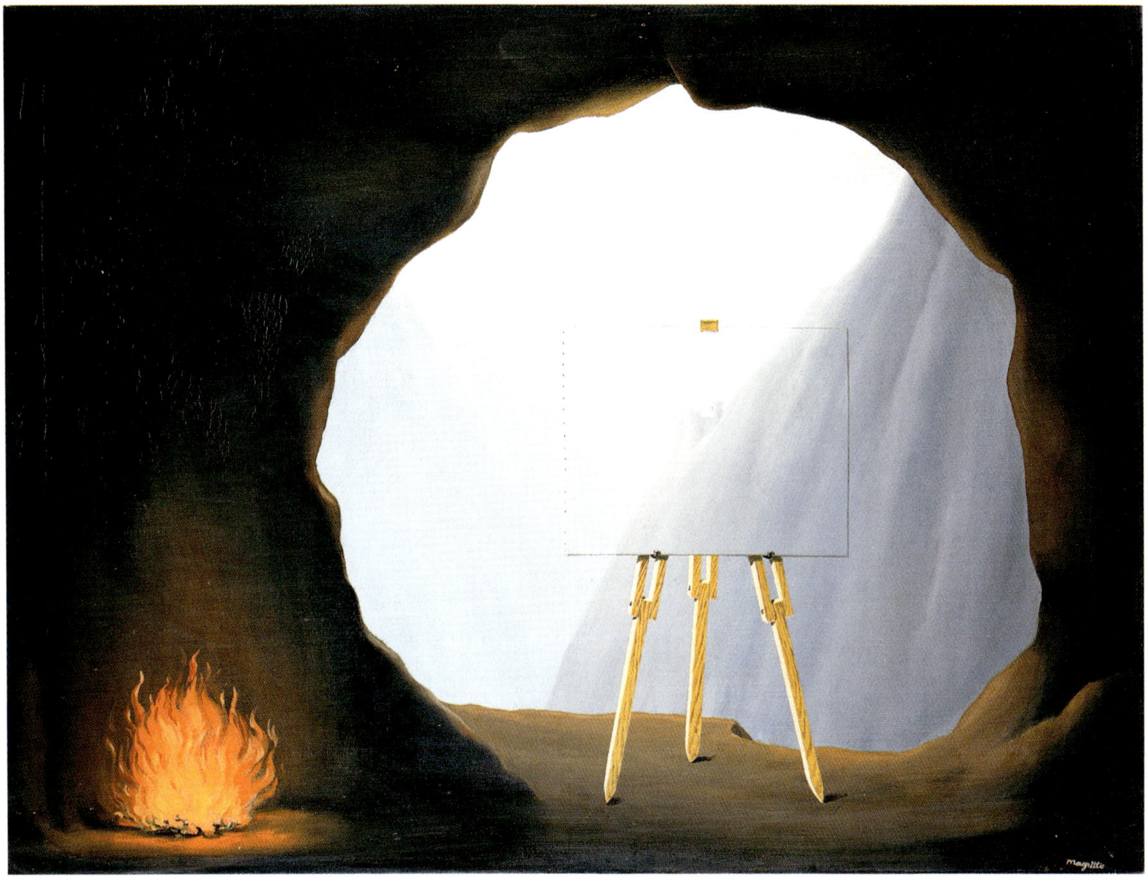

The Human Condition, 1935

RENÉ MAGRITTE (1898–1967)
Oil on canvas, 54 x 73 cm
NWHCM : 1995.88.2 : F
Norwich Castle Museum & Art Gallery, accepted by H.M. Government in lieu of tax and allocated to Norwich Castle Museum & Art Gallery 1995

Rocks and stones are recurring motifs in René Magritte's work, their representation often questioning our understanding of the fundamental nature of stone. Bodies are represented emerging from stone, rocks are brought into inexplicable juxtapositions with everyday objects, and rocky landscapes are used to evoke dreamlike settings for surrealist imagery. In *The Human Condition* the viewer looks through the mouth of a cave across a steep mountainous valley. In the centre of the painting, standing on an easel, is a painted canvas representing a castle. We are led to believe, but can never know for certain, that the painted castle conceals a real castle behind.

Magritte created a number of paintings depicting a canvas upon which a scene is shown, sited against a background replicating that selfsame scene, entitling them *The Human Condition.* In the majority of these the canvas is situated in a domestic setting. In this work, the fourth in the series, 'the indoors' has been transformed into a cave. Magritte simply described this setting as 'a cave like smugglers might use' (David Sylvester and Sarah Whitfield, *René Magritte: Catalogue Raisonné vol.5*, Menil Foundation, Houston and Philip Wilson, London 1993, 212–13). However, Magritte's interests suggest that the cave encourages further interpretation – that the artist is making reference to the parable of the cave from Plato's *The Republic.* In the parable, prisoners trapped in a cave make a philosophical journey through the various levels of Platonic knowledge – from the realm of illusion (represented by shadows cast by a fire against the back wall of the cave) to pure knowledge (represented by the sun).

Such an interpretation is supported by the title chosen for the painting. Plato introduces the parable by stating: 'I want you to go on to picture the enlightenment or ignorance of our human condition...' (Desmond Lee (ed.), Plato, *The Republic*, trans. Penguin, London, 1955, 317). The painting's twin references to the parable, through imagery and title, reinforce a sense of Magritte's interest in the tension or separation between reality and the representation of reality, between knowledge and illusion. Magritte is giving visual representation to questions that have dominated Western philosophy for thousands of years, questions that have helped define the human condition. NT

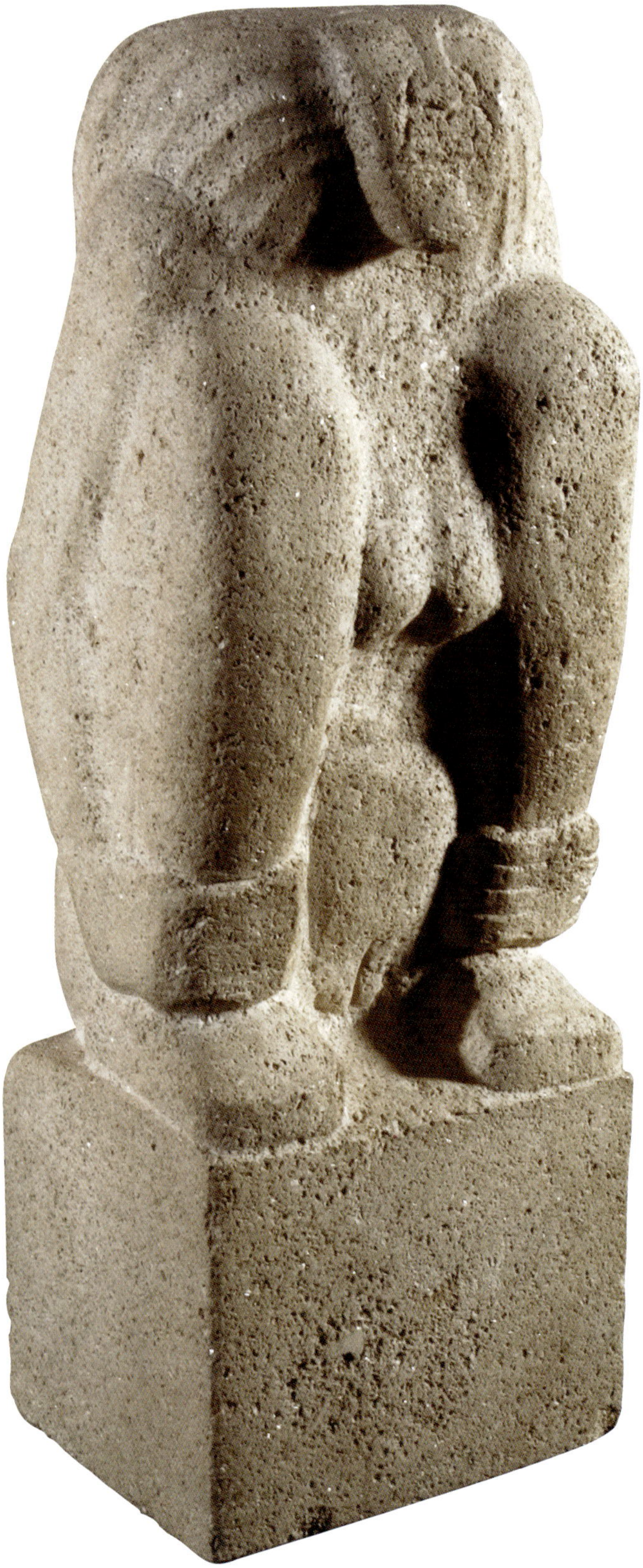

Crouching Sun Goddess, c. 1910

JACOB EPSTEIN (1880–1959)
Limestone, 37.5 x 13 x 10.8 cm

Nottingham City Museums & Galleries: Nottingham Castle

In 1912 Jacob Epstein declared to his patron John Quinn: 'I want to carve mountains' (Richard Cork, 'Image from Stone: Epstein as Carver', in E. Silber and T. Friedman (eds.), *Jacob Epstein: Sculpture and Drawings*, W.S. Manley and Son, 1989, 25). This ambitious statement reveals Epstein's commitment to stone carving. Like other pioneers of modernist sculpture during the early decades of the twentieth century, Epstein favoured 'direct carving'. Rather than being dictated by preparatory sketches or models, the final work would emerge from the artist's understanding and direct engagement with his chosen material. Epstein himself recalled in his autobiography:

> *I always try and get the whole feeling and expression of the work, with regard to the material I am working in. This is important. There are sculptors who treat a figure in stone in exactly the same manner as they do a figure in clay. With an isolated piece of stone they should regard the sculpture as primarily a block, and do no violence to it as stone.*
>
> JACOB EPSTEIN, *LET THERE BE SCULPTURE: AN AUTOBIOGRAPHY*, LONDON, 1940, 176–77

Carved from a single block of limestone, *Crouching Sun Goddess* is an early example of Jacob Epstein's focus on stone carving. The finished work clearly retains the qualities of the original limestone block. The sculpture has a rough-hewn directness – carved surface details are limited to those used to define fingers, facial features and the figure's stylised hair. The pitted surface of the limestone imbues the sculpture with an archaic appearance that firmly links this pagan goddess to Epstein's admiration of ancient and non-Western sculpture.

In particular, *Crouching Sun Goddess* points to the influence of ancient Egyptian and Indian temple sculpture. It is telling that the figure was carved at the same time that Epstein was planning a 'twentieth-century Stonehenge', an outdoor temple to be located on the Sussex Downs. The temple, which was conceived with fellow sculptor Eric Gill, was never realized but the subject and architectural appearance of *Crouching Sun Goddess* suggests that the work was carved with this ambitious and visionary project in mind. NT

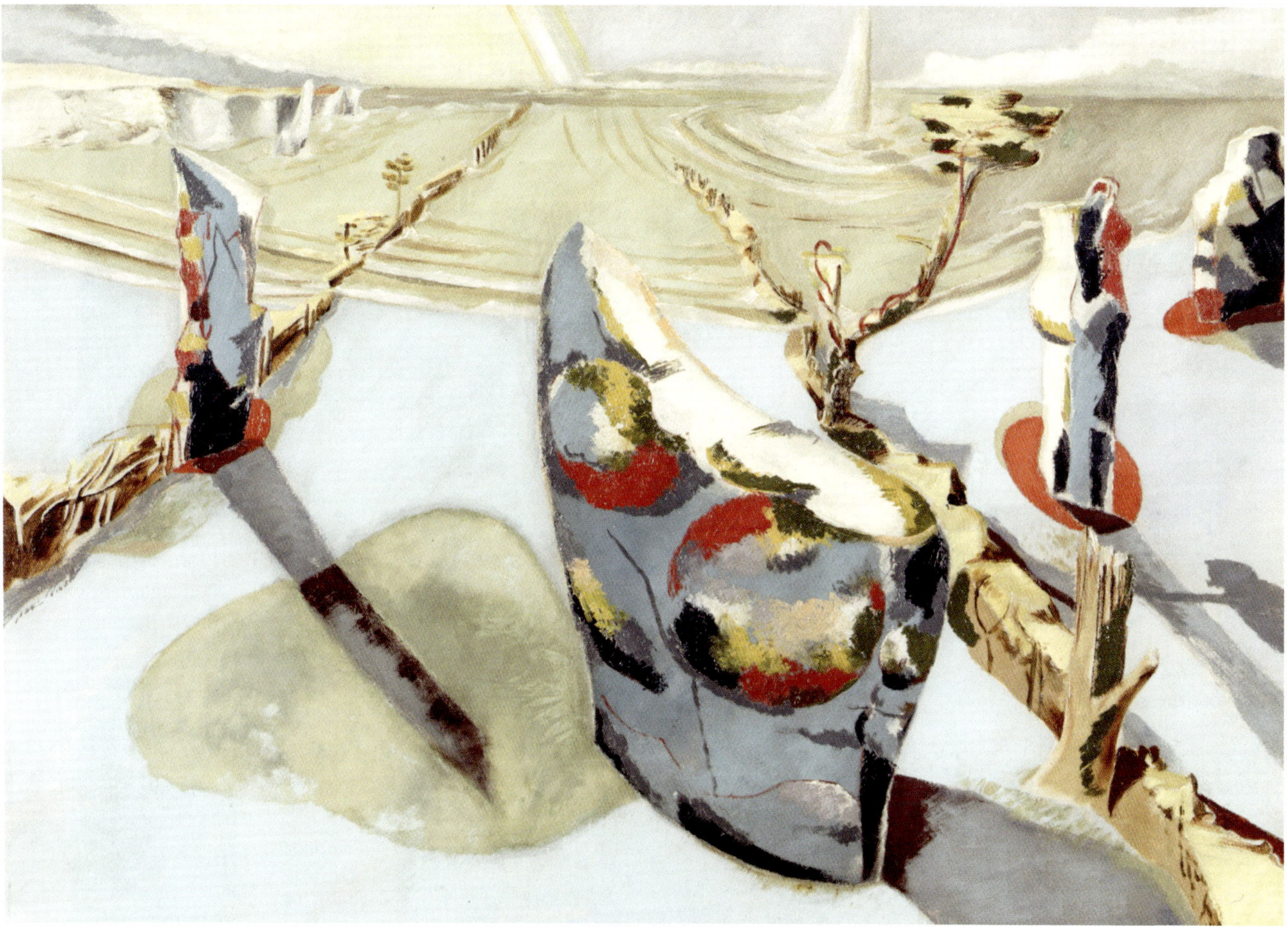

Circle of the Monoliths 1937-8

PAUL NASH 1889–1946
Oil on canvas 78.8 x 104.1
Leeds Museums and Galleries
(City Art Gallery)

In the summer of 1933, whilst taking a recuperative holiday in Marlborough, Paul Nash discovered the prehistoric earthworks and stone circles of Avebury. The sandstone megaliths (Sarsens), collected by Neolithic peoples from the nearby chalk downs and erected to form huge stone circles, had an immediate impact on Nash: 'The great stones were then in their wild state, so to speak. Some were half-covered by the grass, others stood up in cornfields or were entangled and overgrown in the copses, some were buried under the turf...Their colouring and pattern, their patina of gold lichen, all enhanced their strange forms and mystical significance. Thereafter, I hunted stones, by the seashore, on the downs, in the furrows (Paul Nash, Unpublished Manuscript, c.1944, in Jemima Montagu (ed.), *Paul Nash: Modern Artist, Ancient Landscape*, Tate Publishing, London 2003, 76).

Nash's response to the ancient Avebury landscape was a series of paintings featuring megalithic structures that aimed to capture what he described as the *genius loci* or 'spirit of place'. For this reason Nash did not paint the stones in a naturalistic way. He was more interested in conveying their powerful, almost visionary presence in the landscape, rather than their geological or archaeological significance. In *Circle of the Monoliths*, one of Nash's most imaginative renditions of the subject, the megaliths have been removed from the Wiltshire countryside to the seashore of an otherworldly landscape, whilst the surfaces of the stones have been imbued with a mysterious reflective quality.

Nash commented that the stones in *Circle of the Monoliths* had 'a character influenced by the conditions of Dream' (Montagu, 2003, 76). The painting certainly demonstrates the influence of surrealism, together with Nash's neo-romantic reworking of the English landscape tradition. The Avebury megaliths, markers or witnesses for an unknown mythological past, were the perfect subject for Nash as projections of mystical and spiritual significance. NT

Two Figures (Menhirs), 1964

BARBARA HEPWORTH (1903–75)
Slate, 82.5 x 63.8 x 32 cm
Tate, London. Purchased 1964

Barbara Hepworth was a key figure in a generation of sculptors who worked in relation to the modernist doctrine of 'truth to materials'. Of central importance to this idea was the exploration of the properties unique to different sculptural materials. Although a relatively late carving, *Two Figures (Menhirs)* is one of the first examples of Hepworth's use of slate. It demonstrates her lifelong willingness to experiment and explore the sculptural properties of different types of stone.

The structure of slate makes it prone to splitting and as a result a challenging material to carve. In 1971 Hepworth described how the geology of Cornwall, where she had lived and worked since 1939, provided slate that was particularly suited to carving: 'I found that if they quarried it very deeply in the slate quarry here at Delabole (in Cornwall) they could get a reasonable thickness for me, and a very fine quality....The slates from these deep beds are very beautiful' (Matthew Gale and Chris Stephens, *Barbara Hepworth: Works in the Tate Gallery Collection and Barbara Hepworth Museum St Ives*, Tate Publishing, London, 1999, 229). The prehistoric origins of these slate beds are embedded in this work: on one of the forms a fossil leaf can be clearly seen on the polished surface of the stone.

As the title suggests, *Two Figures (Menhirs)* relates to the human figure, yet simultaneously references the granite standing stones (or menhirs) that are such a feature of the landscape of west Cornwall. This conflation of figure and landscape, an important theme in Hepworth's work, came to the fore during the 1950s and '60s. She had long held an interest in the sculptural and associative power of Neolithic standing stones: as early as 1937 she had selected photographs of Stonehenge to accompany an article on her work (Gale and Stephens 1999, 231). Standing stones themselves can also be viewed as a figure/landscape metaphor; they 'belong' to the landscape and evoke timeless, universal values, all qualities to which Hepworth aspired in her own sculpture. NT

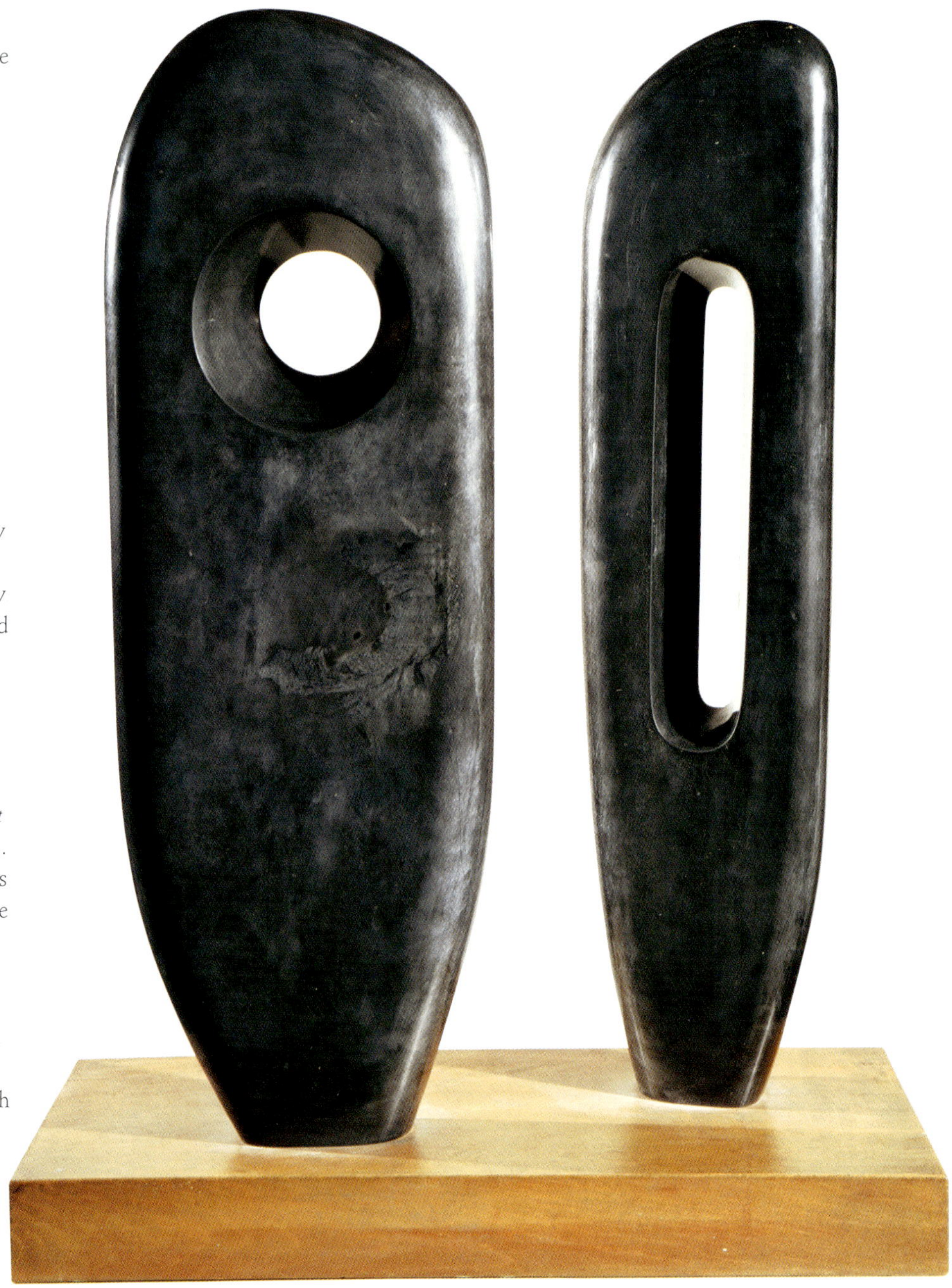

Photographic Credits and Copyright

Andrew Moore is Keeper of Art and Nigel Larkin is Curator (Geology) of the Natural History Department at Norwich Castle Museum & Art Gallery.

Specialist contributing authors include Francesca Vanke Altman, Curator of Decorative Arts, Norma Watt (British Watercolours) and Giorgia Bottinelli and Nicholas Thornton (Modern and Contemporary Art).

Andrew Smith is author of the bestselling book *Moondust*.

Further Reading

Bartholomaeus Anglicus, *De Proprietatibus Rerum*, translated John Trevisa, Oxford, 1975

Phillip Ball, *Bright Earth – The Invention of Colour,* Penguin, 2002

Mohamed ibn Ahmad Al Biruni, *A Book Most Comprehensive in Knowledge on Precious Stones,* translated Hakim Mohamed Said, Islamabad, 1989

Robert Boyle, *An Essay About the Origin and Virtues of Gems,* London, 1672

Wally Caruana, *Aboriginal Art,* Thames and Hudson, 193

John Cherry, *Medieval Decorative Art*, London, 1991

T. Clark, *100 Views of Mount Fuji*, London, 2001

Dominique Collon, ed. *7000 Years of Seals*, London, 1997

E. T. Cook and Alexander Wedderburn eds., *The Works of John Ruskin*, 39 vols, London, 1903–12.

Kamala Dongerkery, *Jewellery and Personal Adornment in India,* New Delhi, 1971

Joan Evans, *Magical Jewels of the Middle Ages and the Renaissance particularly in England*, Oxford, 1922

Wendell Frerichs, *Precious Stones as Biblical Symbols,* Dusseldorf, 1969

R. J. Gettens & G. L. Stout, *Painting Materials*, Dover Publications, 1966

S. Hackney, R. Jones and J. Townsend, ed., *Paint and Purpose: A study of technique in British art*, London, 1999

Michael Harrison (ed.), Sophie Bowness, Judith Collins, *Carving Mountains, modern stone sculpture in England 1907–37*, Ketlle's Yard, 1998

David Hinton, *Medieval Jewellery*, Aylesbury, 1982

Samar Najm Abul Huda, *Arab Roots of Gemology, a translation and commentary on Ahmad ibn Yusuf Al Tifashi's Best Thoughts on the Best of Stones,* Maryland and London, 1998

Camillus Leonardus, *Speculum Lapidum*, translated J. Freeman, London, 1750

Tessa Murdoch, ed., *Treasures and Trinkets: Jewellery in London from pre-Roman Times to the 1930s*, London, 1991

Thomas Nicols, *A Lapidary, or the History of Pretious Stones,* Cambridge, 1652

Venetia Porter 'Islamic Seals: Magical or Practical?', in *Magic and Divination in Early Islam*, ed. Emilie Savage-Smith, Aldershot, 2004

William Rowlands, *A Chymical Dispensatory*, London, 1669

Allen Staley, *The Pre-Raphaelite Landscape*, 1973

Allen Staley and Christopher Newall, with contributions by Alison Smith, Ian Warrell, Tim Batchelor, *Pre-Raphaelite Vision Truth to Nature*, Tate, London, 2004

D. C. Starzecka ed., *Maori Art and Culture*, British Museum Press, 1996

Paul H. Walton, *The Drawings of John Ruskin*, Oxford Studies in the History of Art and Architecture, 1972

Andrew Wilton and Tim Barringer, *American Sublime Landscape Painting in the United States 1820-1880*, London, 2002

Index